IMAGES
of America

MOORESVILLE

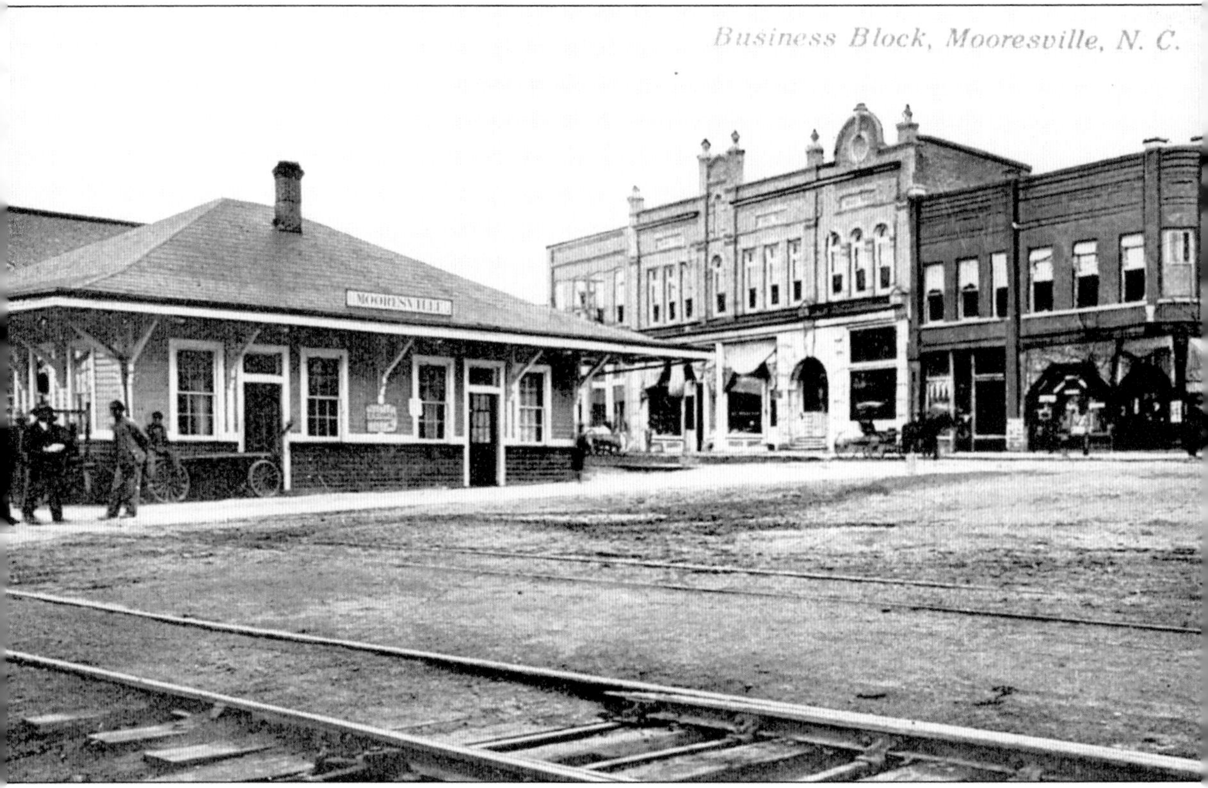

It was at the depot that all growth started in Mooresville. The corporate limits stretched in all directions from the site. This George C. Goodman postcard shows the busy intersection of Main Street, Broad Street, and Center Avenue, with a view of the depot. Freight trains loaded cotton and other products from a platform in the small lot across Center Avenue. People crossed the railroad tracks many times each day to conduct business and shop in the many stores. Pictured in this early postcard are Goodman Drug, the United States Post Office, First National Bank, and the Atlantic, Tennessee, and Ohio Railroad depot.

ON THE COVER: Scouting started in Mooresville as early as 1912, when Zebulon Vance Turlington and Side Mack organized a troop for boys. Lorine Price started a troop for senior high girls in the late 1930s. Frances Craven and Mary Mitchell Norman met with the girls at the Community House to develop citizenship skills. Camping trips to Lake James and other "safaris" were a focus of the activities. Bernice Melchor became a leader and organized activities in the 1960s for Brownies and Girl Scouts in their teens. Campers in 1950 include, from left to right, Anne Bittinger, Margaret Ferry, Frances Gilladette, Joan Morrow, Carolyn Skeen, Barbara Klepfer, Ann Crowell, Mary Barner, Patsy Skeen, Carol Ann Brown, Barbara Smith, Jan McNeely, and Barbara Groom. (Courtesy of Deanna Stallings Gabriel.)

IMAGES
of America

MOORESVILLE

Cindy Jacobs

ARCADIA
PUBLISHING

ISBN 978-0-7385-4402-1

Published by Arcadia Publishing
Charleston, South Carolina

Printed in the United States of America

Library of Congress Catalog Card Number: 2006935670

For all general information contact Arcadia Publishing at:
Telephone 843-853-2070
Fax 843-853-0044
E-mail sales@arcadiapublishing.com
For customer service and orders:
Toll-Free 1-888-313-2665

Visit us on the Internet at www.arcadiapublishing.com

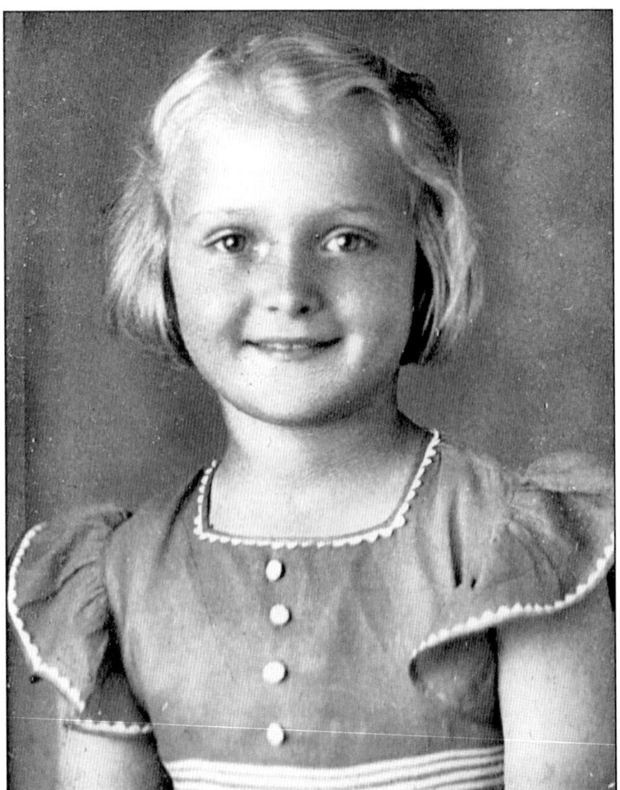

This effort to tell a story of Mooresville is dedicated to my mother, Kathryn Jeanette Stallings Jacobs, and my friends, Ray Boone and James Jennings. Their love of learning and appreciation of Mooresville inspire me to search for knowledge about this community we call home and find ways to share it with others.

Contents

Acknowledgments

A simple thank you is not adequate to describe my appreciation to the people who have shared part of their lives with me so that I may share it with others. These fellow citizens shared their collections of images as well as their recollections to support this effort to make Mooresville history available to those who seek knowledge and information. I hope that this collection of images will add to the pioneering efforts of W. J. Haselden, Dr. Bill Brown, and the Mooresville Centennial Corporation to record Mooresville history for future generations. Thank you to Pearl Troutman Alexander, Francella Craven Kerr, Bobbie Johnston Powers, Kay Kipka Jones, Side Mitchell Mack, Lynda Robinson Mack, Bernard Christenbury, Erleen Mills Christenbury, Rodney Benfield, Virginia Hart Edmiston, Bobby Leagon, Charlie Roberts, Mike Barnhardt, Janet Kerr Ramey, Leigh Lowder Whitfield, Bill Edmiston, Betty Jo Gabriel Lowrance, Rick Gibson, United Daughters of the Confederacy Battle of Bentonville Chapter, Lenore McNeely Hathcock, Karen Brown Smith, Rena Bishop, Sarah Kipka Sides, Bernice Bishop, Fannie Kipka, Richard Newton, Betty Jo Newton, Bill Keeter, Robert J. Holthouser, the Stallings-Sigmon family, Deanna Stallings Gabriel, Jane Marlow Cagle, James V. Houston, Lisa Alexander Lewis, H. Mike Cook, Betty Puckett, Sylvia Smith, Mary Gabriel, Alice Lee, Elizabeth Owens Whitlow, and the Mooresville High School class of 1947. Getting to know you better has been my pleasure. My thanks for support of the project to record and share Mooresville history goes to Dr. Boen Nutting, Dr. Bruce Boyles, Kathy Story Whitehead, Sylvia Spury, Dan Wallace, Mooresville–South Iredell Chamber of Commerce, Dolores Koury Mack, Lake Norman Regional Medical Center, Jean Young, Charles L. Jones, Bill Lowrance, Al Jones, Christa McElveen Owens, Mary Kipka Brawley, Frank J. Owens, Tina Czarnecky, Billie Stutts, South Iredell Senior Center, Vickie Morrow, Danielle Knowland, Charles Mack Citizen Center staff, and John Pritchard. Unless otherwise noted, images are part of the Stallings-Sigmon Collection.

Introduction

The story of Mooresville is about people who, finding themselves together in one place, built a dynamic community. There were good times and recession, business growth and decline, as well as government excellence and political bickering. Through it all, the bold, benevolent leadership of John F. Moore set the standard for citizenship. In 1856, people got excited about starting a town because the railroad offered an opportunity to interact with neighboring communities, towns, and cities. Since those early days, the 25 original residents have been joined by those who arrived by horse, train, and car to get involved in business, provide educational and religious training, and build families.

The early citizens were the descendants of Scotch, Irish, German, English, African American, and Lebanese immigrants. They found themselves in the rich farmland of Piedmont North Carolina, near an excellent source of water, the Catawba River, and railroad transportation. A plank road connected the village to points north and south, and a macadam road led to the Catawba River. Travel was not easy, but it was possible. Crops were sold in markets near and far, thanks to the Atlantic, Tennessee and Ohio Railroad. Later a line connecting Mooresville to Winston-Salem through Mocksville improved the transportation network. Goods came into town over the same rails and highways.

Churches were established almost immediately, with Centre Presbyterian leading the way in 1774. Schools soon followed, with Crowfield Academy offering education as early as 1837. North Bend School was established in 1845 with a land gift from James W. Moore. Baptist, Presbyterian, and Methodist ministers held services there while planning buildings for their congregations. Valuing education and religion, citizens worked together to built a stable government and a dynamic economy.

Mooresville-area farmers were joined by "town dwellers" whose businesses provided necessities and markets for local and regional products. The McPherson Roller Mill used the power of McPherson Creek (now Reed Creek) to grind corn into meal and by-products into feed for animals. In 1887, the Melchor brothers started the Big Oak Roller Mill on North Main Street. The mill was steam powered with boilers fired by wood. Farmers brought their harvest to the mill, where flour, corn meal, and mill feed were manufactured and sold to local stores. After a fire in 1924, Espy Brawley bought the property and rebuilt the company as the Mooresville Flour Mill.

When James E. Sherrill and a group of investors started the first powered cotton mill, the character of the community changed. Sales of cotton goods were brisk, and the mill was able to make use of homegrown cotton to support the active local market. Former farmers were able to develop a wide range of mechanical skills to use the modern machinery. New business emerged to supply specialized machinery to the mill. Mill marketing put Mooresville on the national stage as a source for high-quality goods. In 1906, Espy Brawley organized the Dixie Cotton Mill, later Cascade Cotton Mills, to produce cotton yarn north of the depot along the railroad tracks, in an area now known as Cascade. The Great Depression caused the business to fail, and in 1933, the mill was purchased by Burlington Industries. The neighborhood was revitalized by the new operations, named Cascade Weaving Company. Both mills provided houses for workers near the plants.

Mooresville was a place for merchants and professionals as well as farmers. The Templetons and Williamses ground wheat, corn, and cottonseed. The McNeelys provided livery services and offered groceries and goods. The Rankins provided everything from notions to Sunday dresses to shoes. The Macks sold clothing, confectioneries, and ice cream. The Troutmans sold wood, brick, and furniture. The Turners sold hardware and the Johnstons ice and coal. Zeb Turlington practiced law, and Squire Voils took care of teeth. All combined their skills and expertise to add something to the community.

It all started when the smoke cleared and the rumble of the train faded. John Moore and his neighbors prepared for the future. Trains traveling the 44 miles from Charlotte to Statesville would stop near their fields at a place called Moore's Siding.

Their crops could travel to other markets, and locals would have access to a wide variety of goods from the entire region. New citizens and business owners could make their way to the village to set up shops, establish homes, and ply their trade.

The railroad and its tracks leading to other towns brought prosperity and opportunity to the village. Those same tracks, when removed during the Civil War, brought economic recession.

On July 1, 1864, J. F. Gilmer, major general and chief of the Engineer Bureau of the Confederate States of America, wrote to CSA secretary of war James A. Seddon about the destruction of the Danville (Virginia) railroad:

> On my arrival at this place four or five days ago I found the enemy had destroyed a part of the Richmond and Danville Railroad south of Burkeville. To aid in making the repairs vital to the working of the road and the supply of General Lee's army, I sent Lieut. Col. John J. Clarke, engineer, to Charlotte, N. C., with orders to remove iron from the Charlotte and Statesville road [the Atlantic, Tennessee and Ohio Railroad] and forward it to Danville, the same being a military necessity.

Nothing moved by rail and Moore's Siding was quiet.

The village survived and economic disaster was averted. When the tracks were returned in 1872, the community grew and prospered. Soldiers returning from the Civil War found opportunities to get involved in a growing community.

A U.S. post office, churches, and schools added to the community. The North Bend School, established in 1845 on land donated by James W. Moore, was in operation, as well as the Oak Institute and a school operated by Stephen Frontis and Augustus Leazer.

By 1873, the community was ready to become a town. John Robert McNeely, Issac Harris, Robert McPherson, John Melchor, John Moore, and Joseph Templeton met and developed a charter for a town. On March 3, 1873, the North Carolina General Assembly enacted legislation to incorporate Mooresville, named in honor of John Franklin Moore.

Dramatic change came, with streets that were paved and lighted, electricity, telephone service, municipal water and sewer, police and fire protection, and industry. The bold steps of John F. Moore and his neighbors paved the way for a community of individuals who work hard each day to make Mooresville a great place to live, work, and raise a family.

The images in this book allow us to see fleeting glimpses of the town's history. The people, individuals and families, are at work, worship, and play in places that are still alive with activity today.

One

From the Farm to Town

After a meeting at the North Bend School, the leaders of Moore's Siding prepared to present a charter to the North Carolina Legislature for incorporation of the village. It was ratified on March 3, 1873, and John Robert McNeely was named mayor by the legislature. He served until the 10 eligible voters, out of a population of 25, elected Issac Harris mayor. Harris and his commissioners got down to work by levying a tax to open streets within the corporate limits, which were "one mile everywhere from Moore's Depot." Their work continued with the addition of streetlights and the first public well. The town grew with business enterprises designed to meet the needs of citizens and visitors. The first newspaper, the *Gazette*, was published in 1880. The *Mooresville Monitor* was published by G. P. Jones in 1885, followed by J. F. Starrette's *Mooresville Record* in 1895 and the *Record-Times* and the *Enterprise* in 1899. Of these, the *Enterprise*, published by Harry P. Deaton, was the only success. The Mooresville Academy, Oak Institute, the Frontis-Leazer School, and the Institute served the community. In 1905, the North Carolina General Assembly established the Mooresville Graded School District. The first stores—Moore and McLean, Rankin's, W. C. Johnston, and Goodman Drug—opened on Main Street near the depot. Broad Street was the site of even more business development, including Turner Hardware, W. P. Carpenter, H. N. Johnston, and Miller Drug. Their goods and services ranged from medicines to hardware to produce, ice, coal, and clothing. Cotton, dairy, and cattle farmers joined forces to process and market their crops. W. M. Neel and Company started in 1890 with an order for an eight-pound bucket of butter and a crate of eggs. He traded with local citizens and became the largest shipper of eggs, butter, and chickens to outside markets. Lorene Cotton Seed Oil Mill established a busting market on Broad Street, with a siding to load cotton products onto waiting trains. Roller mills like the Big Oak, McPherson, and Templeton-Williams processed wheat and corn into flour, meal, and animal feeds. The town grew in population and economic prosperity with the addition of new citizens, new businesses, and technology.

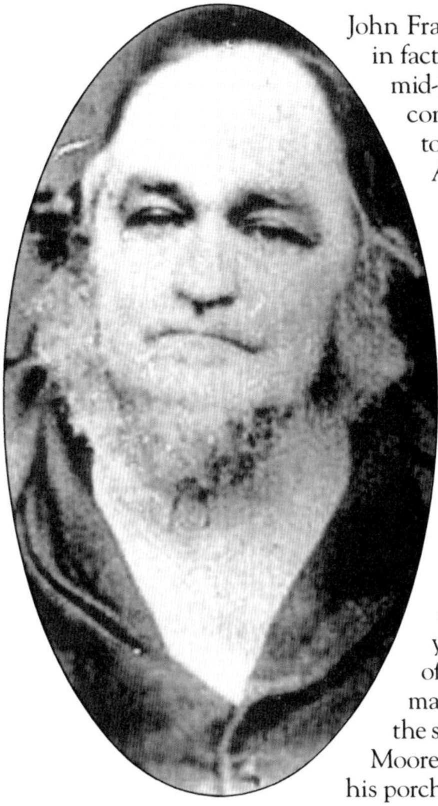

John Franklin Moore (1822–1877) had a farm as big as a town; in fact, most of what is Mooresville was part of his farm in the mid-1850s. He viewed the crops he and his neighbors grew as commodities to be sold in markets near and far. He saw a town in the future and looked for a way to get started. The Atlantic, Tennessee, and Ohio Railroad paved the way for Moore's dream. After donating land for a depot and cotton-loading platform at Moore's Siding, he opened a store with Bert McLean and provided lots for businesses and homes in the emerging downtown. His civic pride asserted itself when he donated land for the Mooresville Academy, the First Presbyterian Church, and Central Methodist Church. Later he provided six acres for a town cemetery, Willow Valley. At 55, Moore became the first person buried there. John and Rachel Summerow Moore had five daughters, Victoria (Shepherd), Mary (Connally), Jane (McNeely), Kate (McNeely), and Alice. John had one brother, James, and two sisters, Estelle Templeton and Polly McNeely. Their daughters and sons-in-law carried his vision forward, providing economic and political leadership through the present day. Over the years, Moore never hesitated to contribute to the well-being of his fellow citizens and the town. Nor did he hesitate to make his wishes known, as he did to Dr. Stevenson when the streets were laid out. The bend in the "Public Road" at the Moore home remained as a wagon road so that he could sit on his porch and have a clear view of the traffic and activities.

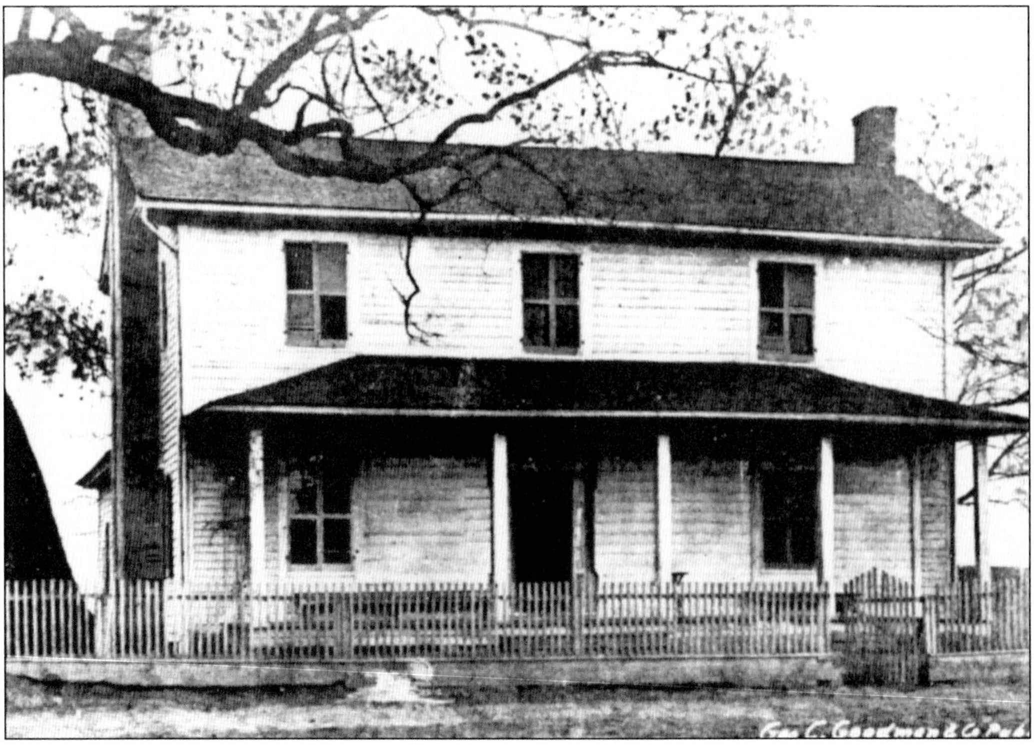

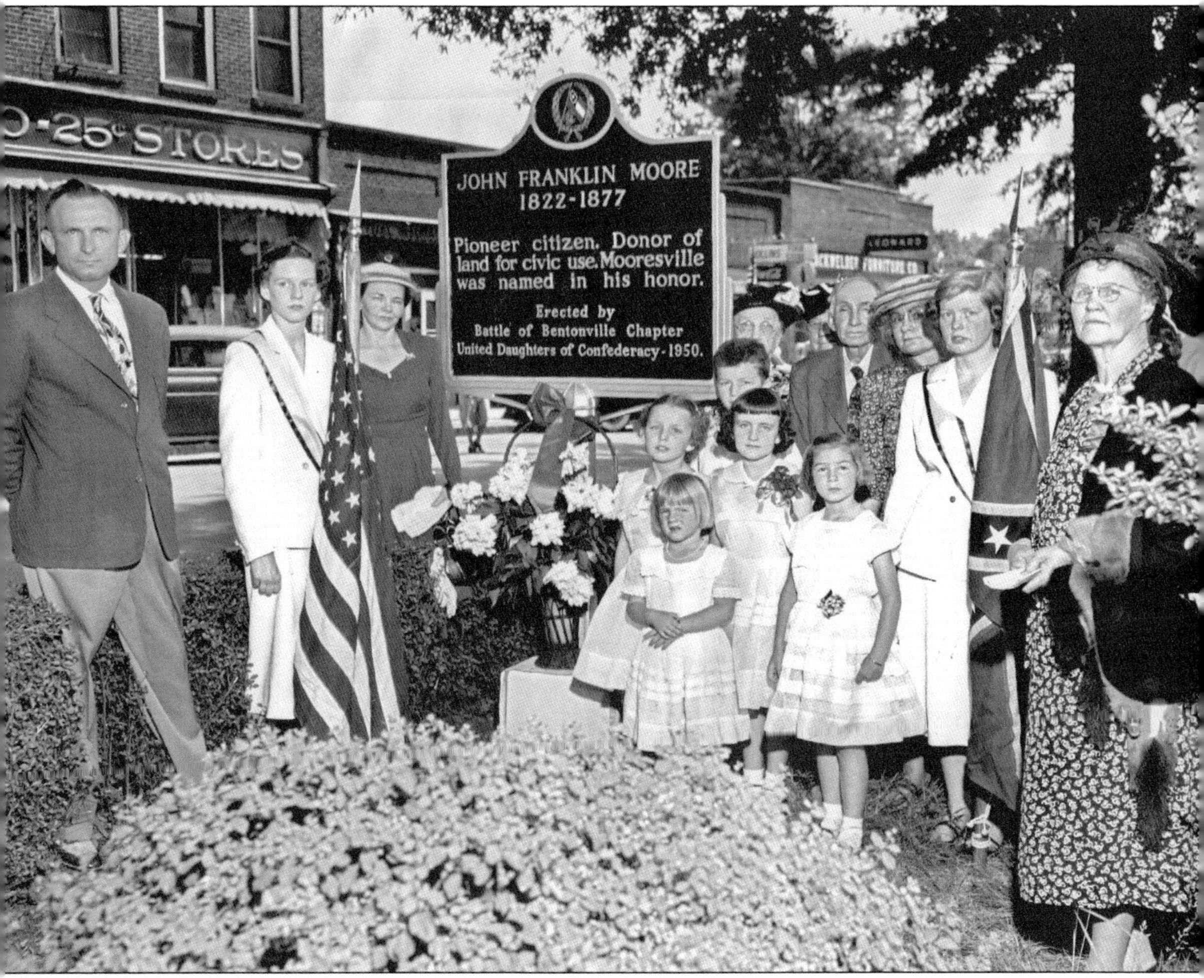

In 1951, a marker was placed in the civic park near the depot to honor the contributions of John F. Moore by the UDC Battle of Bentonville Chapter. Mayor Robert J. Holthouser (left) and Anne McNeely (second from left) led the service. In attendance were some of Moore's great-grandchildren, including (from left to right) Frances, Jane, and Harriett Brantley, Jean Brawley, and Nancy Lytle. Also included were, from left to right, Octa Brown, Catherine and J. E. McKey, Doris McKey and Giles Lytle, Mary McNeely Rogers, Cornelia Kendrick, Rachel Allred, and Mamie Houston. (Courtesy of UDC Battle of Bentonville Chapter 818, original photograph by Blake Studios.)

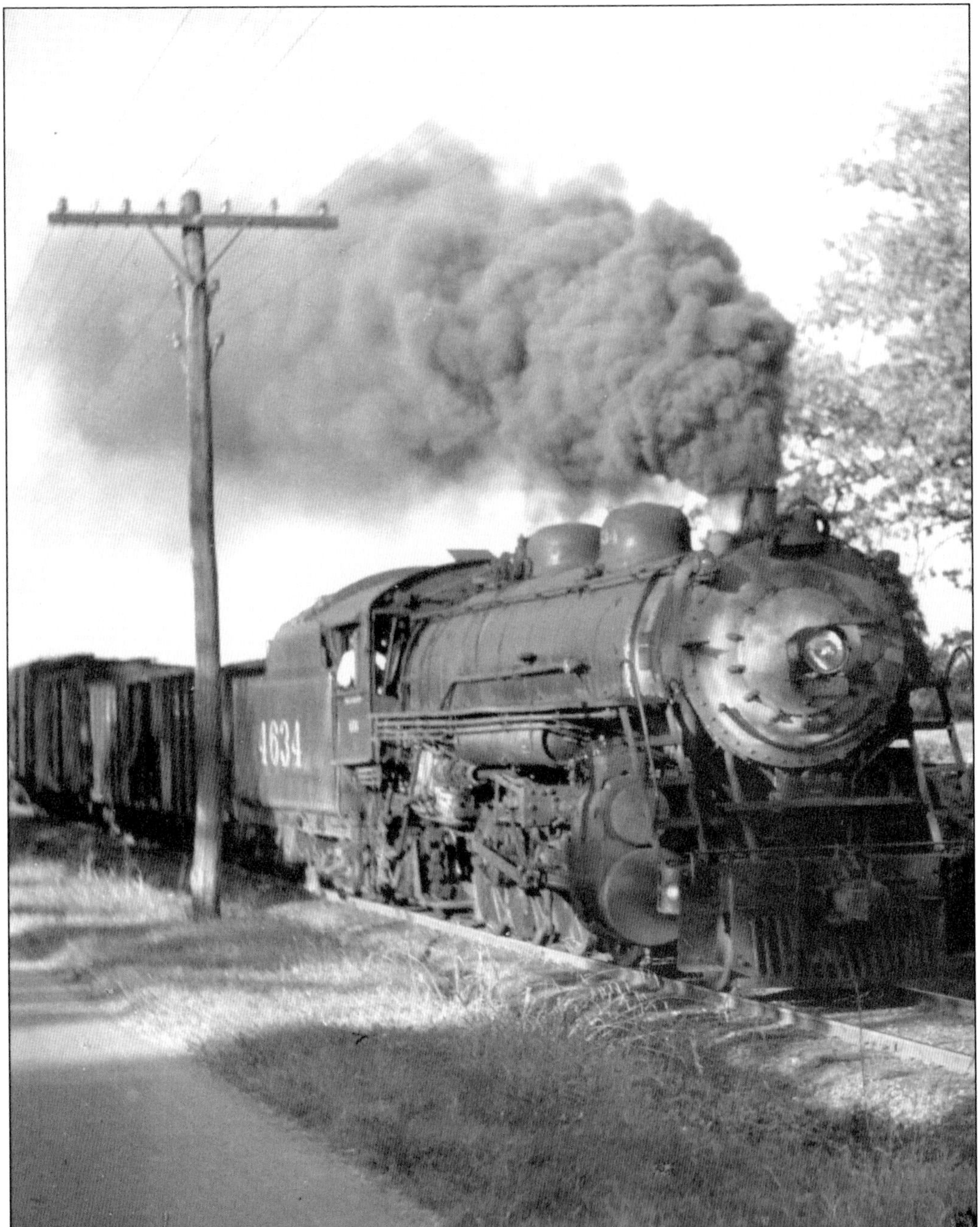

Atlantic, Tennessee, and Ohio Railroad trains brought passengers and freight to Moore's Siding and opened markets to local farmers and merchants. A second line was opened to Winston-Salem through Mocksville in 1886. Proximity to transportation was essential in making the town grow and prosper. The rumble of locomotives became part of the character of the community. (Courtesy of Edward Kipka Family.)

The one-acre lot housing the depot was established as the center of town at an elevation of 918 feet above sea level, measured from the center of the first crossing street at the depot door. A cotton platform was located on the property across Center Avenue from the depot, allowing farmers to load their crops onto waiting trains. The corporate limits of the town extended one mile in every direction. The Public Road became Main Street, and the first crossing road was Center Avenue. Main Street was wider than the original roadway, and Broad Street followed the same design to provide space for pedestrians and vehicles of all kinds.

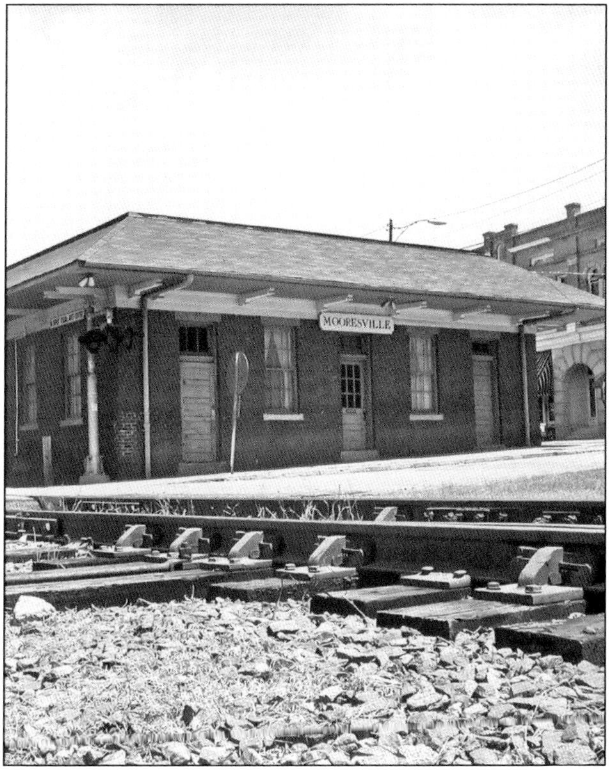

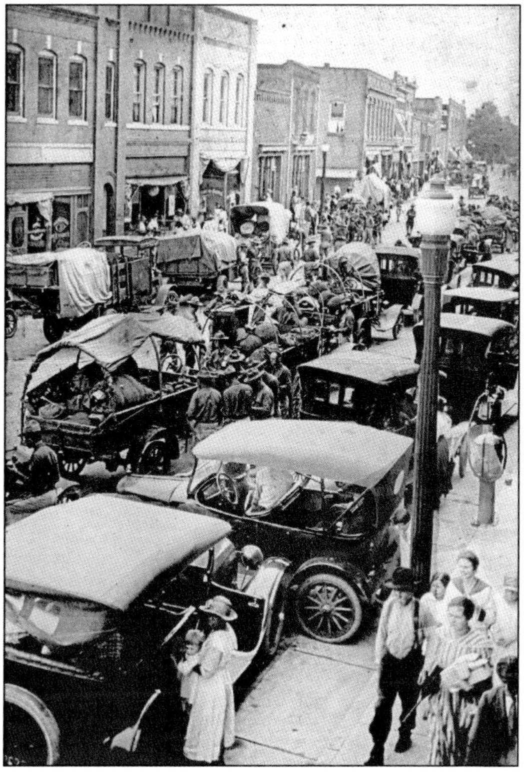

Locals gathered at "the square" for activities and events, being close to business, government, and transportation. Citizens could take advantage of the close proximity of banking, postal service, shopping, druggists, livery, and trains in the Main Street–Broad Street block. Main Street was often crowded with visitors, such as this army truck convoy after World War I.

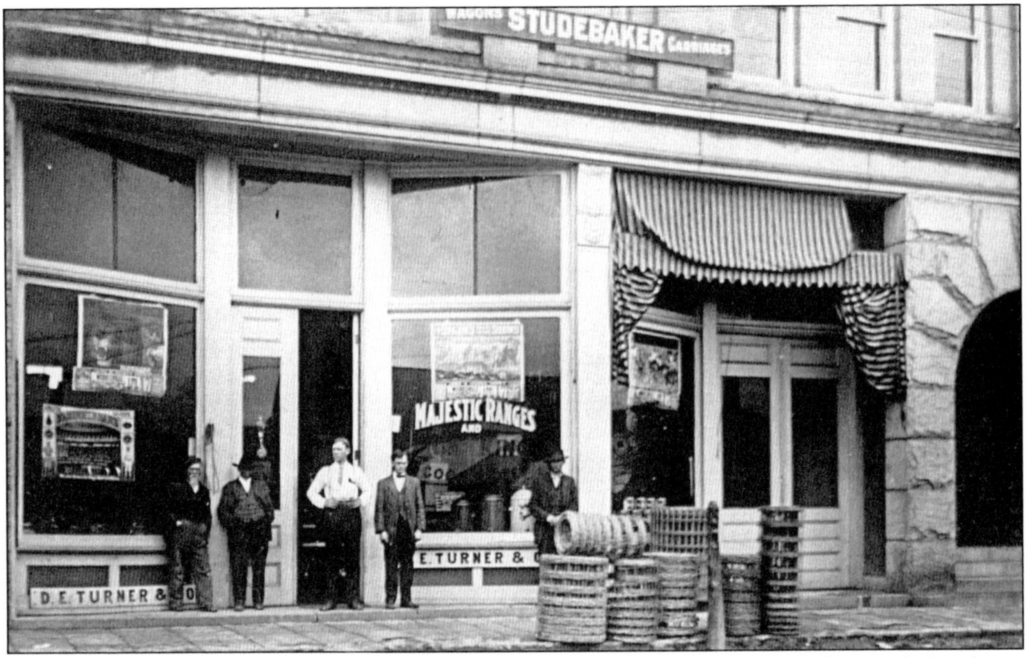

The Turner brothers—D. E., W. W., and A. M.—formed a partnership in 1899 and opened a hardware store on Broad Street. In 1900, they moved the store to Main Street across from the depot. Their goods included buggies, stoves, ranges, and an extensive line of shelf and heavy hardware. Turner's supplied much of the farm equipment used by cotton, dairy, and cattle farmers in the area. It was the site of the first gasoline pump in the area. Its proximity to the Salisbury-to-Asheville highway made Turner's the place to fill up Model T Fords traveling toward the Catawba River.

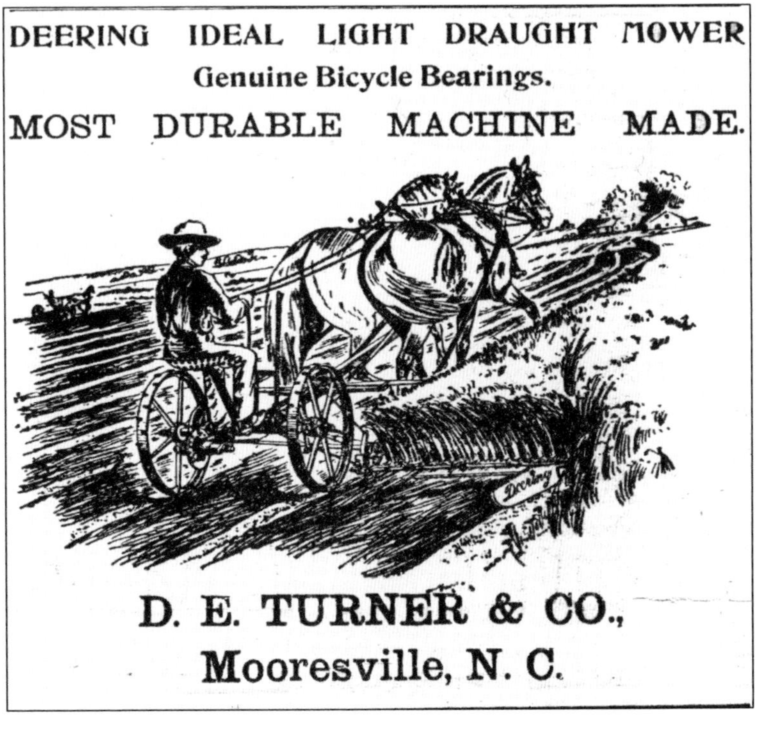

Turner Hardware was a significant member of the local economy and provided a wide variety of goods and services to farmers and those involved in agriculture. Only the finest-quality hardware was offered for sale, as seen in this 1901 advertisement in the *Mooresville Enterprise*.

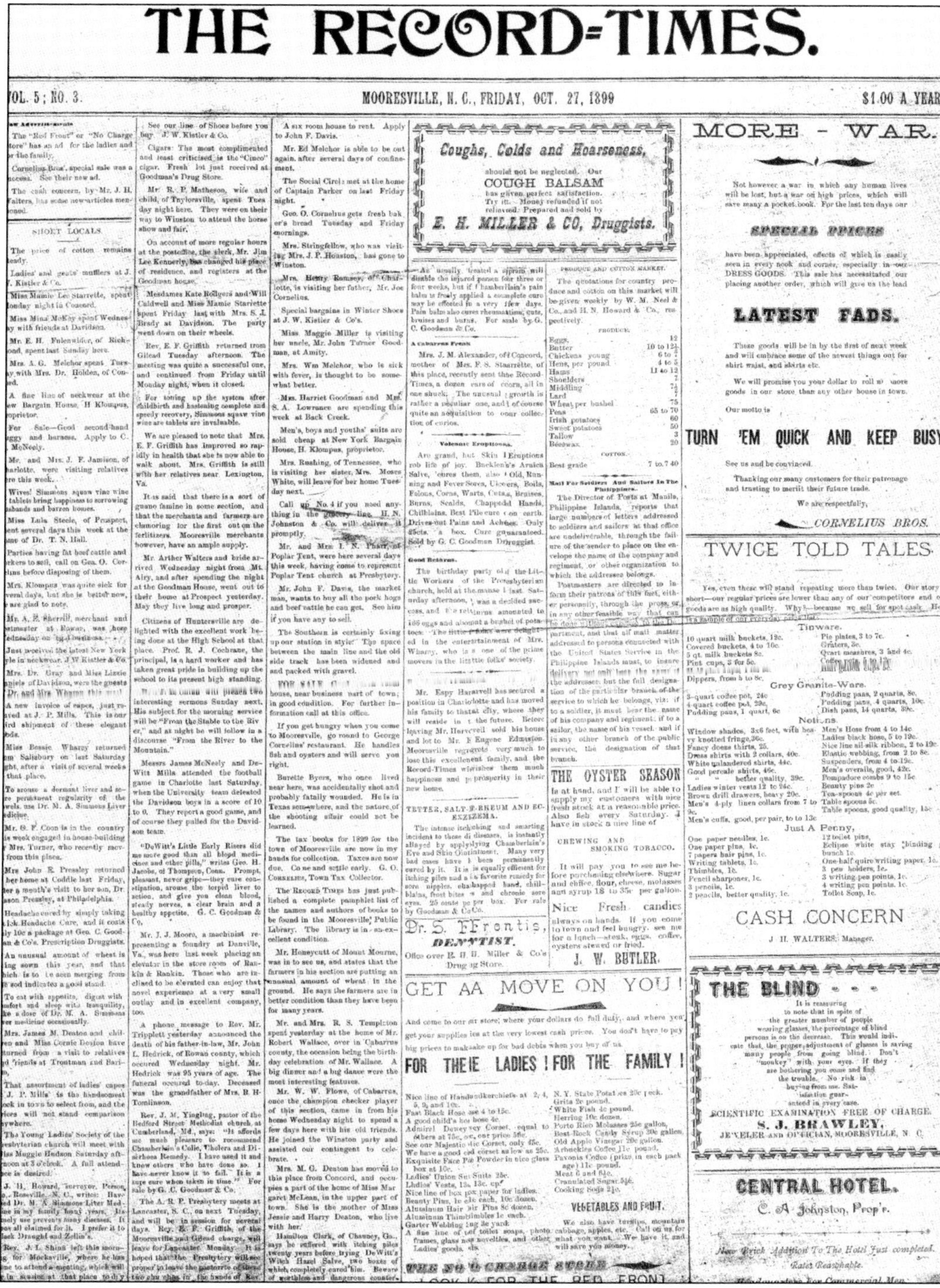

THE RECORD-TIMES.

VOL. 5; NO. 3. MOORESVILLE, N. C., FRIDAY, OCT. 27, 1899 $1.00 A YEAR.

Coughs, Colds and Hoarseness, should not be neglected. Our COUGH BALSAM has given perfect satisfaction. Try it. Money refunded if not relieved. Prepared and sold by E. H. MILLER & CO, Druggists.

MORE - WAR.

Not however a war in which any human lives will be lost, but a war on high prices, which will save many a pocket-book. For the last ten days our SPECIAL PRICES have been appreciated, effects of which is easily seen in every nook and corner, especially in our DRESS GOODS. This sale has necessitated our placing another order, which will give us the lead

LATEST FADS.

These goods will be in by the first of next week and will embrace some of the newest things out for shirt waist, and skirts etc.

We will promise you your dollar to roll no more goods in our store than any other house in town.

Our motto is

TURN 'EM QUICK AND KEEP BUSY.

See us and be convinced.

Thanking our many customers for their patronage and trusting to merit their future trade.

We are respectfully,

CORNELIUS BROS.

TWICE TOLD TALES.

THE OYSTER SEASON

GET AA MOVE ON YOU!

FOR THEIE LADIES ! FOR THE FAMILY !

CASH CONCERN

J. H. WALTERS, Manager.

THE BLIND

SCIENTIFIC EXAMINATION FREE OF CHARGE.

S. J. BRAWLEY,

JEWELER AND OPTICIAN, MOORESVILLE, N. C.

CENTRAL HOTEL.

C. A. Johnston, Prop'r.

J. W. BUTLER.

The *Mooresville Record* and the *Record-Times* were published by F. S. Starrette beginning in 1895. They contained news and advertising for all kinds of businesses, including the Mooresville Academy, offering room, board, and instruction for only $10 per month. Anna W. (Mrs. George C.) Goodman led the music department, while Lula Gray took charge of primary students. In the February 27, 1897, edition, L. Goodman offered his seven-room house on easy terms for $1,000.

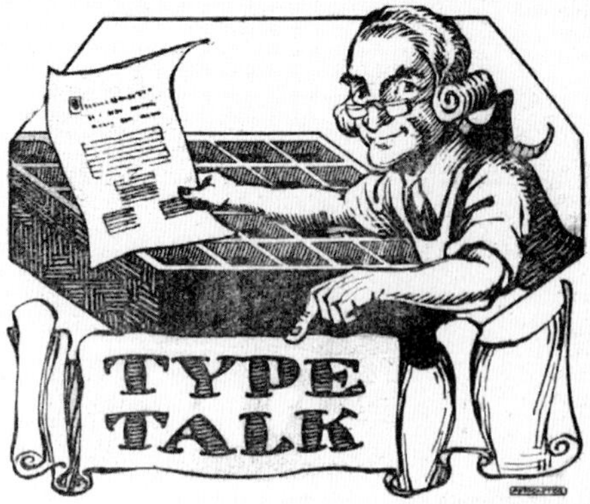

Almost everyone ordering matter feels that they want "something different." They sense that to obtain such printing they must have either one or two things—special cuts or type. To outline or specify "just what they want" is a task beyond one inexperienced in the craftsmanship of printng.

When you let us do your prnting you get all of this service free o fextra charge. We know just which type faces to use to carry your message in the most effective way. In addition to this we have a complete line of cuts to illustrate your message—pictures which will attract readers and make them read.

No matter what kind of printing you want we can do it—deliver the job promptly—and at a price far below what you may pay

The Mooresville Enterprise

Printers *Publishers*

The *Mooresville Enterprise* was founded in 1899 by Harry P. Deaton. Working with Frank P. Freeze, Deaton published the newspaper continuously until his death in 1945. In the 1930s, Fred Hudson and Guy Shook started the *Rounder*. Tom McKnight purchased the paper in 1935 and continued to use the name until 1937, when he determined that the paper had attained status as a source for information and that the name simply did not fit the character of the publication. McKnight said, "Advertising people are not apt to think well of a newspaper named the *Rounder*. It rhymes with 'bounder,' smacks of yellow journalism, scandal sheets and connotes something which is far from the plans and ideals for this newspaper." The *News Leader* emerged as the name of choice. In 1940, McKnight became the sole owner and changed the name to the *Mooresville Tribune*.

Mooresville Telephone Co.

Exchange Directory.

BROWN, J. W. Res.,	No. 15
BROWN, W. O. Res.,	No. 39
BANK,	No. 55
BROWN, J. E. Res.,	No. 7
BROWN, D. M. Res.,	No. 56
BRAWLEY, D. C. Res.,	No. 63
CENTRAL HOTEL,	No. 25
CORNELIUS, G. O., Market,	No. 19
CALDWELL, W. L., Res.,	No. 28
CARPENTER, W. P., Res.,	No. 38
COTTON MILL NO 1,	No. 13
COTTON MILL NO. 2,	No. 45
DEPOT.	No. 6
DEATON, J. M., Stable,	No. 12
DEATON, J. M., Res.,	No. 12a
DAVIS, JOHN F., Market,	No. 3
DAVIS, J. F., Res.,	No. 53
DEATON, P. E., Res.,	No. 54
ENTERPRISE OFFICE,	No. 51
FRONTIS, DR. S., Office,	No. 10
GOODMAN, GEO. C. & CO.,	No. 1
GOODMAN, G. C., Res.,	No. 17
HUDSON, J. W., Res.,	No. 11
HAWTHORN, C. E., Res.,	No. 36
HALL, T. N., Res.,	No. 43
JOHNSTON, H. N., & CO.,	No. 4
JOHNSTON, W. N., Res.,	No. 18
JOHNSTON, W. C., & CO.,	No. 5a
KISTLER, J. W. & CO.,	No. 33
KISTLER, J. W., Res.,	No. 32
LENTZ, W. M., Res.,	No. 23
LOWRANCE, S. A., Res.,	No. 20
LEAZAR, A., Res.,	No. 41
MILLER, E. H., & CO.,	No. 9
Mills, J. P., & CO., Store,	No. 34
MELCHOR BROS. ROLLER MILL,	No. 48
MURRAY, REV. J. G., Res.,	No. 30
MAYOR'S OFFICE,	No. 50
McNEELY, C. K., Res.,	No. 35
McLELLAND, DR., J. R., res.,	No 8
McGHEE, REV. W. P. Res.,	No. 37
NEEL, W. M. & CO.,	No. 5
POSTOFFICE,	No. 2
PRESSLEY, S. J., Res.,	No. 61
PRESSLEY, B. W., Res.,	No. 59
RANKIN, W, W., Store,	No 42
" W. W., Res.,	No. 47
" S. C., Res.,	No. 31
RANKIN, HARRIS & CO.,	No. 57
ROGERS, L. B., Store,	No. 52
SHERRILL, J. E. Res.,	No. 16
STEVENSON, DR. S. W. res.	No 14
SMITH, T. B., Store,	No. 22
TEMPLETON, WILLIAMS & CO., ROLLER MILL,	No. 21
TEMPLETON, R. S., Res.,	No, 2a
TEMPLETON, R. L. Res.,	No. 49
TURNER, D. E. & CO.,	No. 26
TOMLINSON, R. H., Res.,	No. 44
TROUTMAN, B. A., Res.,	No. 40
TROUTMAN, J. D., Res.,	No. 46
WHITE, M W., Res.,	No. 29
WHAREY, REV. J. M., Res.,	No 27
WALKER, A. M., Res.,	No. 58
YOUNG, DR. JAS., Res.,	No. 24

The first telephone book was published on a single sheet of cardboard with 31 subscribers listed. George C. Goodman Drug Company had the first phone with the number 1. The U.S. Post Office, located next door to Goodman, was number 2. The third directory was an eight-page book, with H. N. Johnston Company advertising on each page. It is noted that there is no number for either the police or fire departments, since town offices had yet to be constructed. (Courtesy of Alice Lee.)

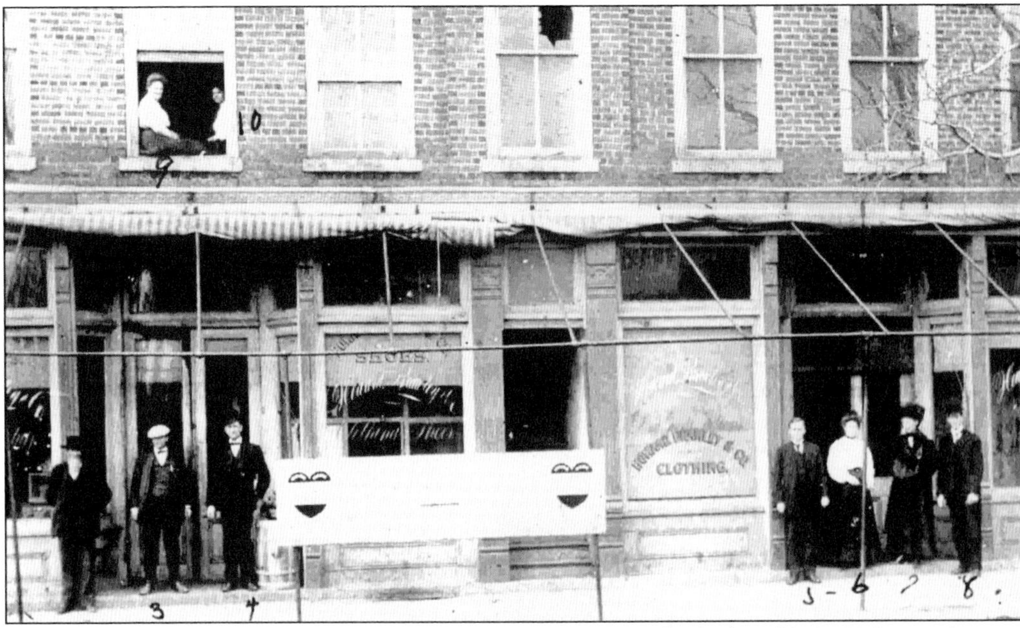

According to W. J. Haselden's review of town records, W. E. Shuford and J. A. Helving obtained a franchise to provide 25 telephones to businesses and individuals. The franchise terms specified that the company would furnish business phones for $2 per month for a private line and $1.50 for party lines. Over the next two months, the commissioners awarded franchises to Sam Brawley and S. A. Lowrance. Brawley installed lines and provided service. The Mooresville Telephone Company is the result of Brawley's efforts. The offices and exchange were located on the second floor of the Johnston building on the corner of Broad Street and Center Avenue. "Hello Girls" answered customer calls and made connections. (Courtesy of Alice Lee.)

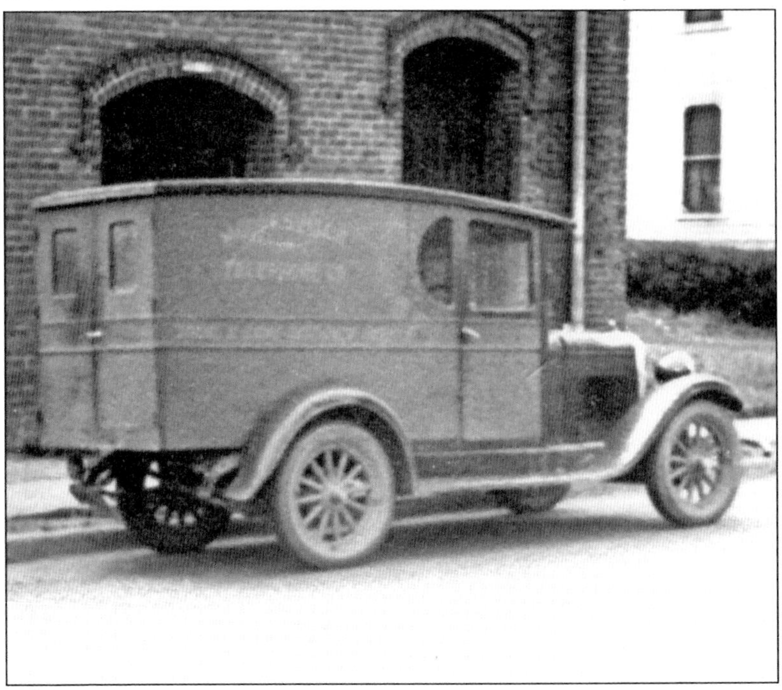

The telephone company warehouse was located 50 yards from the exchange office on Center Avenue. From there, trucks and equipment traveled throughout the town to install equipment and phone lines. (Courtesy of Alice Lee.)

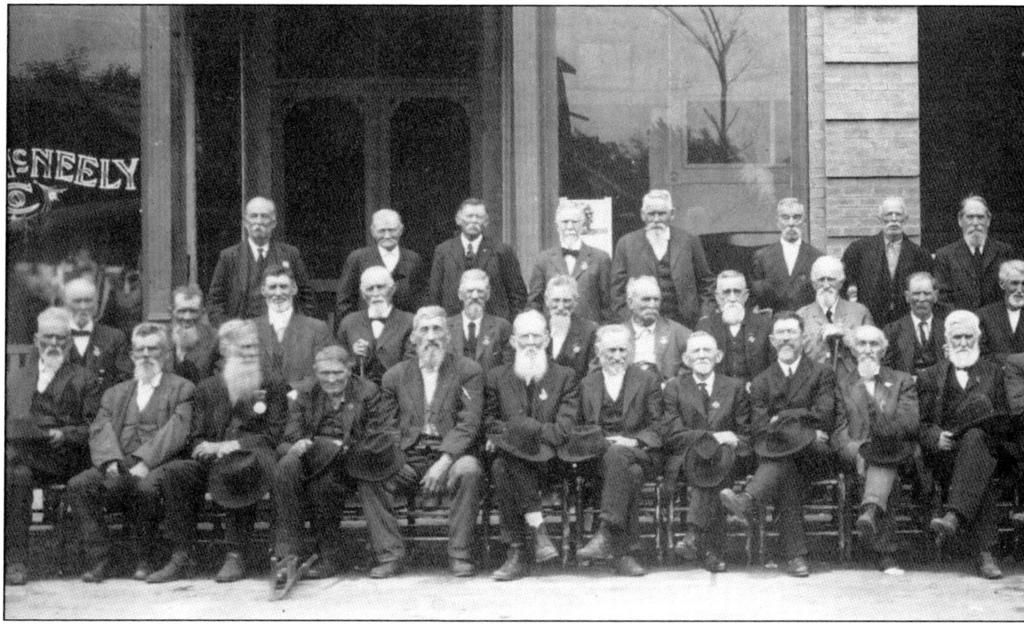

Soldiers returning home from the Civil War found a struggling but strong community. Many got involved in the business community by working for existing firms or using their skills to open their own businesses. J. I. Goodman, writing in the Rounder in 1930, described them as "much changed" by the war. "Most had lost material possessions and, though defeated and discouraged, they sought to make a fresh start." This May 10, 1920, photograph was taken during the celebration of Confederate Memorial Day sponsored by the United Daughters of the Confederacy Battle of Bentonville Chapter. The list of veterans participating in the event incudes Sam Hart Sr., Peter Kistler, Adam Albert McNeely, Augustus Leazer, John R. Stirewalt, R. W. McKey, and W. N. Johnston. The veterans shown in this photograph are not identified individually.

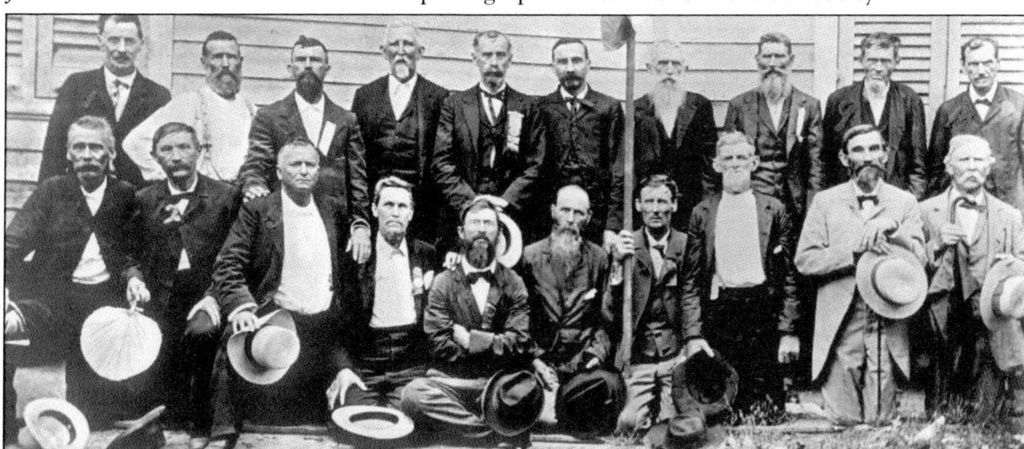

A reunion of Confederate veterans in August 1898 included 20 members of the 56th North Carolina Infantry, Company K: John Martin, Samuel Lowrance, Albertus Kennerly, H. J. Warsham, Dr. Walter Craven, R. J. Stough, A. H. Alexander, Allison Christenbury, I. W. Barnette, M. A. Emmerson, W. D. Barnhardt, Robert S. Templeton, B. D. Brown, John Kennerly, W. T. Cashion, John Hays Johnston, C. T. Deweese, S. R. Andrews, and J. C. Bell. (Courtesy of the UDC Battle of Bentonville Chapter.)

PROTECT YOUR CASH !

Buy Your Goods From the
CHEAP CASH STORE.

CLOTHING--CHEAP VERY CHEAP!

$10.00 Suits to go for $5.50
$8.50 Suits to go for $4.50
$4.50 Suits to go for 2.50
50 Job Suits at ½ price.
Boy wash Suits only 48c
PANTS, fine pants at half price.
$1.50 pants only 98c
$2.50 pants only $1.50
Job in Overalls
$1.00 Overalls only 58c
50ct Overalls only 29c
Boys' Overalls 25c
2000 Yds. Ba[illegible]r's Bleached at a low price
2000 Yds. Calico, per yd. 3c
500 Yds. god Lawn, 3c
Fine Organdies and Lawns to go at cost.
2,000 yards of good Alamance at 4c

NOTIONS.

25c Sailors, big job, at 5c
Children's 25c Soilors, big job, at 5c
Men's Fine Hats, big job, at 48c
Ladies Hats to close out cheap.
Umbrellas, good quality, at 32c
Umbrellas, fine quality, 39c
Umbrellas, finer quality, 48c
$1.50 Parasols for $1.15
150 Fine Shirts, job, 38c
75c Shirts for 48c

$1.50 Fine Shirts for 98c
Big job in Work Shirts at 39c
Fine Sox 3c
Home-made Fine Sox 8c
Men's Heavy Coarse Sox 6c
Men's Heavy Slips, per pair, 20c
Hair Brushes 5c
Shaving Brushes 1c
Tooth Brushes 3c
Pins, 280 for 1c
5 papers of needles for 3c
Blacking per box 1c
Soap per cake 1c
2 balls of thread for 1c
Envelopes, good, per pack, 3c
Sewing machine oil 4c per bottle.
Big lot of Hamburg and Insertions to arrive Friday.
Good Brooms 19c
Crocks, Jugs and Jars cheap.
Big lot of Trunks CHEAP.
Big lot of Telescopes CHEAP.
Big lot of Grips VERY CHEAP.

GROCERIES.

17 lbs Standard Granulated Sugar for $1.00.
10 lbs Best Green Coffee for $1.00.
15 lbs of Soda for 25c.
20 lbs of Rice for $1.00.
Schnapps Tobacco 36c.

"More Goods for the Same Money, and the Same Goods for Less Money,"
AT THE MOORESVILLE RACKET STORE,

W. P. CARPENTER, Owner.

W. P. Carpenter opened the first department store on Broad Street in 1901. After moving to a new building on Main Street in 1910, the W. P. Carpenter store housed two floors containing groceries, dishes, and kitchen utensils. Glass showcases on the main floor displayed a wide range of furnishings and fancy goods. Customers could find dry goods, clothing, and ladies' ready-to-wear garments. The attractive balcony area featured millinery, rugs, trunks, suitcases, and art squares. Carpenter operated the store until 1940, when it was purchased for the expansion of Belk's.

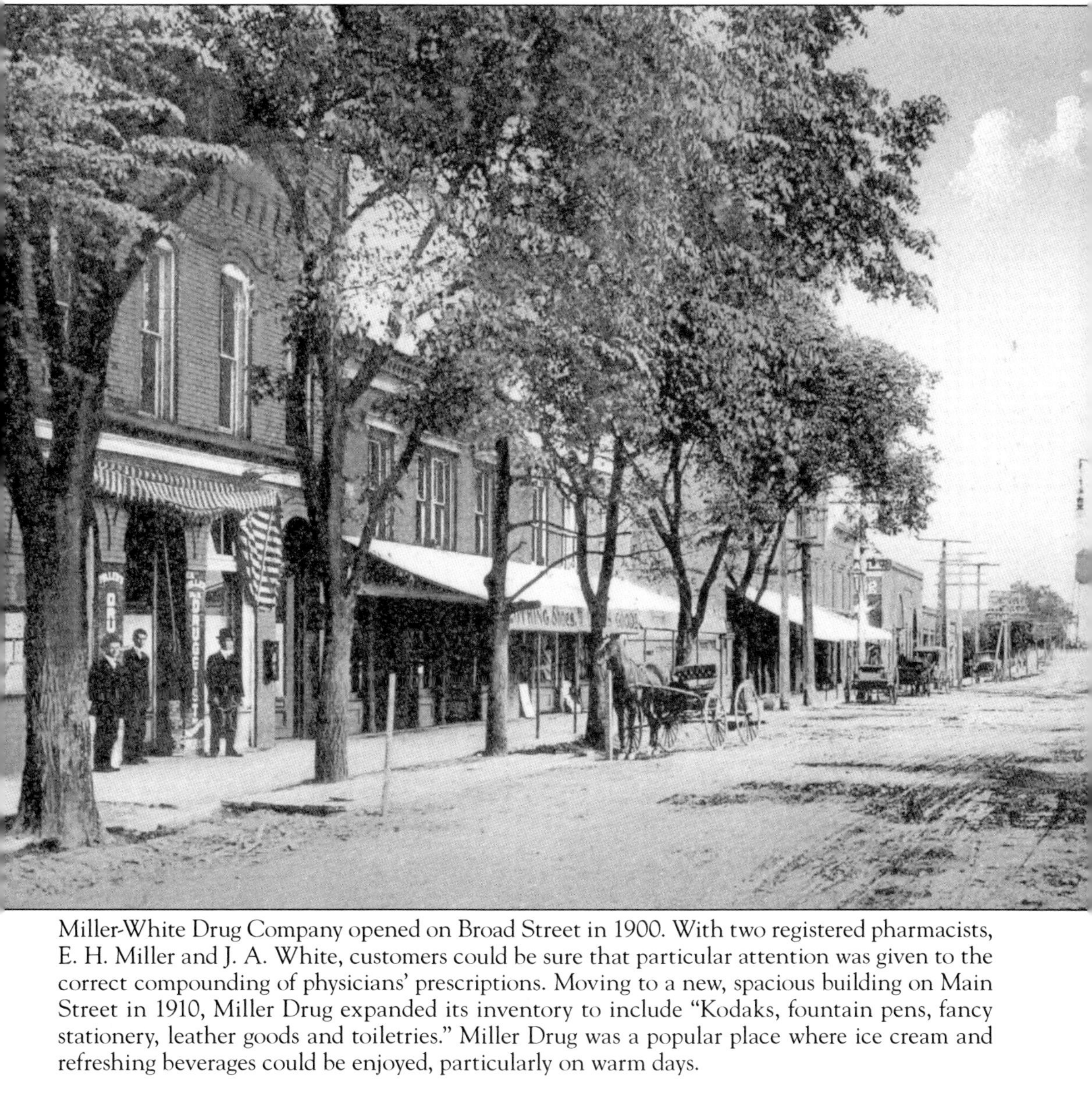

Miller-White Drug Company opened on Broad Street in 1900. With two registered pharmacists, E. H. Miller and J. A. White, customers could be sure that particular attention was given to the correct compounding of physicians' prescriptions. Moving to a new, spacious building on Main Street in 1910, Miller Drug expanded its inventory to include "Kodaks, fountain pens, fancy stationery, leather goods and toiletries." Miller Drug was a popular place where ice cream and refreshing beverages could be enjoyed, particularly on warm days.

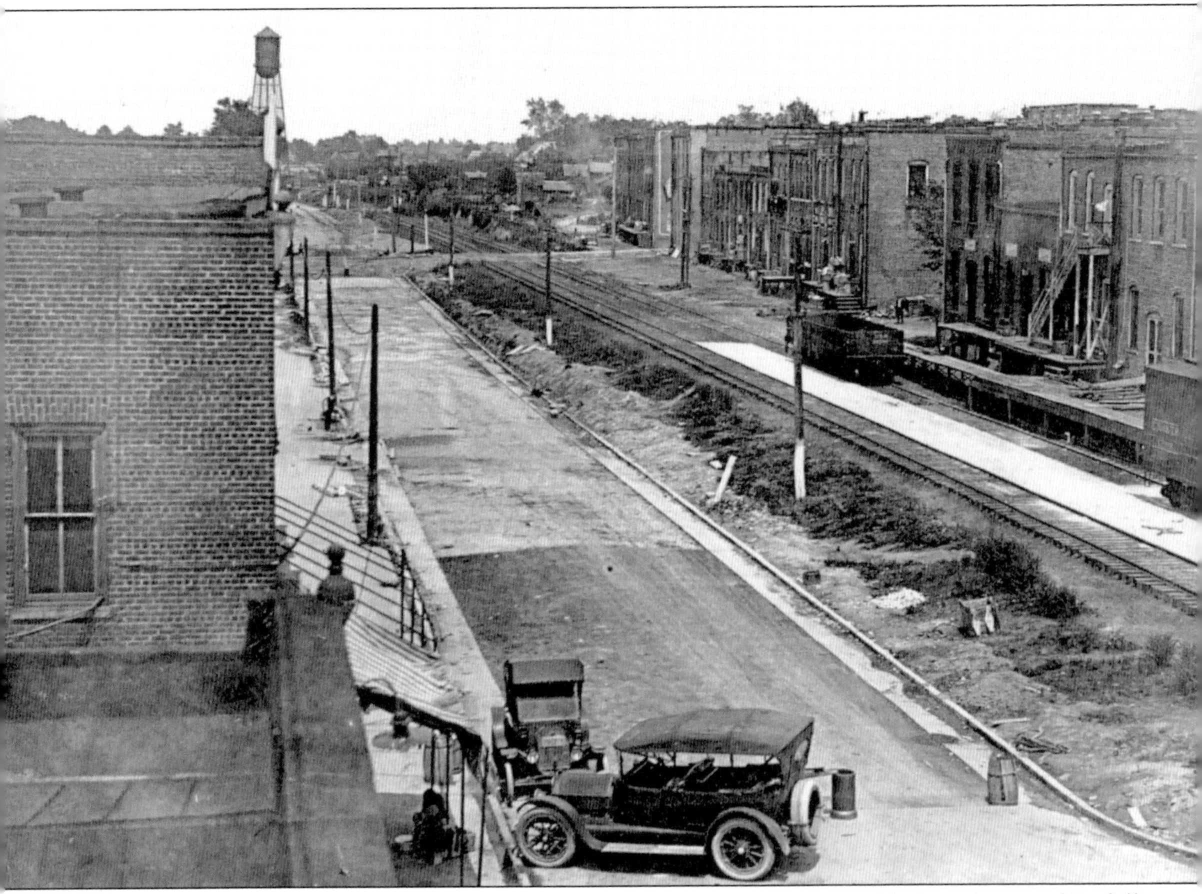

Development along Broad and Main Streets was steady, with buildings added north toward Iredell Avenue. H. N. Johnston and Company offered groceries, coal, and ice to the community. The Mooresville Cooperative Creamery was built on the corner of Broad Street and Moore Avenue. Center, Moore, and Iredell Avenues provided easy cross streets linking Main and Broad.

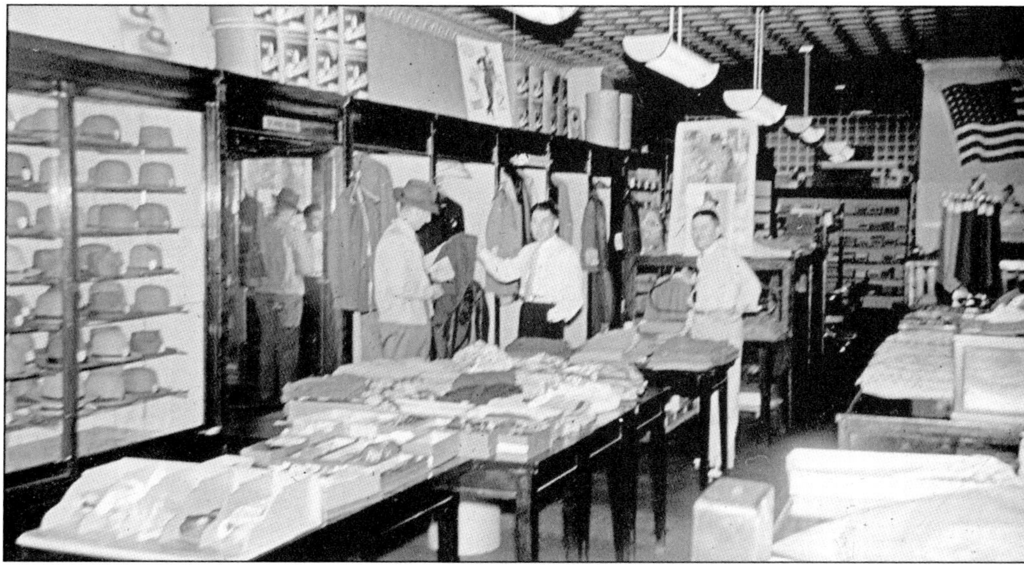

C. L. Kelly Sr. opened Kelly Clothing Company on Main Street in 1911 catering to men and young men exclusively. Kelly's featured the finest apparel, including such brands as Hart, Schaffner, and Marks suits; Stetson hats; Manhattan shirts; and Bayden shoes. Men's suits were displayed in a revolving glass cabinet, along with a complete line of collars and neckwear. A biography in the *Rounder* and *News Leader* described him as a "businessman with a splendid reputation and one that is interested in the development of this section of North Carolina."

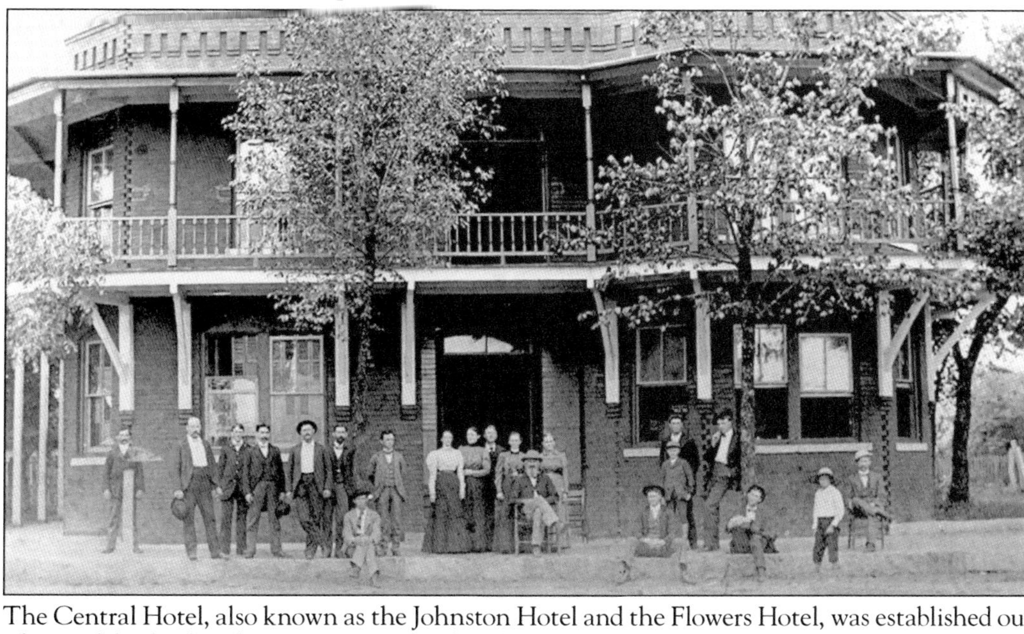

The Central Hotel, also known as the Johnston Hotel and the Flowers Hotel, was established out of a need for food and services among railroad conductors and trainmen stopping at the depot. Lillie Harrison Johnston Melchor, daughter of Cyrus Johnston, was married to John Angus Melchor in 1888. Widowed in the 1890s, she returned to her father's home on Main Street. As requests for food increased, she began selling lunches and eventually served meals in the family dining room. Expanded by eight rooms and renovated to accommodate guests, the hotel was a popular gathering place for locals and visitors.

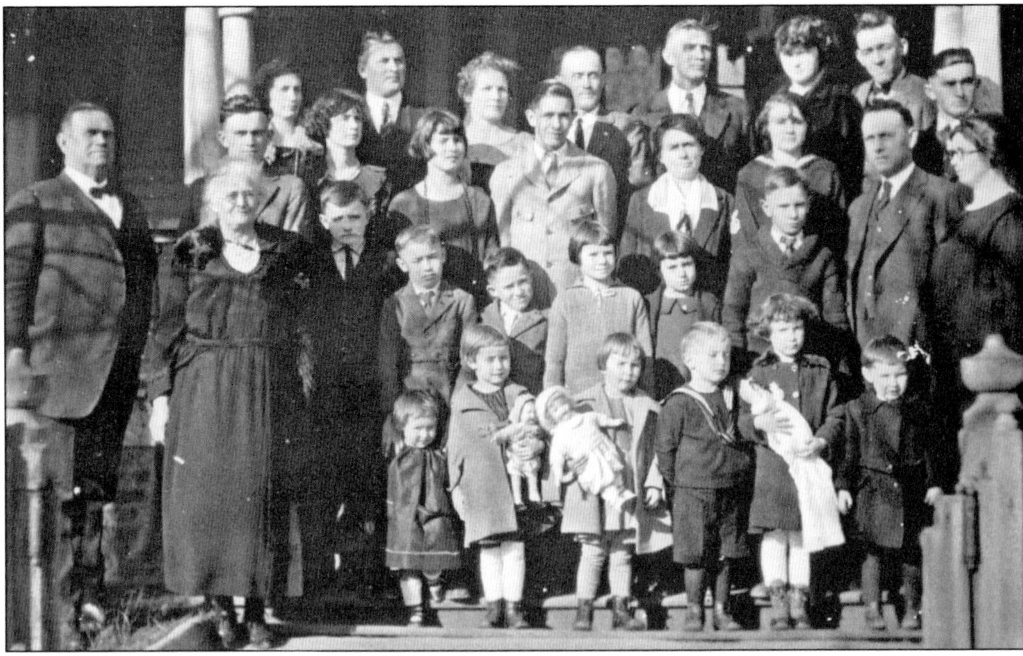

Farm families moved to town, and new citizens arrived to take part in the building of a new town. Buretta Augustus Troutman and Martha Louise Jones Troutman moved to Mooresville in 1890. They opened a saw and planing mill on North Main Street and started making furniture, bricks, and other building essentials. His large farm included a spring from which he could pipe water into a large wooden tank for his home and businesses. It was adjacent to Troutman's mills, water tank, brick-making yards, and farm. (Courtesy of Pearl Troutman Alexander.)

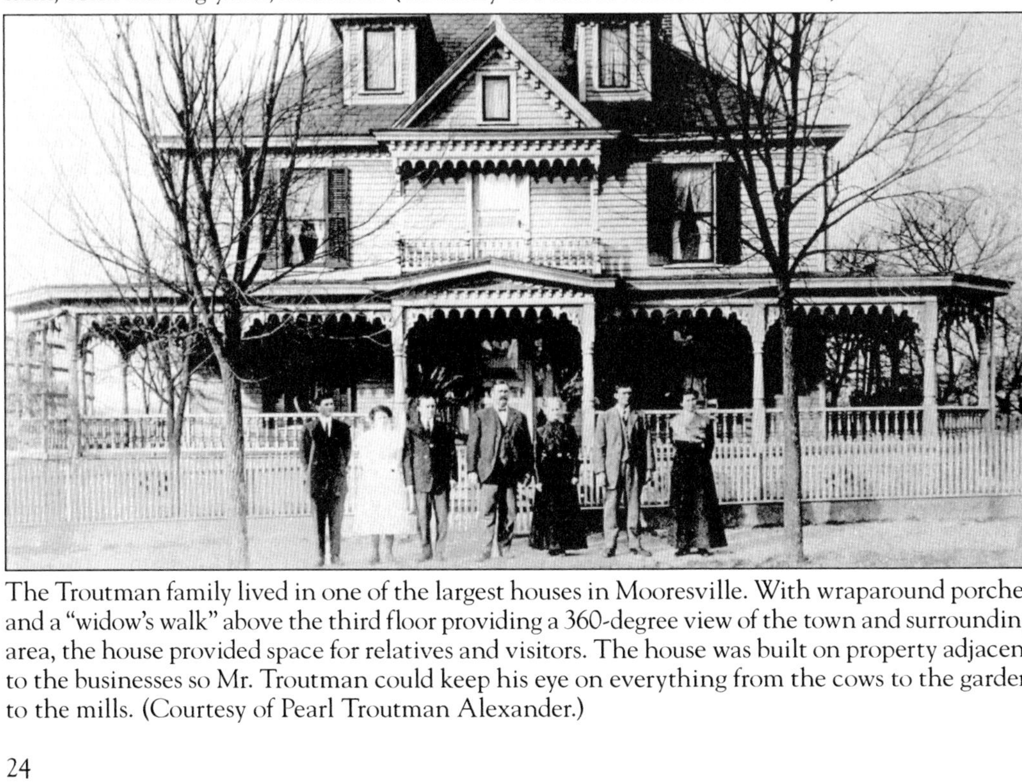

The Troutman family lived in one of the largest houses in Mooresville. With wraparound porches and a "widow's walk" above the third floor providing a 360-degree view of the town and surrounding area, the house provided space for relatives and visitors. The house was built on property adjacent to the businesses so Mr. Troutman could keep his eye on everything from the cows to the garden to the mills. (Courtesy of Pearl Troutman Alexander.)

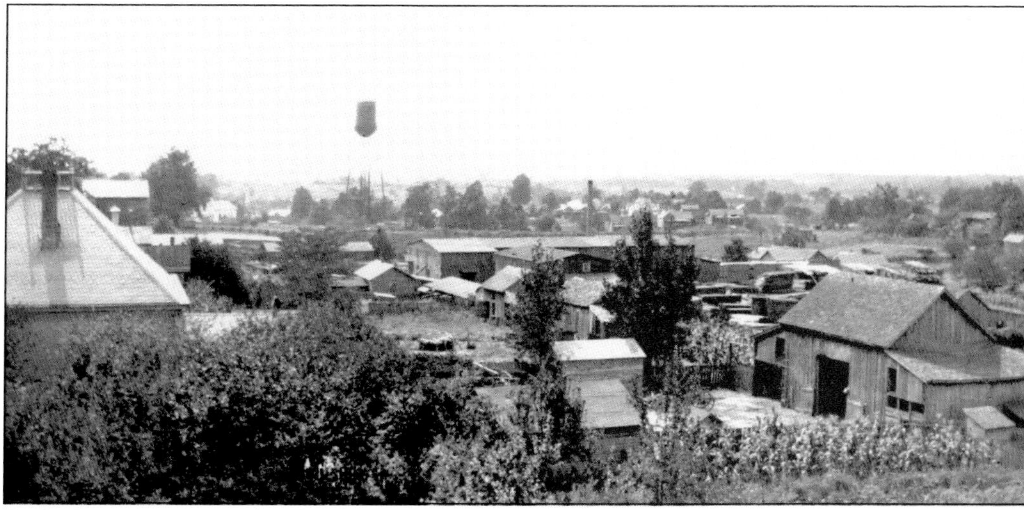

B. A. Troutman's sons lived in homes on the same property, with a wide view of the area. The barns, mills, and storage areas extended over 11 acres. Troutman's cows and large garden were located near the creek at the edge of the property. (Courtesy of Pearl Troutman Alexander.)

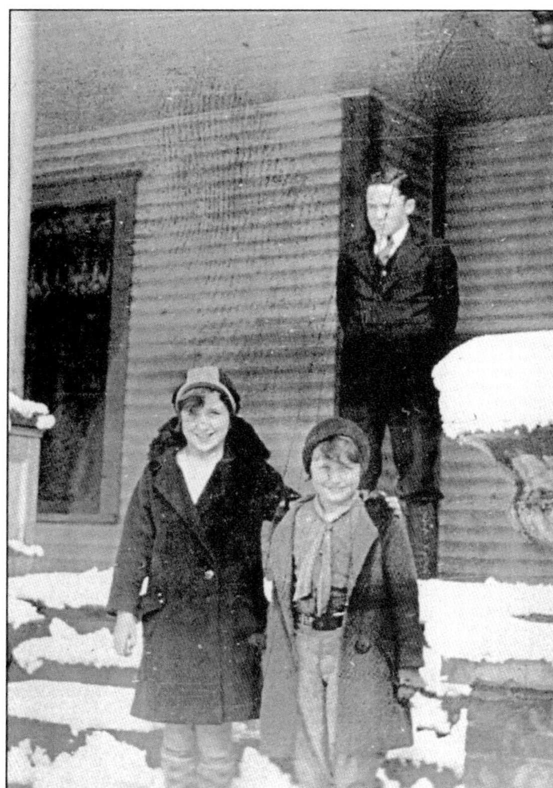

Charles Troutman's children, Pearl (left) and Carolyn, visited their grandparents as much as possible, always looking forward to surprises from their grandpa. (Courtesy of Pearl Troutman Alexander.)

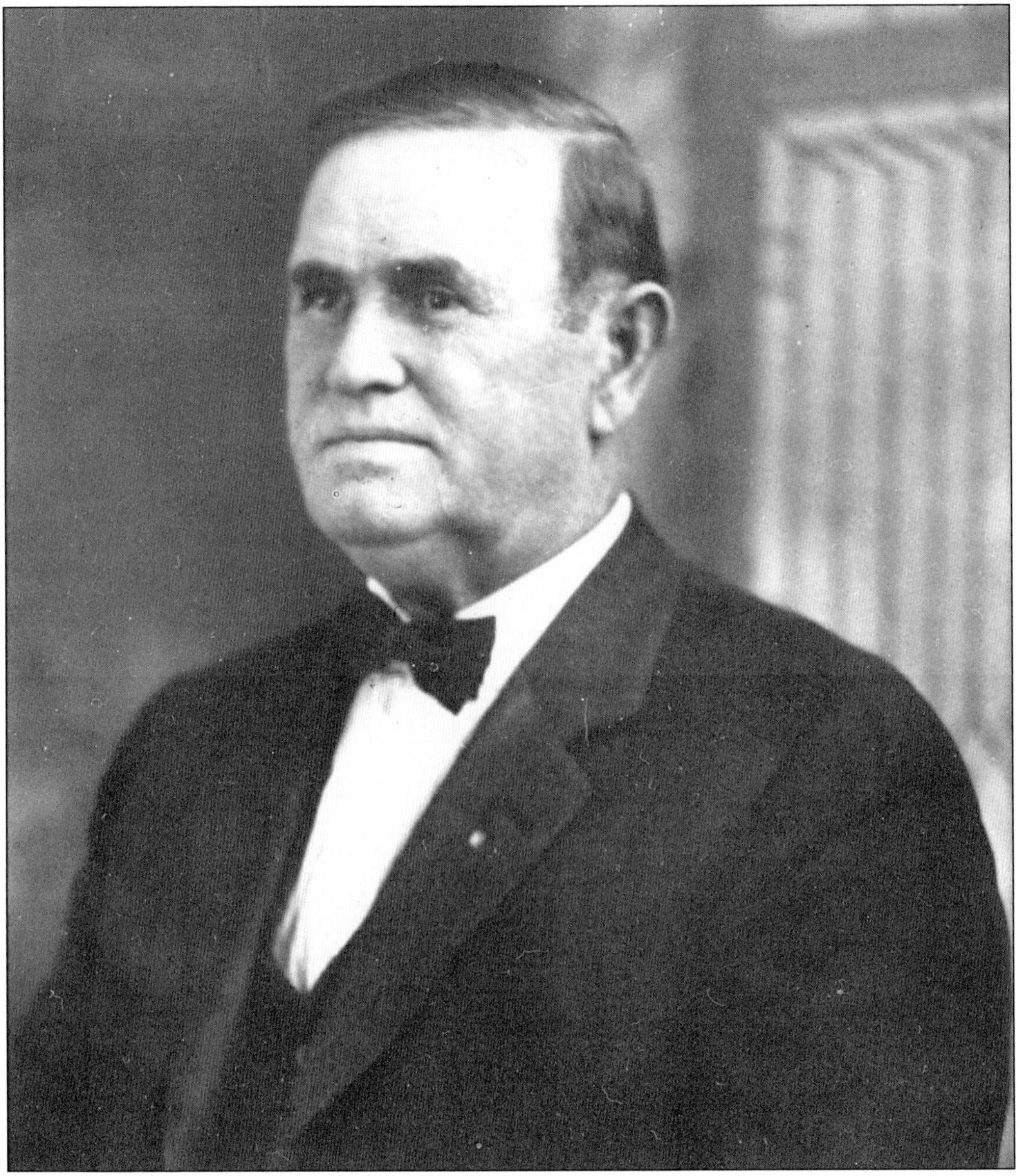

B. A. Troutman, one of Mooresville's pioneer contractors, described himself as a "lumber man" to an *Enterprise* reporter in 1931. He worked for J. W. Brown and learned the construction business before branching out on his own, building a sawmill to prepare timber for homes and businesses. People started coming to him to build their homes. He said, "I would stop my sawing and draw up a plan, asking the number of rooms, the sizes of windows and doors and all the other details." Troutman said, "I have two rules for myself. One was to finish the job when I promised to, and the other was to give just a little more than I had contracted to give." He was the first president of the Mooresville Ice Cream Company, providing milk from his own cows for the confection. Troutman said, "I sell the best milk you ever drank, most of it to the ice cream plant." (Courtesy of Pearl Troutman Alexander.)

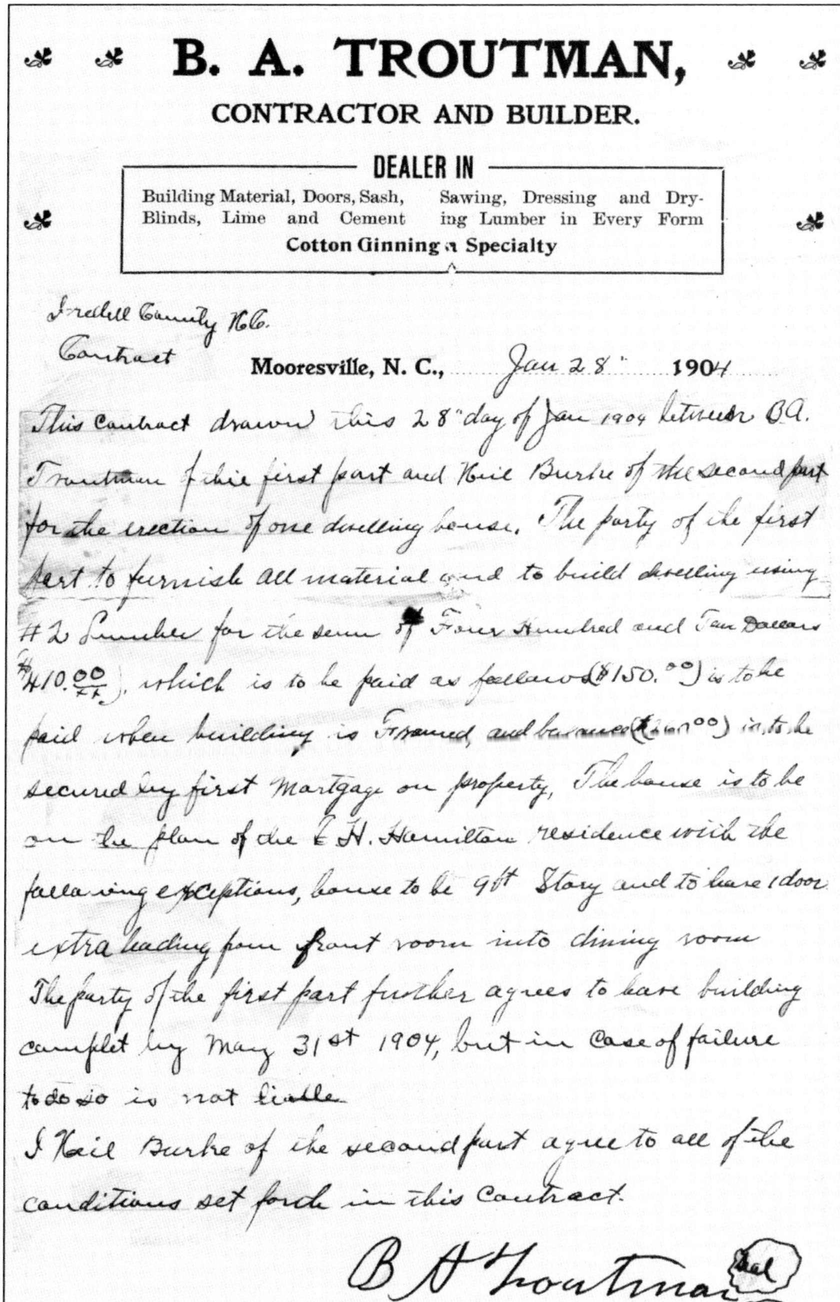

B. A. TROUTMAN,

CONTRACTOR AND BUILDER.

DEALER IN

Building Material, Doors, Sash, Blinds, Lime and Cement

Sawing, Dressing and Drying Lumber in Every Form

Cotton Ginning a Specialty

Iredell County N.C.
Contract

Mooresville, N. C., Jan 28th 1904

This Contract drawn this 28th day of Jan 1904 between B.A. Troutman of the first part and Neil Burke of the second part for the erection of one dwelling house. The party of the first part to furnish all material and to build dwelling using #2 Lumber for the sum of Four Hundred and Ten Dollars $410.00/xx, which is to be paid as follows ($150.00) is to be paid when building is Framed, and balance ($260.00) is to be secured by first Mortgage on property. The house is to be on the plan of the E.H. Hamilton residence with the following exceptions, house to be 9ft Story and to have 1 door extra leading from front room into dining room. The party of the first part further agrees to have building complet by May 31st 1904, but in Case of failure to do so is not liable.
I Neil Burke of the second part agree to all of the conditions set forth in this Contract.

B A Troutman (Seal)
Neal Burke (Seal)

On January 28, 1904, Neal Burke (father of Selma Burke) hired Troutman to build "one dwelling house" for $410. The home design followed the Hamilton residence plan and was to be constructed with No. 2 lumber. Burke paid $150 when the structure was framed and financed the remaining $260 secured by a first mortgage. The home was completed on May 31, 1904. (Courtesy of Pearl Troutman Alexander.)

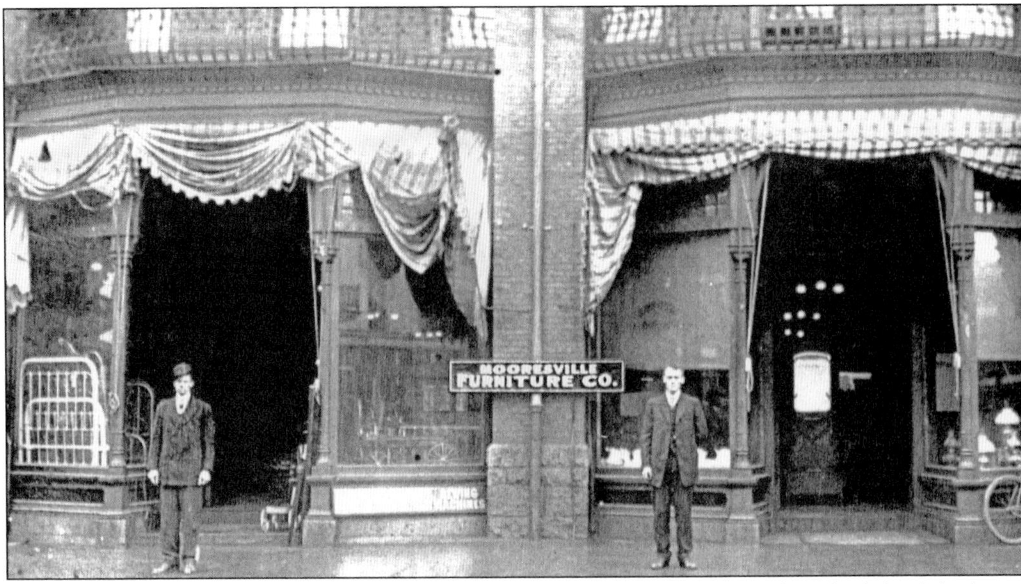

Mooresville Furniture Company, owned by B. A. and L. L. Troutman, produced solid oak bedroom suites, sideboards, chiffoniers, and mantels. The company's business included dressed lumber and building materials of all kinds, including lime, cement, bricks, and plaster. Four sawmills supplied an extensive list of customers. "Mr. Gus," as B. A. Troutman was known, was involved in home construction and real estate in the Mooresville area and estimated that "he owned 11 or 12 acres" on the North Main Street property. Pictured in front of the Main Street store are Roy Troutman, left, and Charles A. Troutman Sr. (right). (Courtesy of Pearl Troutman Alexander.)

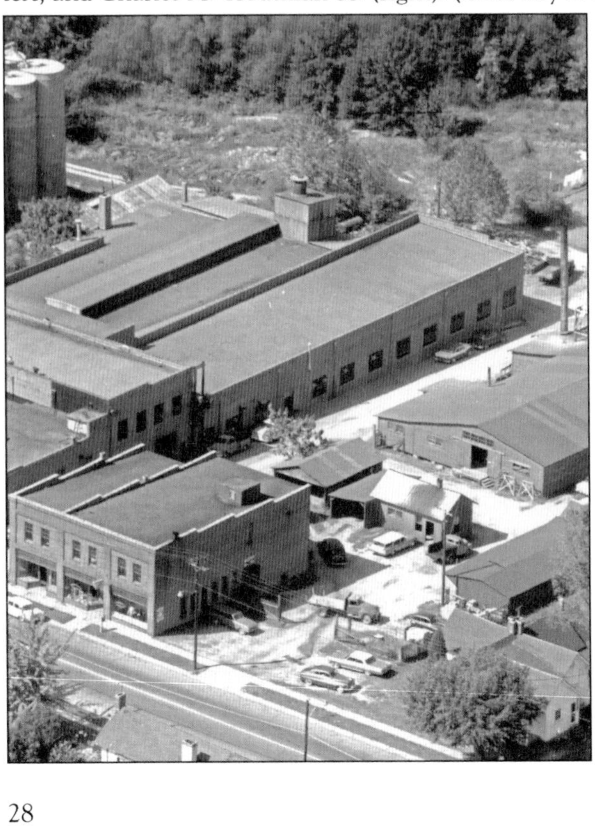

The Troutman family operated their furniture store, planing and sawmills, construction operations, and farm from a single location on North Main Street. This aerial photograph taken by Fletcher Davis shows the buildings and warehouse. (Courtesy of Robert Holthouser Jr.)

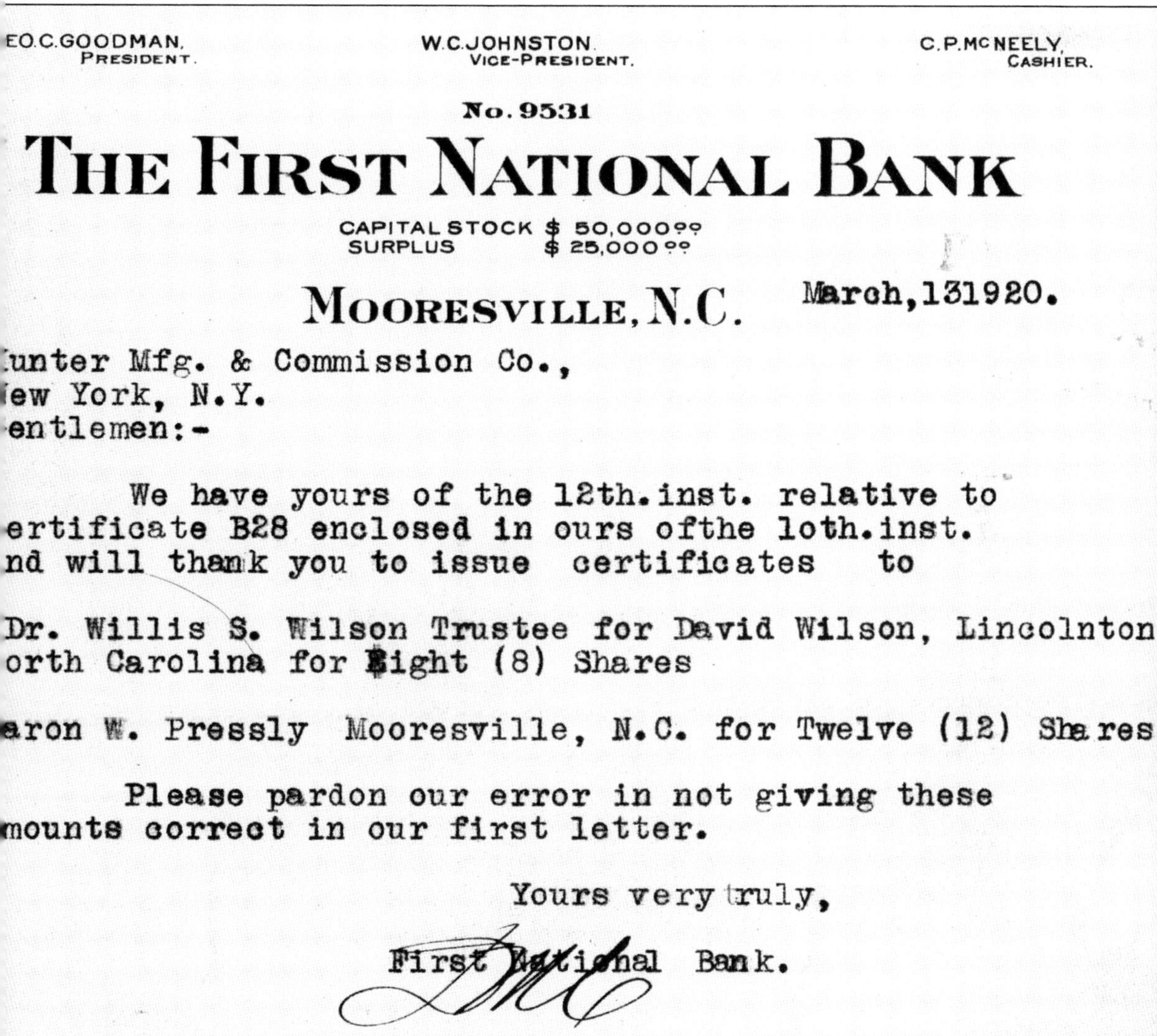

EO.C.GOODMAN, PRESIDENT. W.C.JOHNSTON, VICE-PRESIDENT. C.P.MCNEELY, CASHIER.

No. 9531

THE FIRST NATIONAL BANK

CAPITAL STOCK $ 50,000.00
SURPLUS $ 25,000.00

MOORESVILLE, N.C. March,131920.

:unter Mfg. & Commission Co.,
ew York, N.Y.
entlemen:-

We have yours of the 12th.inst. relative to ertificate B28 enclosed in ours ofthe 10th.inst. nd will thank you to issue certificates to

Dr. Willis S. Wilson Trustee for David Wilson, Lincolnton orth Carolina for Eight (8) Shares

aron W. Pressly Mooresville, N.C. for Twelve (12) Shares.

Please pardon our error in not giving these mounts correct in our first letter.

Yours very truly,

First National Bank.

The Bank of Mooresville (First National Bank) was started in 1900, organized under a state charter with an initial capital of $15,000. Located on Main Street beside Turner Hardware, the institution played a large role in the development and expansion of the community. In 1914, the officers included George C. Goodman, W. C. Johnston, C. P. McNeely, C. F. Melchor, and J. F. Dorroh. It was described by Waters in 1914: "The career of the bank has been one of steady progress, with dividends being paid since the first year of its organization."

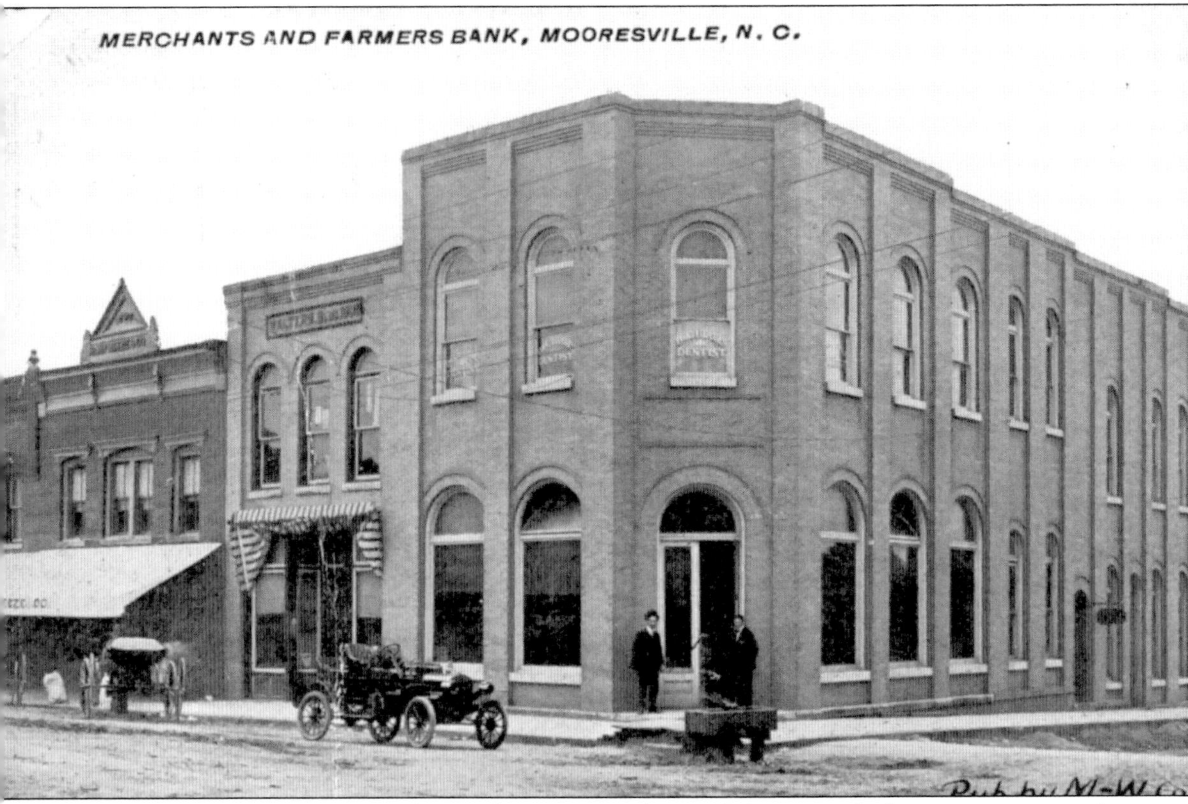

Merchant's and Farmer's Bank joined First National in 1907. It occupied a "conspicuous corner" on North Main Street. Officers include E. W. Brawley, W. C. Johnston, H. D. Mills, Mort McKnight, B. A. Troutman, and G. M. Kipka. Starting with a capital of $20,000, it continued to do a brisk business until the Great Depression, when it closed in 1933. Piedmont Bank and Trust Company opened for business in 1946 in the corner location.

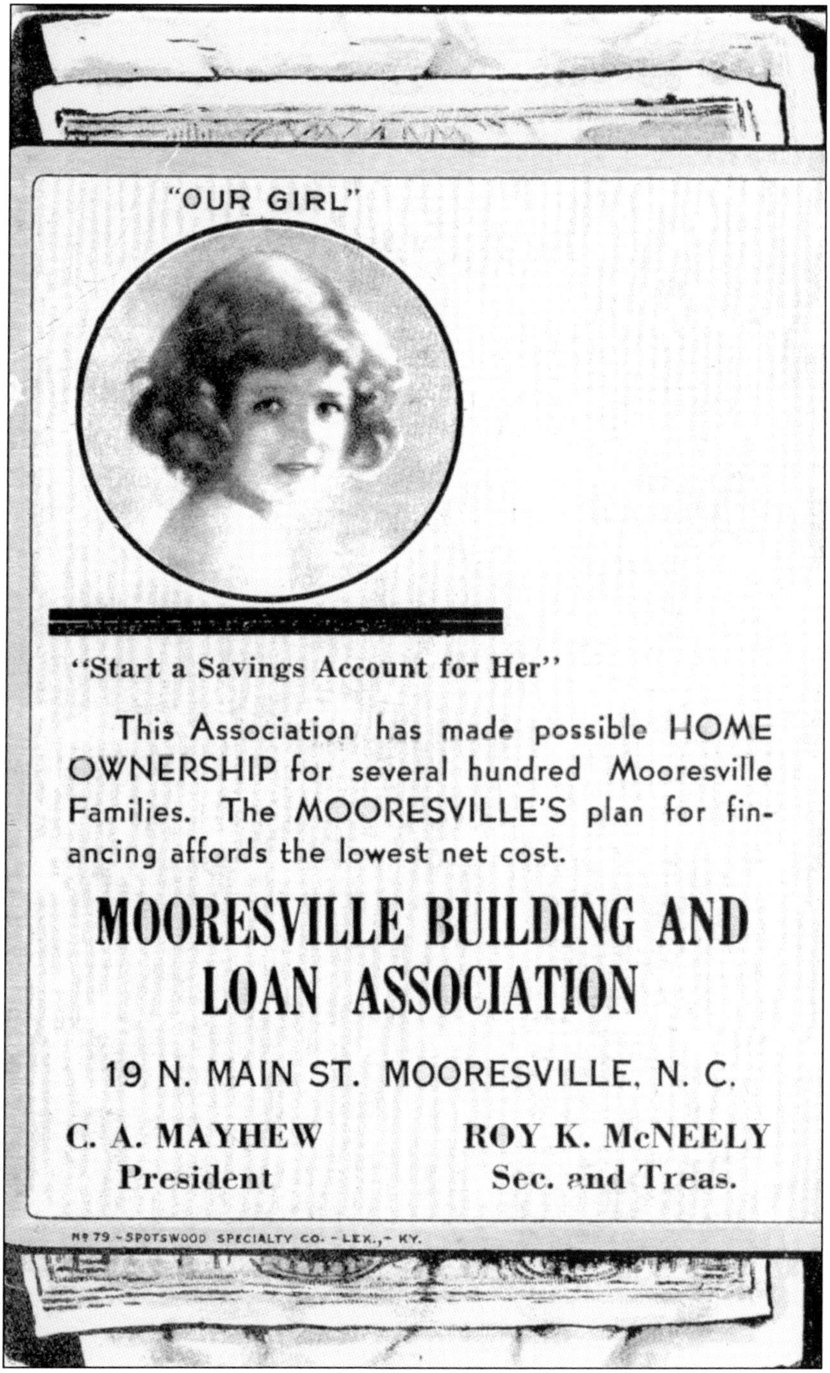

Mooresville Loan and Trust and Mooresville Building and Loan Association, both organized c. 1900, provided financial support for the building of homes and other structures in town. The "building and loan" was responsible for about 200 structures in and around town. Mooresville Loan and Trust offered insurance, loans, and management of rental and real estate transactions. Both companies were organized by community leaders like George C. Goodman, Zebulon V. Turlington, and J. P. Mills. (Courtesy of Sloop Collection.)

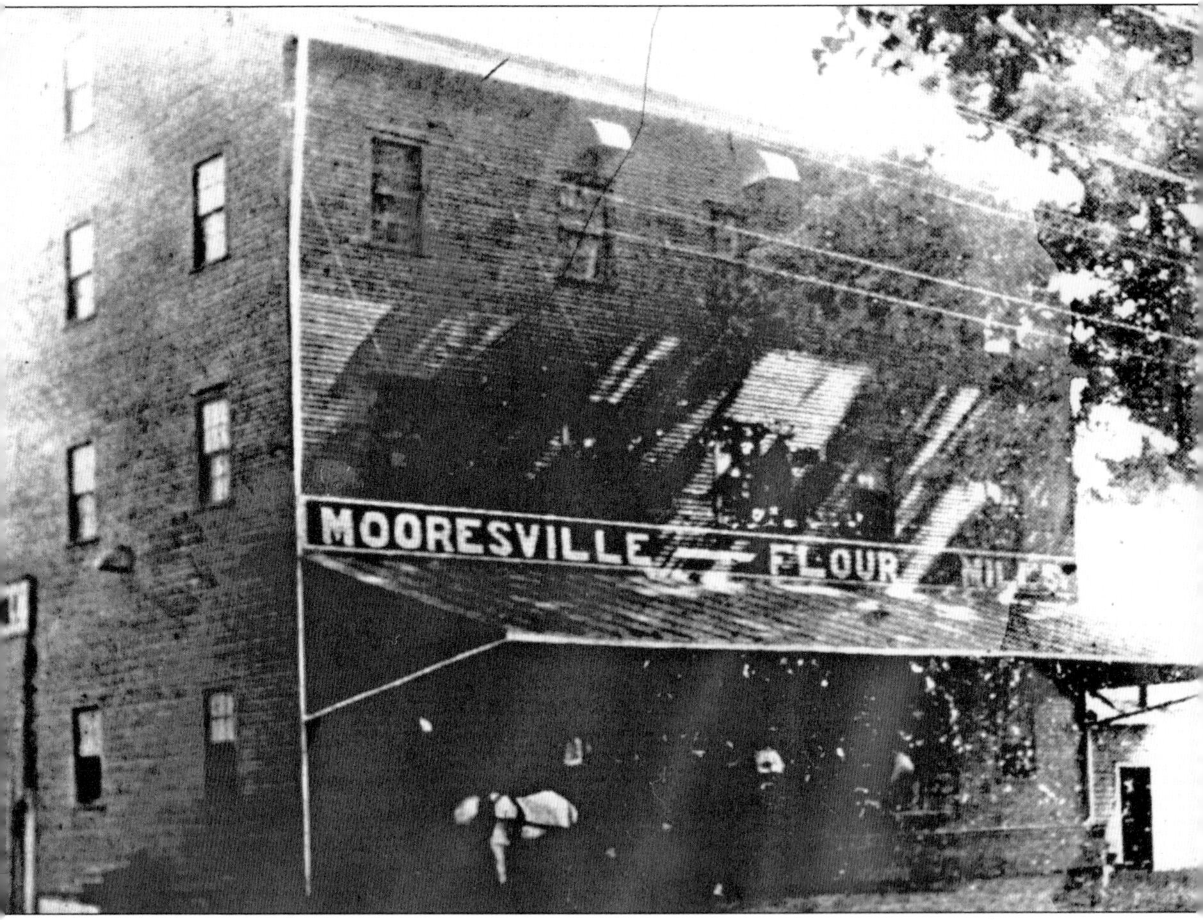

W. W. Melchor operated the Big Oak Roller Mill in the late 19th century on North Main Street next door to the home of John F. Moore. The water tank on the property provided water for both the mill and the Melchor home across the street. When Melchor entered the grocery business in 1914, he sold the mill to Espy Brawley, who produced specialty flour and meal as well as feed for livestock. A fire in 1924 destroyed the original mill. Brawley built a new building in 1926 and produced patented flour known as the "Up to Date" brand. In 1928, Mooresville Flour Mills was incorporated by Brawley, W. N. Lentz, and Dr. A. E. Bell.

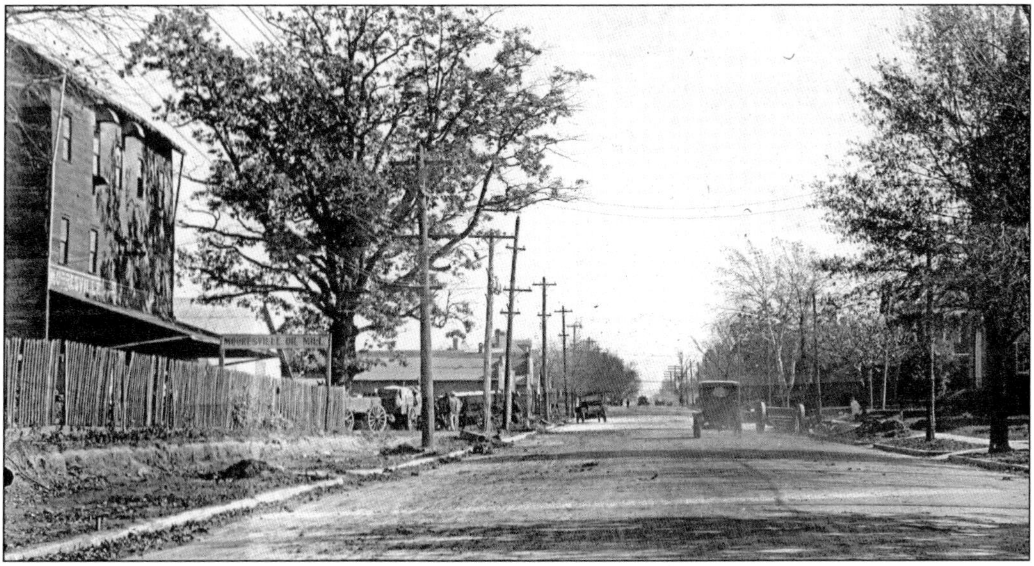

The site of the flour operations was adjacent to a railroad siding and enjoyed a prime location on the wide North Main Street. Farmers from southern Iredell and other counties brought their corn and wheat to be processed into flour and meal. The mill had a daily capacity of 125 barrels of flour and 250 bushels of corn. All products delivered to the mill went through a thorough cleaning and purifying process. Advertising later boasted that the products were "untouched by human hands."

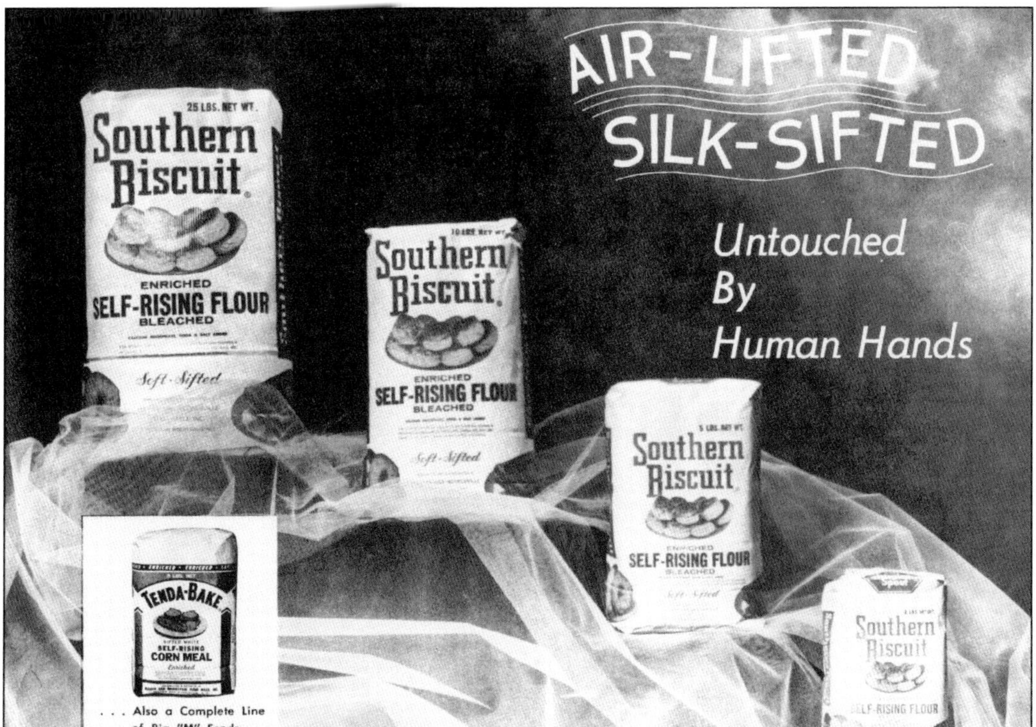

Mooresville Flour Mill products began to have regional prominence and offered yet another fine product to come from Mooresville producers.

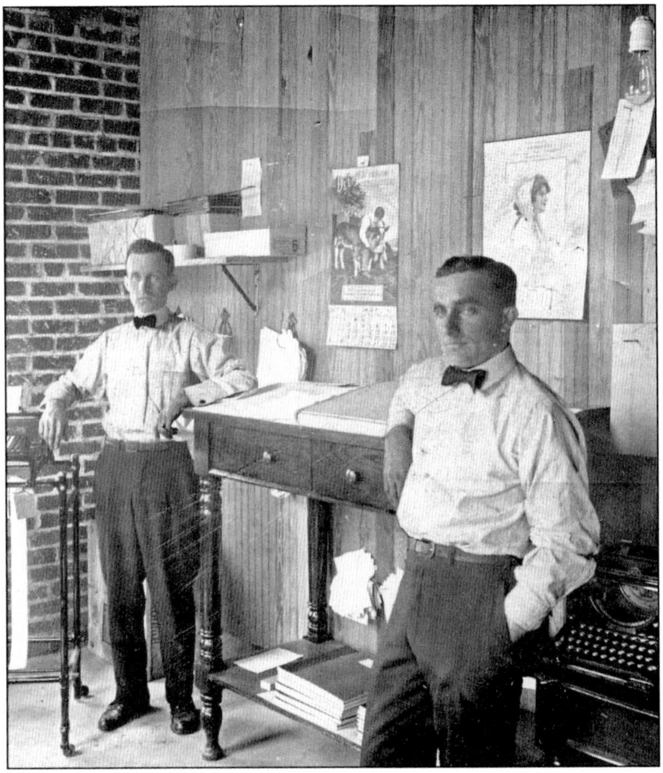

Southern Iredell dairy farmers joined forces in 1914 to operate a creamery in Mooresville. Much of the butterfat sold in Hickory was coming from Mooresville and Iredell County, so it seemed prudent to the local farmers to organize their own creamery. Stock was sold for $25 per share, and $6,000 was raised in two days. To insure that the operation was truly a "cooperative," stockholders were limited to four shares each. The Mooresville Cooperative Creamery produced large quantities of butterfat and sold it in regional markets. Autumn Leaf butter was produced in the plant at the corner of Moore Avenue and Broad Street and was available in local grocery stores. Eugene Johnston (left) and William Perry are shown in the creamery office.

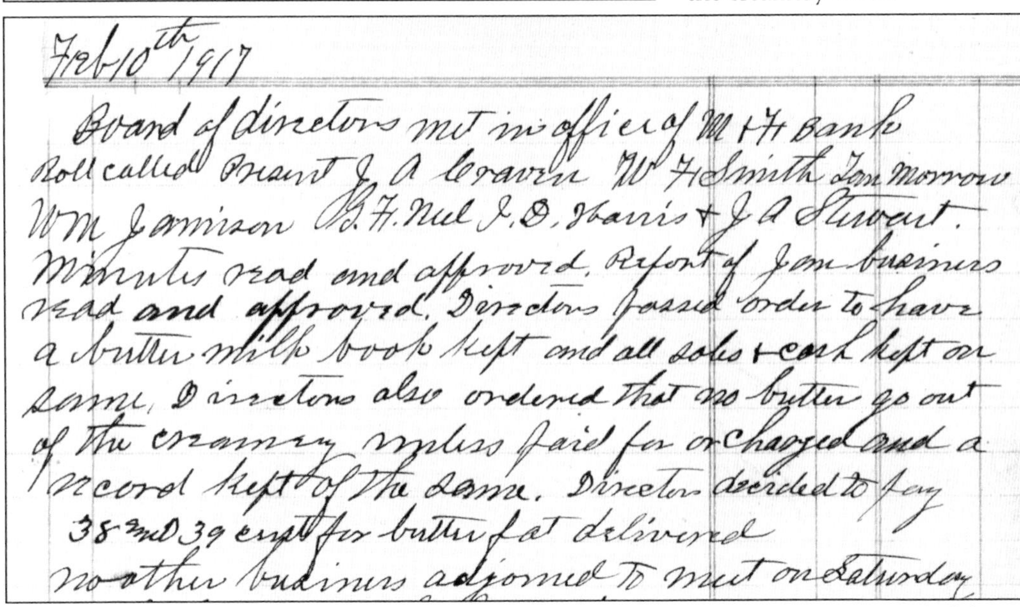

Feb 10th 1917
Board of directors met in office of M & F Bank
Roll called Present J. A. Craven W. F. Smith Jon Morrow
W M Jamison B. F. Neel J. O. Harris & J A Stewart.
Minutes read and approved. Report of Jan business
read and approved. Directors passed order to have
a butter milk book kept and all sales & cash kept on
same. Directors also ordered that no butter go out
of the creamery unless paid for or charged and a
record kept of the same. Directors decided to pay
38 and 39 cents for butter fat delivered
no other business adjourned to meet on Saturday

J. A. Stewart kept meticulous records of all creamery activities and the minutes of all board meetings. The price of butterfat was the single most important subject for each meeting, as this determined the success of the creamery operation. The directors were actively involved in the growth and management of the town and supported organizations like the chamber of commerce with funds and involvement. On March 12, 1921, they voted to improve and beautify the building in an economical way.

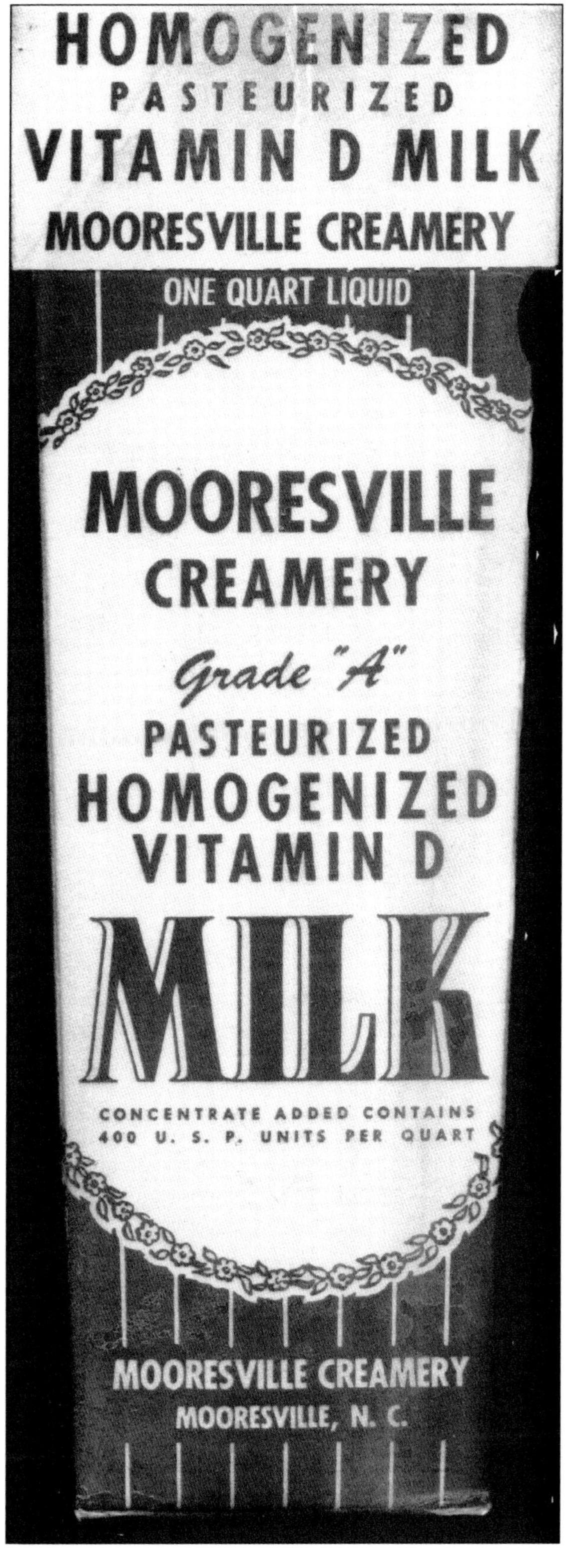

In 1937, pasteurizing equipment was installed to make Grade A milk for local consumption. Whole milk was purchased from farmers in the cooperative and processed in the local plant. Daily delivery from the creamery resulted in additional revenues for the farmers and freedom from the delivery and collection process. The milk produced was of the finest quality, establishing another "Moor" product as the best available. "Pure-Pak" coated paper cartons replaced the standard glass bottles containing the slogan, "I serve healthful Mooresville Creamery milk . . . it's country fresh." Other Moor quality products included homogenized milk, buttermilk, whipping cream, chocolate milk, orangeade, and Autumn Leaf butter.

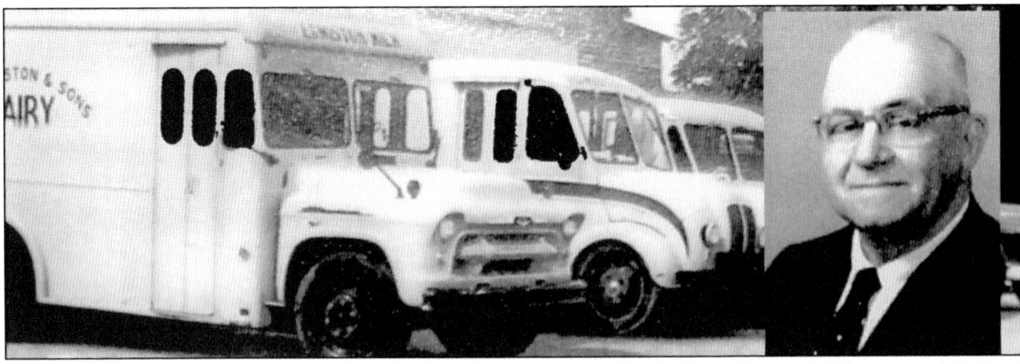

Edmiston and Sons Dairy was founded on June 1, 1924, by Robert Samuel Edmiston. He built his business on the purchase of the J. A. Stewart Dairy. At the time of the purchase, Stewart was delivering 19 gallons of milk to his customers in Mooresville. Edmiston's dairy grew, and daily deliveries increased to 1,500 gallons to 400 homes. During these years, the herd increased from 16 Jersey cattle to 150 Ayrshire cows, with Edmiston becoming a leader in the National Ayrshire Breeders Association. Edmiston Dairy merged with Rowan Dairy on July 1, 1959. (Courtesy of Bill and Virginia Edmiston.)

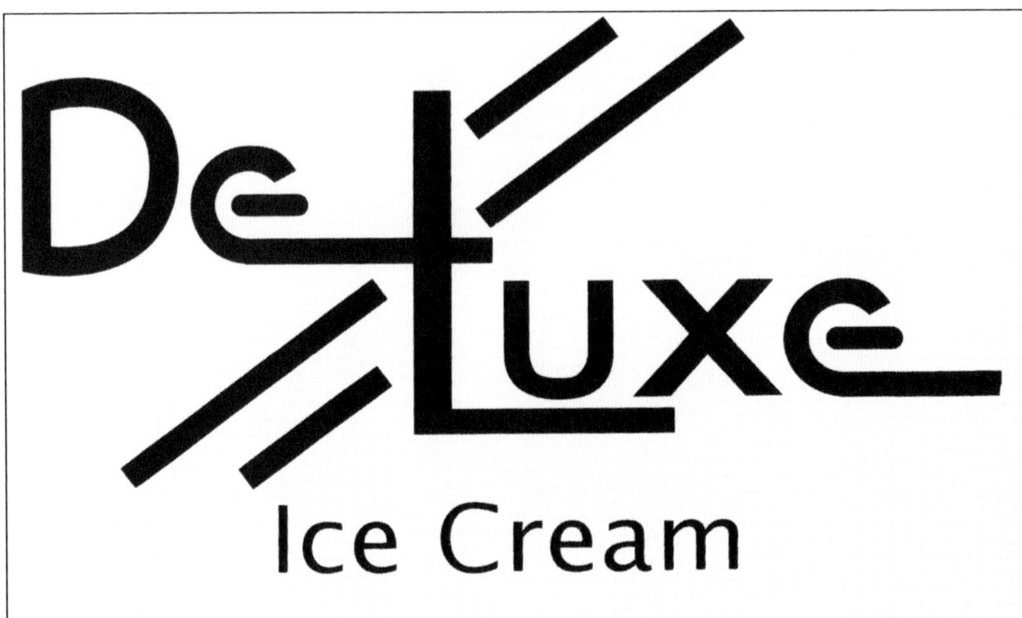

The Mooresville Ice Cream Company was organized on February 9, 1924, to supply high-quality ice cream to the region. The original investors included B. A. Troutman, Tom Morrow, Masoud Salem, E. H. Francis, Joe Ikall, Charles Mack, Side Mack, Hugh Sloop, and Miller Drug Company. Charles Mack developed the original recipe and was the master ice cream maker for the company. DeLuxe became another "Moor" brand that was known for its premium quality. (Courtesy of Mooresville Ice Cream Company.)

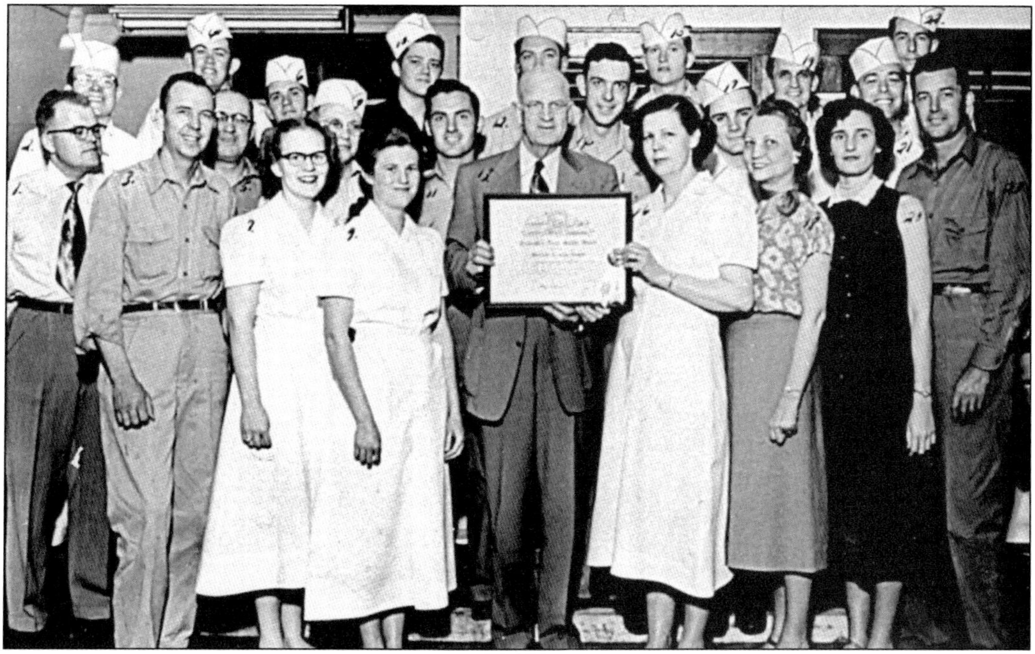

Robert Edmiston succeeded B. A. Troutman as president of the company. Ralph Millsaps served as secretary-treasurer and general manager until 1943, when he became president of the Mooresville Ice Cream Company. The Millsaps family purchased Edmiston's interest in the company in 1947. R. C. Millsaps became president, with his sons Harvey and Clyde serving as vice presidents. (Courtesy of Mooresville Ice Cream Company.)

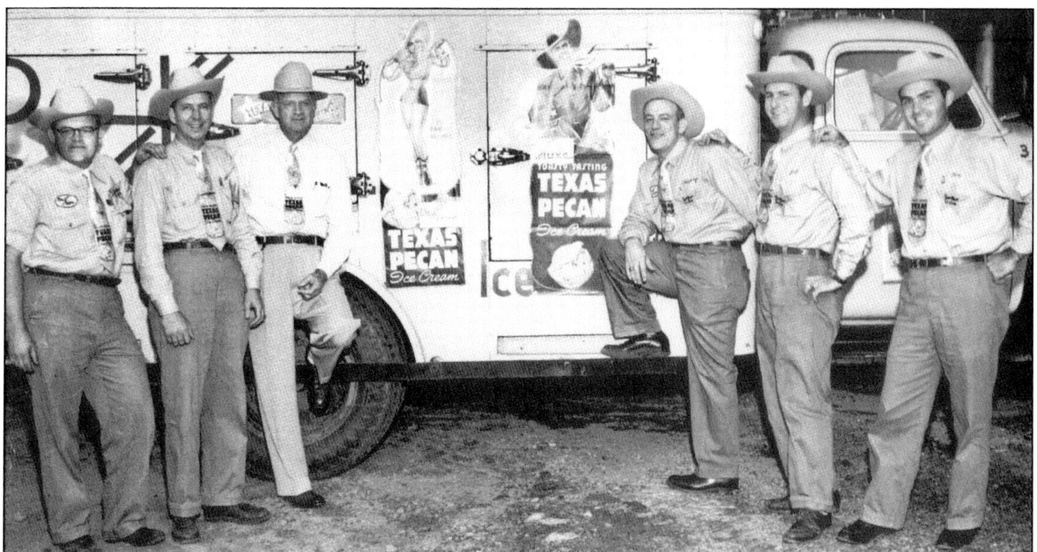

The company broadened its line of products to include more flavors of ice cream, Popsicles, fudge bars, and the Mooresville bar. New products were added and promoted over the years, such as the locally popular Texas Pecan flavor. The company engaged in an extensive promotion of the product in 1954, using a wide variety of visual merchandising materials and marketing strategies. Main promoters were, from left to right, Ralph Millsaps, Harry Bradshaw, R. C. Millsaps, Harvey Millsaps, J. C. Brooks, and Thomas Howard. (Courtesy of Mooresville Ice Cream Company.)

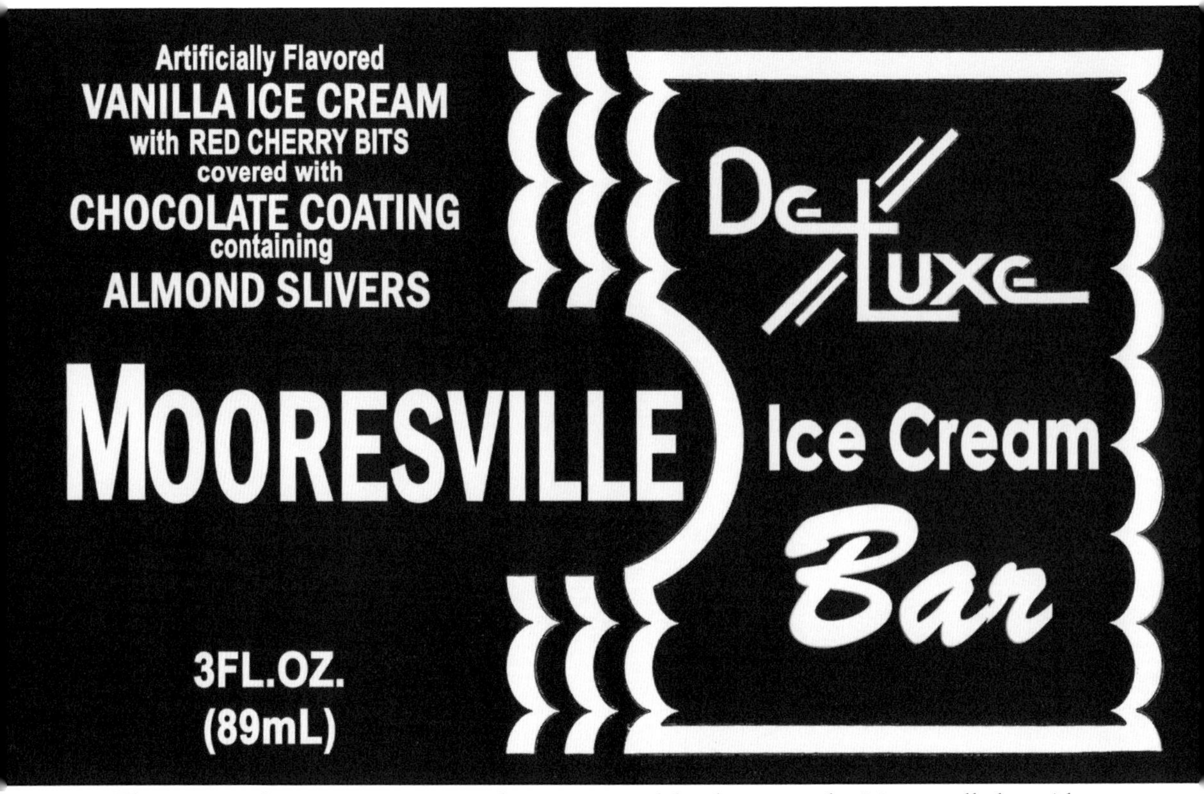

The company's signature ice cream bar was named for the town, the Mooresville bar. Always a favorite of customers, it is part of a product line that strives to provide high-quality refreshment for everyone. (Courtesy of Mooresville Ice Cream Company.)

Two

King Cotton and Moor Quality

Cotton was a minor crop prior to 1793, thanks to the labor-intensive requirement to separate cottonseeds from the cotton. In the 18th century, 25 farm hands working on 25 cotton bales often took 100 days to seed the crop. While widely grown, cotton was a small crop intended for local use in homespun cloth. There were small jenny mills, sometimes on plantations, operated by hand, mules, or oxen, producing a crude yarn suitable for homespun. The Eli Whitney cotton gin did the work of 10 men. As the gin was improved and access spread, it encouraged Mooresville-area farmers to grow the crop, which could be sold easily. Crop was hauled overland or on riverboats to access points north to powered textile spinning mills.

Beginning about 1840, cotton became a leading cash crop for North Carolina farmers. The demand for cotton focused farmers primarily on growing the crop in the South until 1840, when the effort to create new planting areas slowed. This allowed more resources to be diverted to cotton processing. Moreover, pioneering efforts proved that cotton mills could be highly profitable. The lure of being near the fields caused many to think about creating a powered textile mill. Mooresville was ready for the textile industry. It had immediate access to the railroad and vast fields of cotton crops. In 1893, James Elbert Sherrill and a group of investors organized the Mooresville Cotton Mills, the first powered cotton plant in Mooresville. The local cotton economy was strong, and the Lorene Cotton Seed Oil Mill processed cotton from farmers throughout the area, making it available for shipping and sales to local and regional markets. In 1906, the Dixie Cotton Mill began producing yarns for the cotton industry.

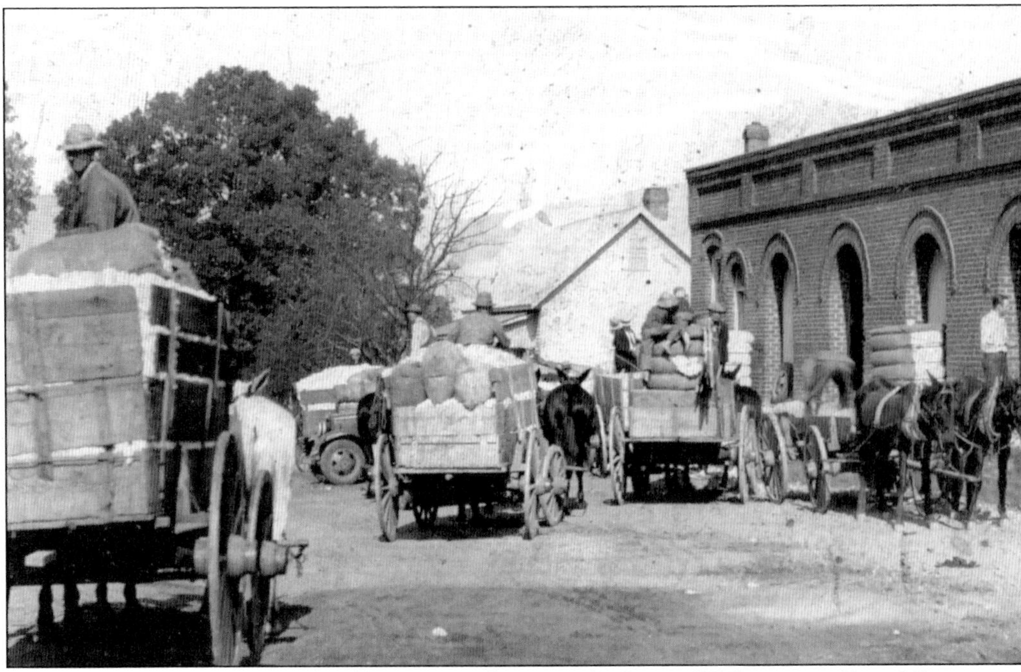

The Lorene Cotton Seed Oil Mill was started in 1906 by James W. Brown on Broad Street near the corner of Iredell Avenue. The mill had a daily capacity of 25 tons of cottonseed. The adjacent warehouse was built for the storage of machinery and heavy loads of cotton. The warehouse had easy access to main roads, particularly Broad Street leading into Mooresville from the Shepherds and Statesville vicinity. The warehouse soon replaced the cotton loading platform across Center Avenue from the depot, making this lot available for a small park. (Courtesy of Harry H. Hart.)

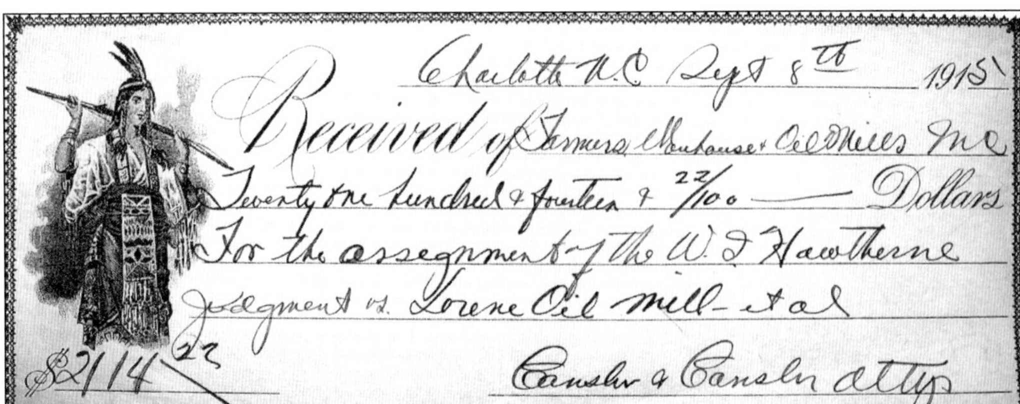

Charlotte N.C. Sept 8th 1915

Received of Farmers Warehouse & Oil Mills Inc

Twenty one hundred & fourteen & 22/100 Dollars

For the assignment of the W. D. Hawthorne judgment vs. Lorene Oil mill et al

$2114 22

Cansler & Cansler attys

COLUMBIA BOND

In 1911, the Farmer's Warehouse and Oil Mills, under the leadership of cotton merchant Steve Hart, purchased the Lorene Mill for $2,114.22. He renamed the facilities Farmers' Warehouse and Oil Mills, Inc., and established one of the most efficient and active cotton processing concerns in the state. Hart was a talented cotton grader and continued in the cotton business as S. A. Hart Cotton, Inc. (Courtesy of Harry H. Hart.)

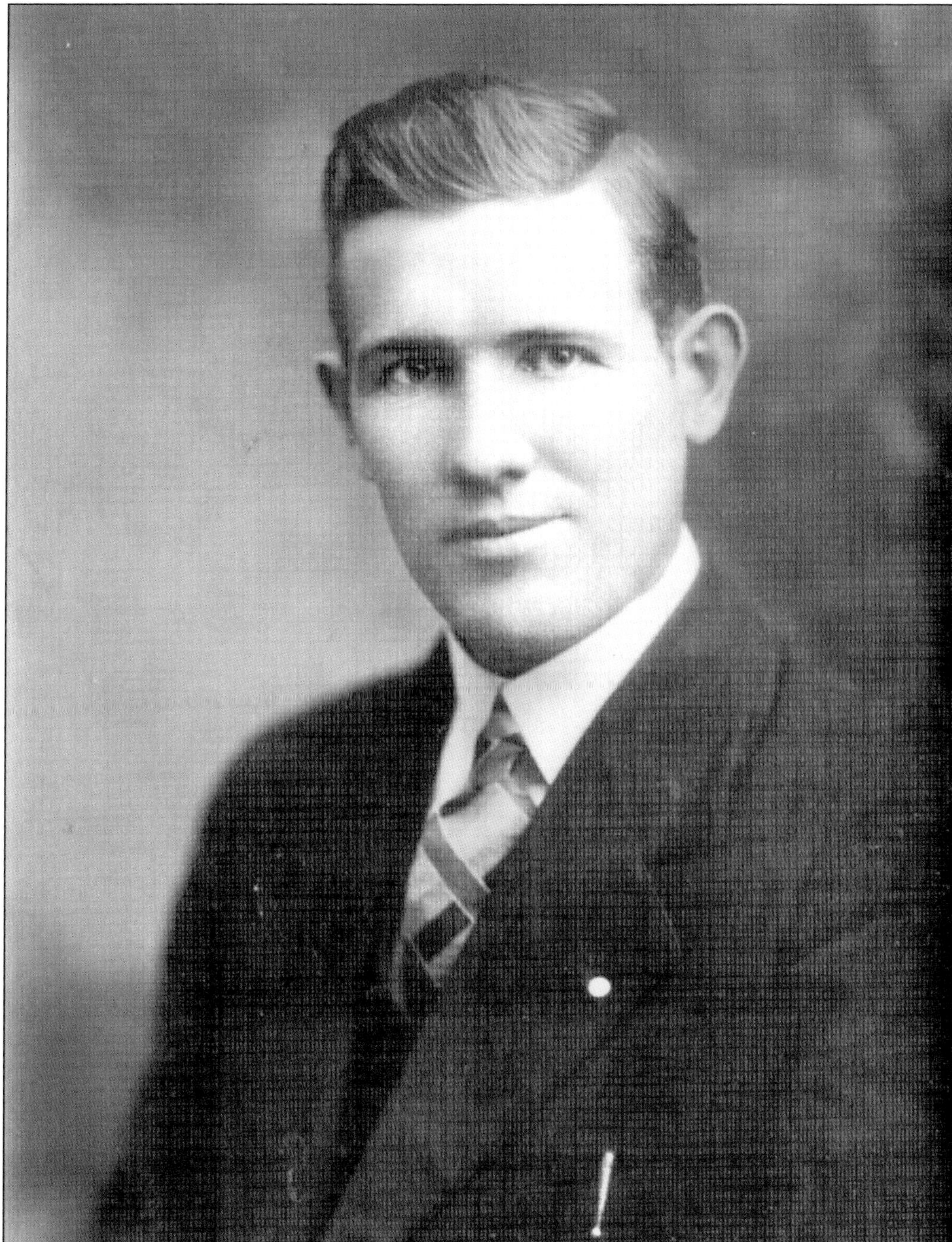

Steve Hart was a young cotton merchant from a family of farmers living at the Rowan County line in the Prospect community. He organized farmers in the area and formed the Farmers' Warehouse and Oil Mills, Inc., Mooresville's oldest active corporation. The warehouse and mill prospered, and tons of cotton left Mooresville for faraway markets from the siding on Broad Street. (Courtesy of Harry H. Hart.)

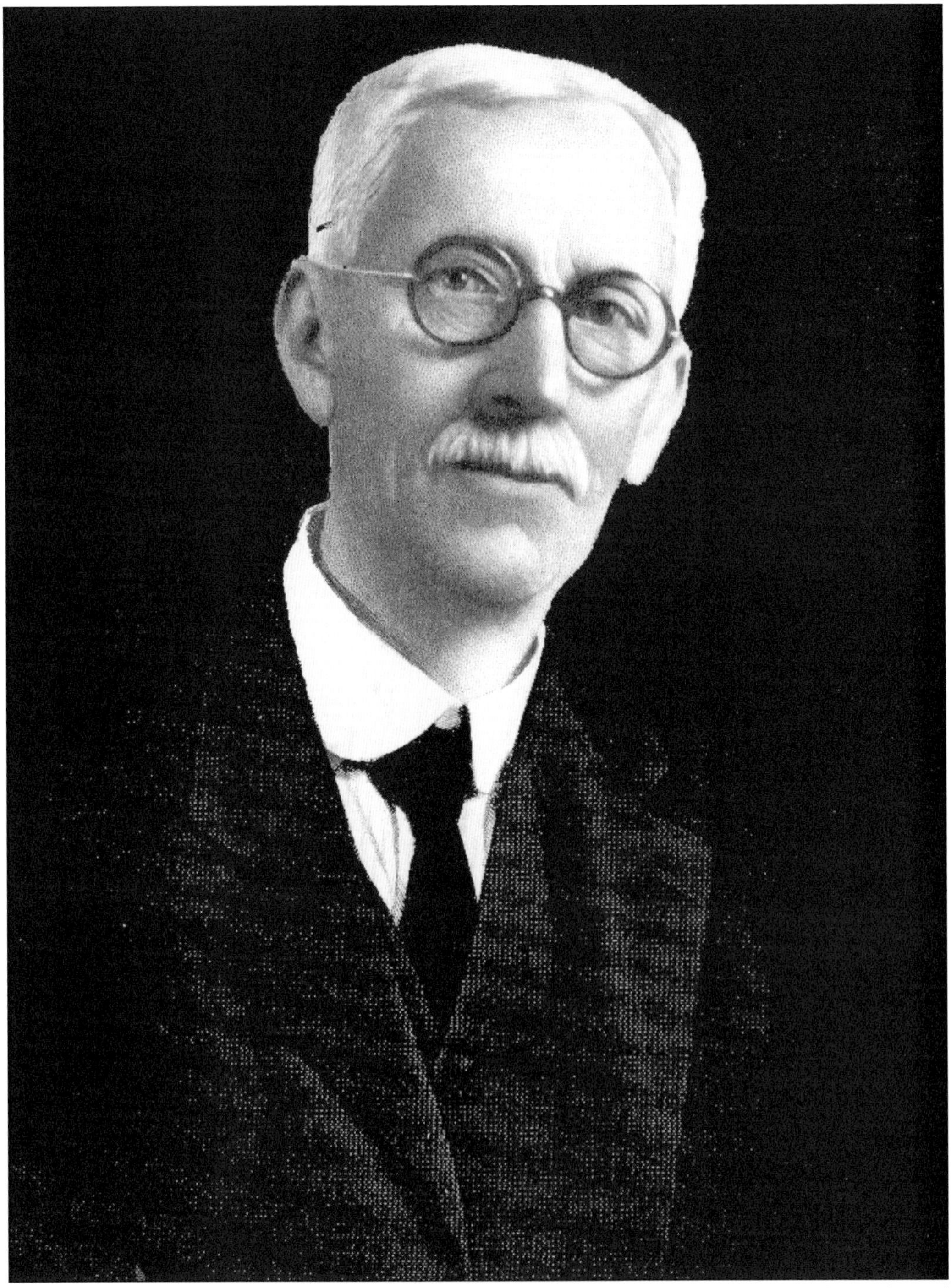

James Elbert Sherrill came to Mooresville from Sherrills Ford in 1874 to work in the Culp and Caldwell store. Described as a clever young man, he joined with Issac Harris to buy the firm and continue operations as Harris and Sherrill. This general merchandise business was located on Main Street adjacent to the depot. Sherrill married Margaret Emma Harris in 1875 and later built a home at 304 South Main Street. (Courtesy of Fletcher Davis Studio.)

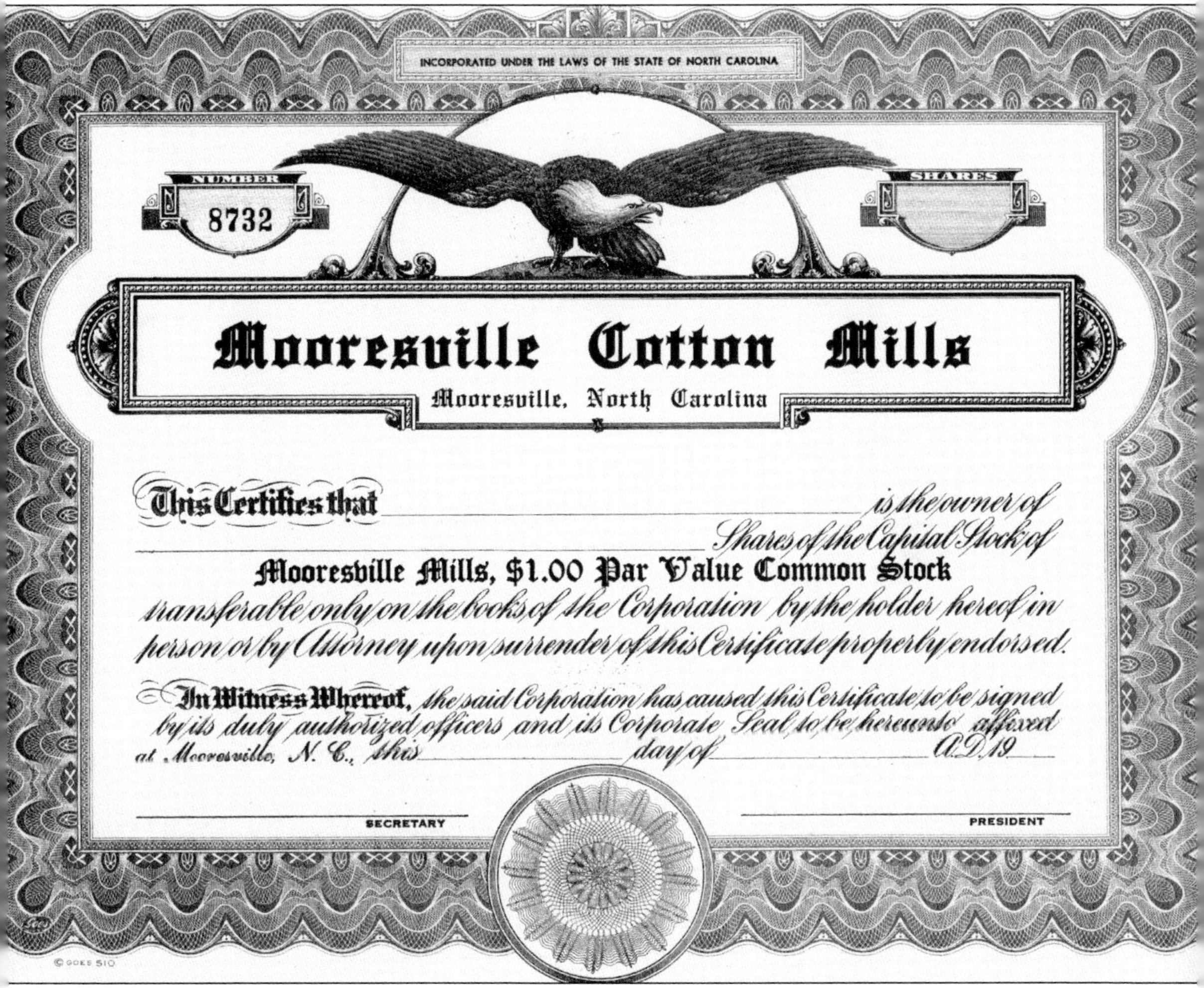

INCORPORATED UNDER THE LAWS OF THE STATE OF NORTH CAROLINA

NUMBER 8732

SHARES

Mooresville Cotton Mills

Mooresville, North Carolina

This Certifies that ______________________ is the owner of ______________________ Shares of the Capital Stock of

Mooresville Mills, $1.00 Par Value Common Stock

transferable only on the books of the Corporation by the holder hereof in person or by Attorney upon surrender of this Certificate properly endorsed.

In Witness Whereof, the said Corporation has caused this Certificate to be signed by its duly authorized officers and its Corporate Seal to be hereunto affixed at Mooresville, N. C., this ____________ day of ____________ A.D. 19___

SECRETARY

PRESIDENT

© GOES 510

Sherrill took a personal interest in both the operations of the mill and the effort to sell stock. Support came from local citizens eager to get involved in a profitable operation that would bring economic stability to the town. During his 30-year presidency, assets grew from $25,000 to more than $5 million. He along with his partners, George C. Goodman and Pascal Boyd, brought job opportunities and employment to hundreds of Mooresville residents. (Courtesy of Burlington Industries.)

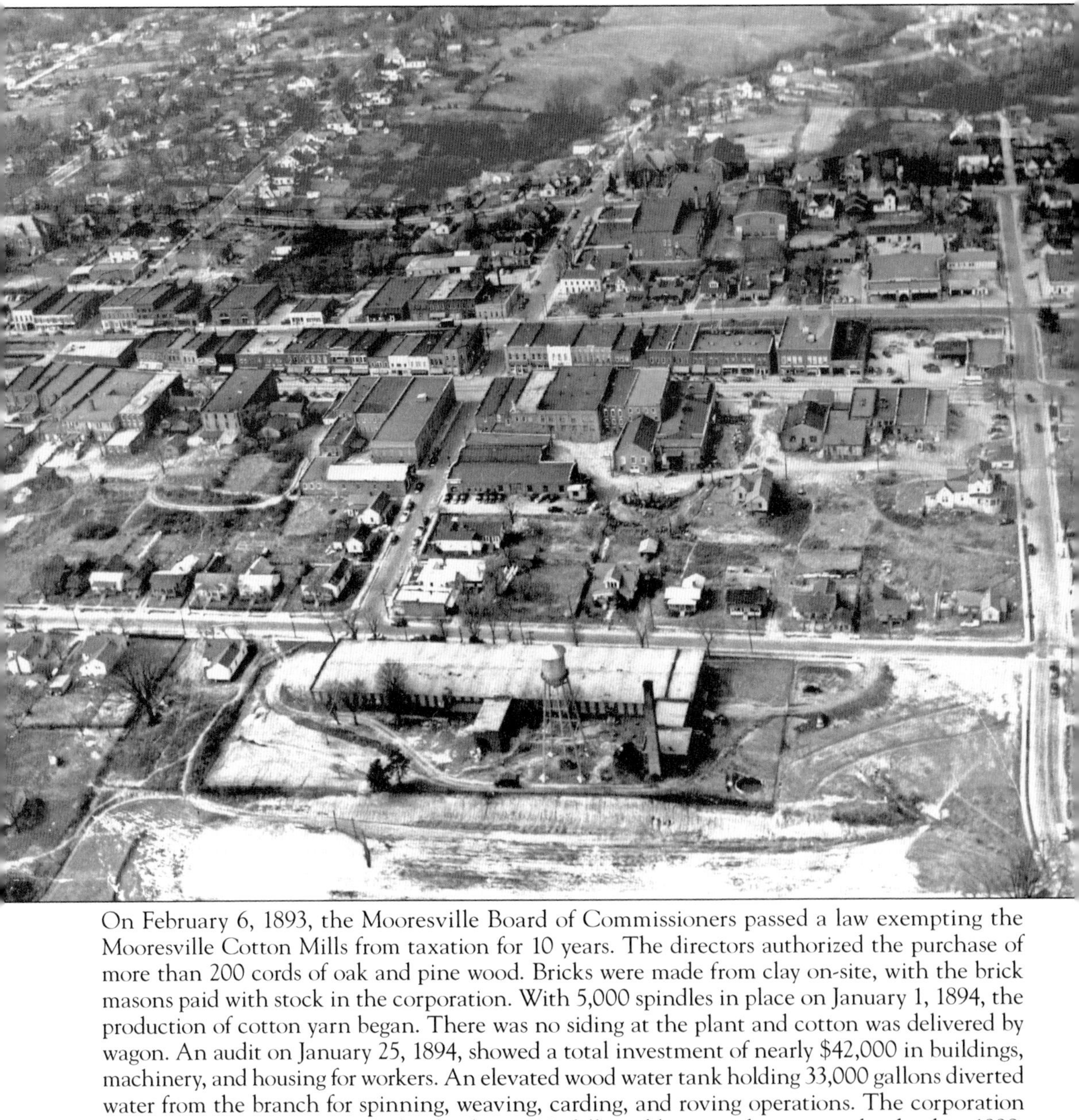

On February 6, 1893, the Mooresville Board of Commissioners passed a law exempting the Mooresville Cotton Mills from taxation for 10 years. The directors authorized the purchase of more than 200 cords of oak and pine wood. Bricks were made from clay on-site, with the brick masons paid with stock in the corporation. With 5,000 spindles in place on January 1, 1894, the production of cotton yarn began. There was no siding at the plant and cotton was delivered by wagon. An audit on January 25, 1894, showed a total investment of nearly $42,000 in buildings, machinery, and housing for workers. An elevated wood water tank holding 33,000 gallons diverted water from the branch for spinning, weaving, carding, and roving operations. The corporation declared its first, four-percent dividend in 1897, followed by an eight-percent dividend in 1898. (Courtesy of Burlington Industries.)

With the advent of Moor Quality towels, the corporate logo was changed to portray the character of the product. Fletcher Davis, photographer and artist, designed the first Moor Quality logo for the successful Turkish towel business. Depicting a Turk on horseback, it seemed to fit the product and was adopted by the Mooresville Mills as its logo. Tom McKnight compared the fighting spirit of the Moors with the fighting spirit and tenacity of the Mooresville Mills' management and employees. The sign of the Moor was used by the mill as its logo until 1955, when the Burlington Industries logo took its place. The Town of Mooresville uses the trademark as its seal today. (Courtesy of Bobbie and Oller Powers.)

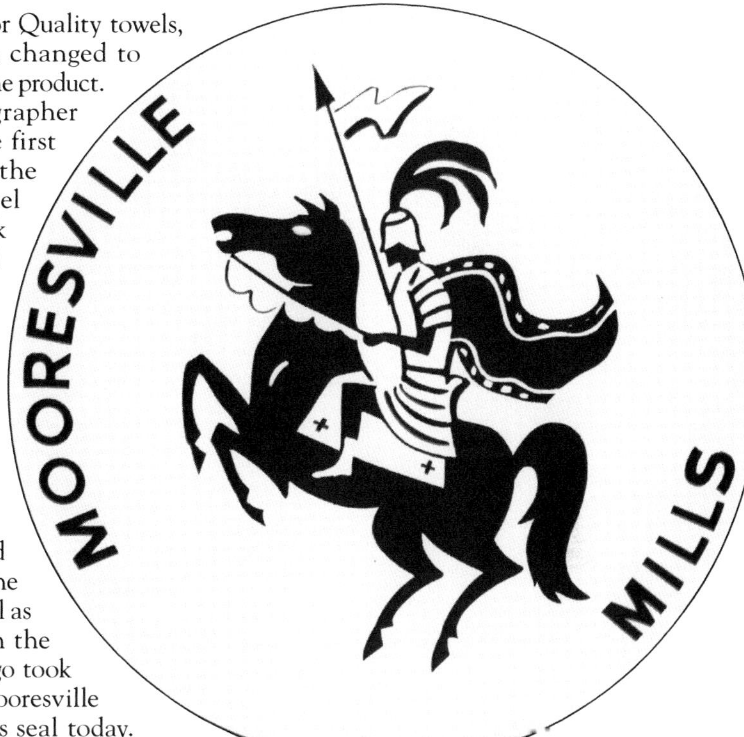

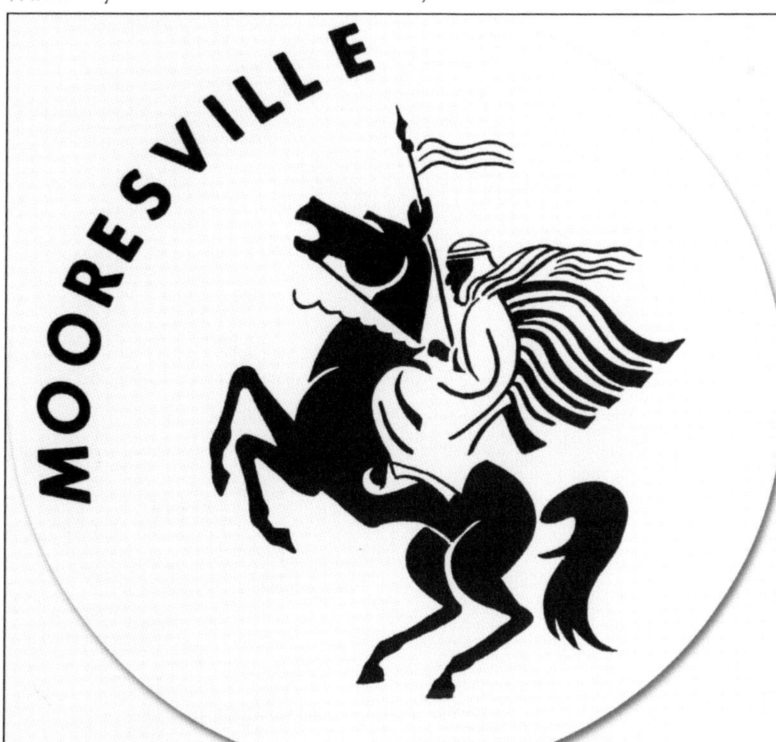

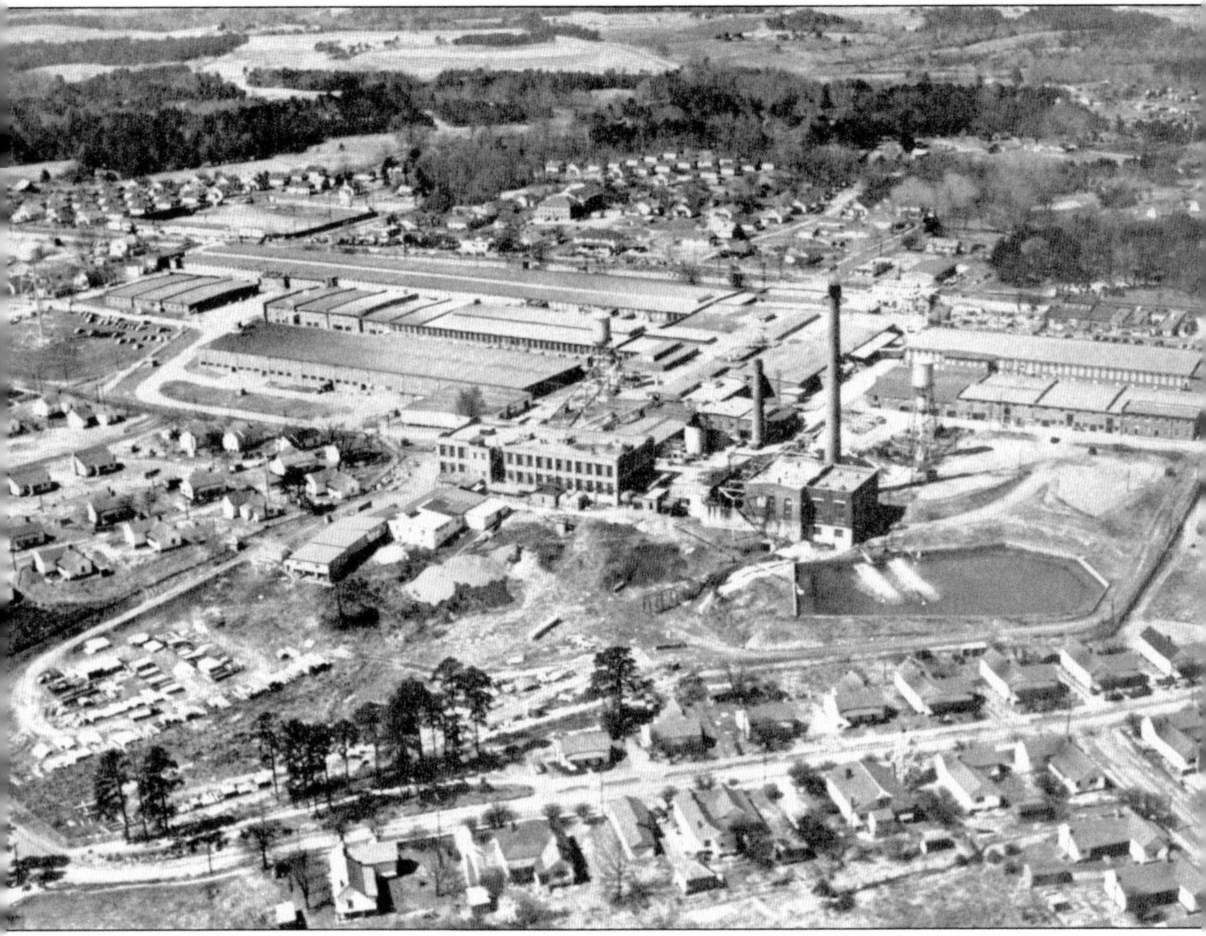

The Mooresville Cotton Mills was Mooresville's first and largest mechanized industry until 1999. It was an industrial revolution for the newly incorporated town, providing opportunities for employment as well as a market for local goods and services. The town grew with the mill, and the economy became dependent on its success. Merchants were aware that when the mill "stood," workers had less money for goods and services. As a result, items like food, ice, and fuel were available on credit until the next paycheck. With the addition of weaving machinery, more than 1.5 million yards of fabric were produced in 1893 from nearly 200,000 pounds of yarn. The mill outgrew the plant and added a location on South Main Street. New buildings housed machinery and equipment to make towels, handkerchief cloth, and flannels. Mooresville Mills became one of the largest producers of Moor Quality towels in the country. (Courtesy of Burlington Industries.)

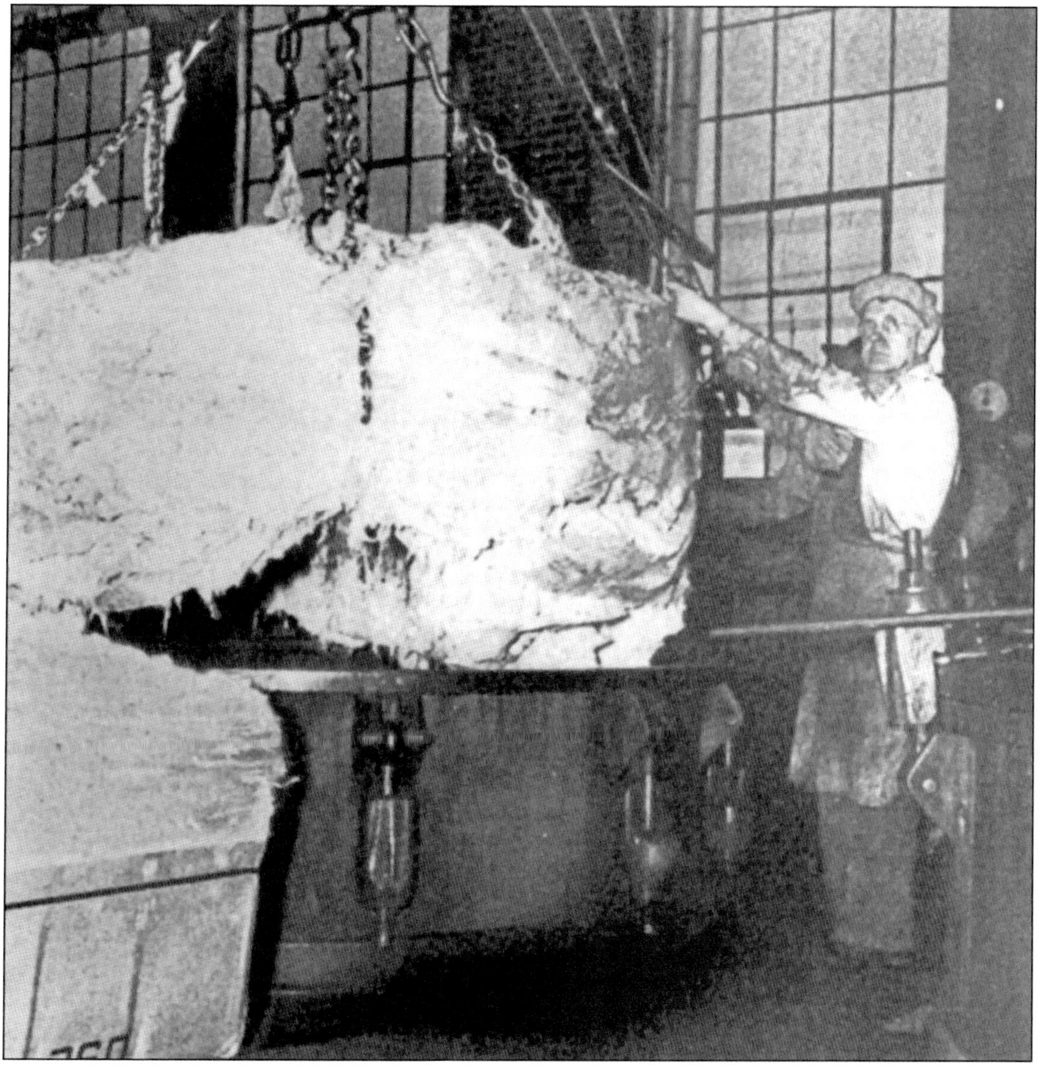

By 1902, Plant 2 was constructed 1.5 miles south of the depot, using 5,000 spindles for spinning, roving, and carding. A 37,000-gallon reservoir supplied water for operations. In 1908, Plant 3, with a railroad siding, added to the production capacity. The mill operated 27,000 spindles and 923 looms by more than 550 employees. The mill received raw cotton from freight cars and processed it into finished yarns and fabrics using machines for dyeing, spinning, roving, and weaving. (Courtesy of Burlington Industries.)

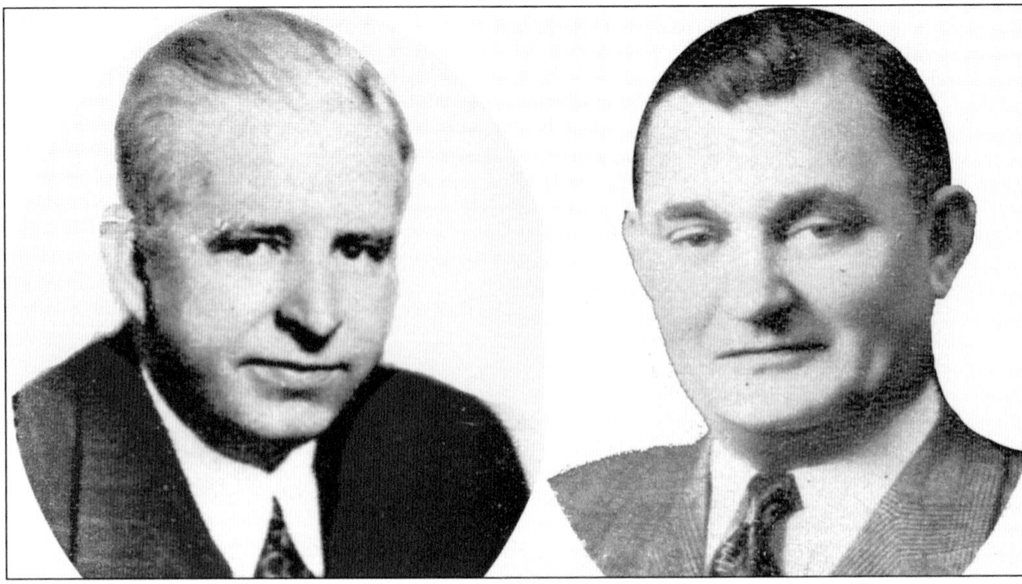

In 1927, a young textile graduate from North Carolina State University came to work in Mooresville. John Matheson (left) worked in cost accounting, served as secretary-treasurer, and was promoted to president in 1932. The mill's selling agent, Hunter Manufacturing Company, failed and the mill went into receivership. Matheson, only 28 years old, took the reins of the leadership team to rejuvenate the industry by marketing products directly to buyers from offices in New York City, Los Angeles, and Chicago. Management wanted to convert Mooresville into a specialty mill and felt that they would have greater flexibility in determining which products to produce. Charles Gunter (right) was superintendent of the mill during Matheson's tenure as president. (Courtesy of Burlington Industries.)

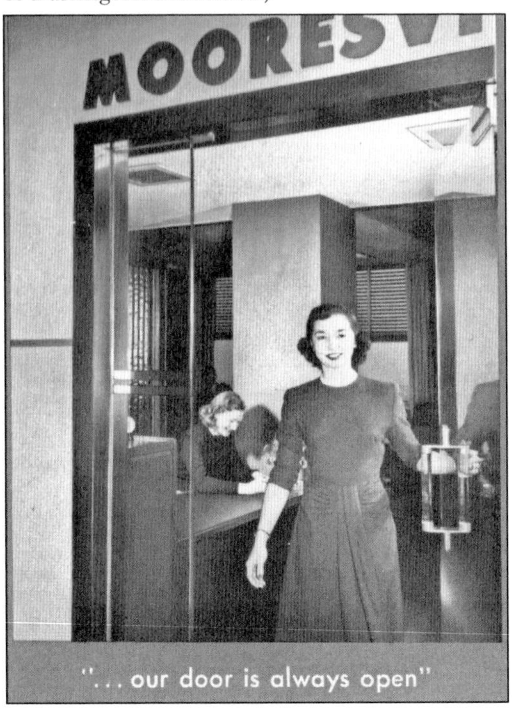

By 1950, the entire marketing and sales operation was headquartered in the Empire State Building. Miniature looms were available to fabric designers and marketing professionals so that ideas generated in meetings with customers could be developed, tested, and physically translated into real fabrics that could be seen and evaluated. (Courtesy of Burlington Industries.)

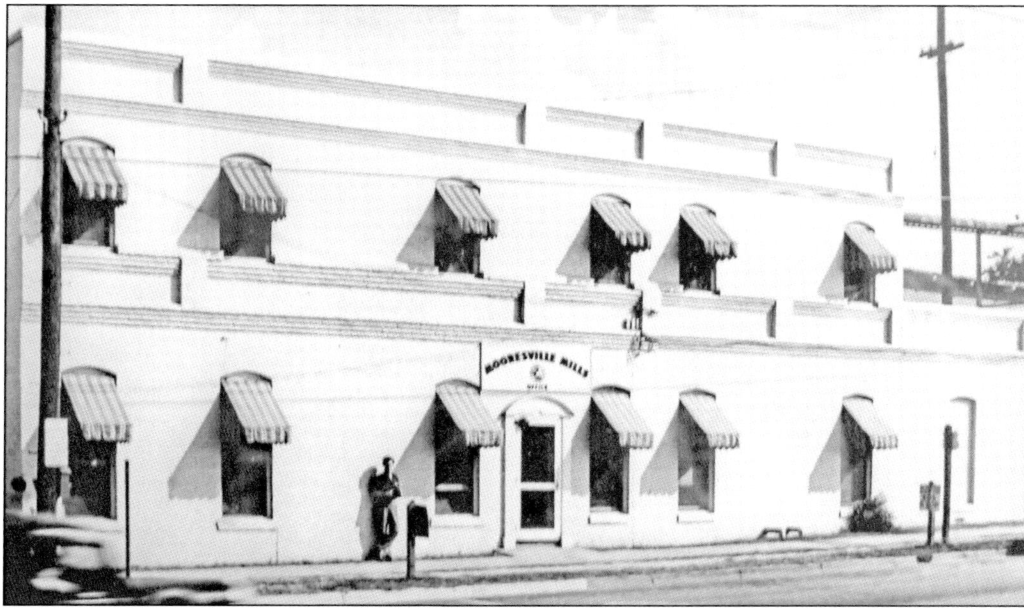

"The Front" was the hub of activity for mill management. Located on South Main Street outside the main gate, these administrative offices served the company until its purchase in 1955 by Burlington Industries. (Courtesy of What-a-Burger.)

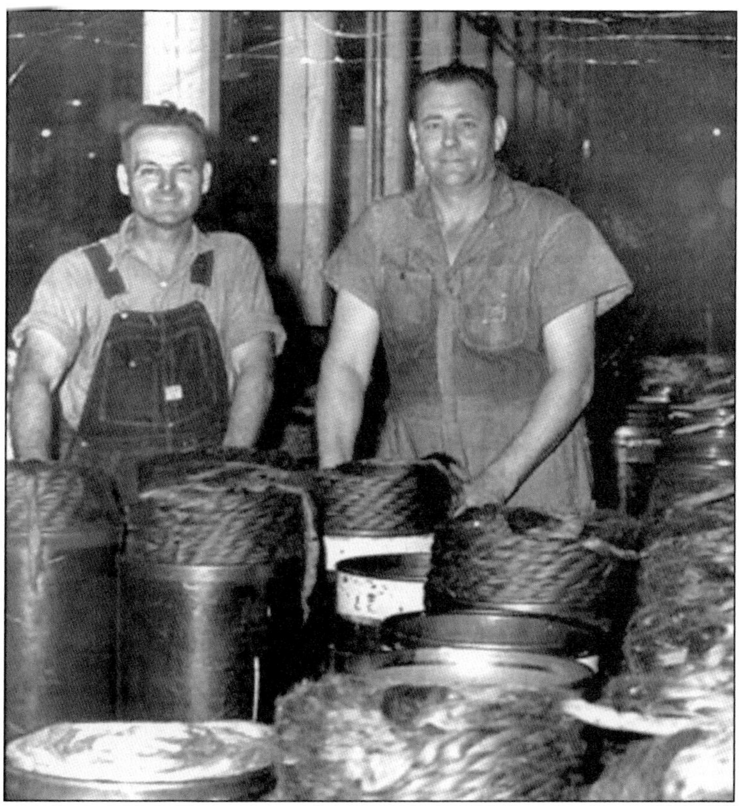

Mooresville Mills developed a completely integrated manufacturing operation that started with the raw fibers, either cotton or synthetic, and carried through to the final stage, when the finished fabric was ready for immediate use of the apparel manufacturer. (Courtesy of Burlington Industries.)

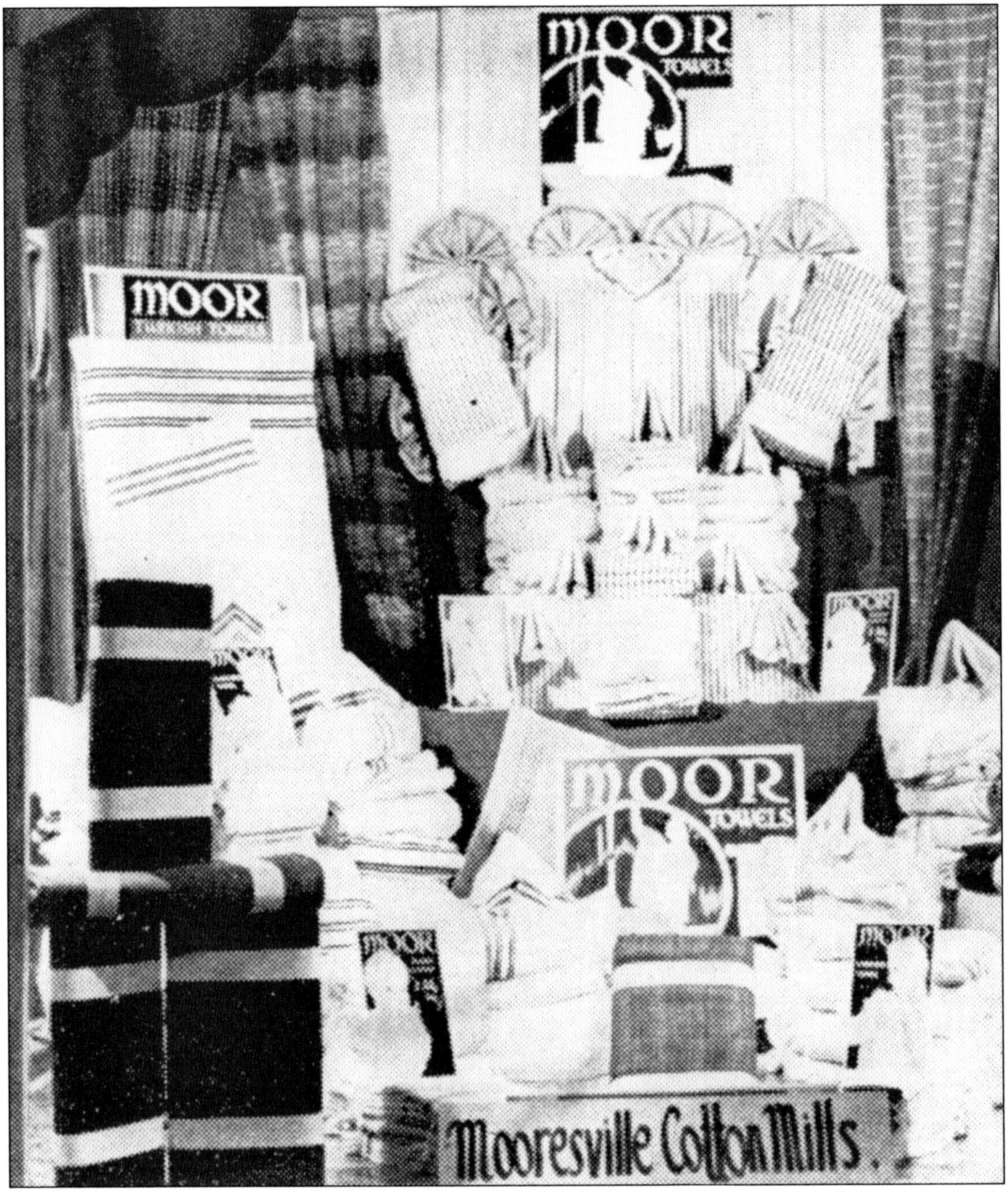

By 1935, the Moor Quality brand was well known for its Turkish towels and ginghams. The Mooresville Mills provided nearly 15 percent of the toweling sold in America. A state fair exhibit shows the variety of products available in Iredell County. (Courtesy of Erleen Mills Christenbury.)

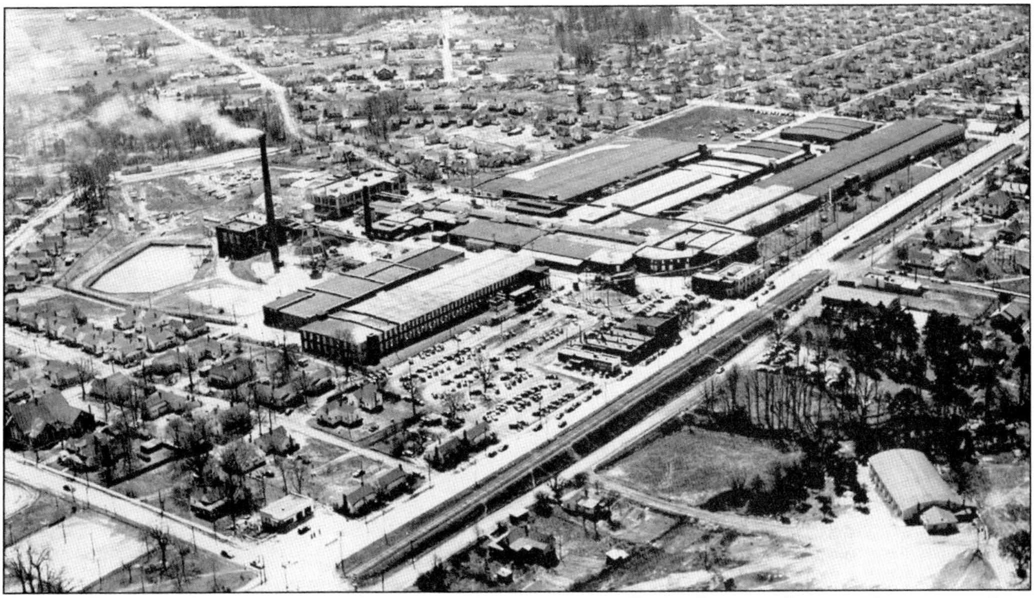

The Mooresville Cotton Mills, later named the Mooresville Mills to indicate a diverse product line, continued to grow and prosper. According to a report in the *Rounder and News Leader* on June 17, 1937, the mill employed approximately 2,000 people in 1936. Approximately 15 percent of the towels manufactured in the United States came from the Mooresville plant, with total sales of $3 million in 1936. After a brief time in receivership, the mill emerged in sound financial condition and grew to be one of the leaders in the textile industry. The mill was sold to Burlington Industries in 1955. (Courtesy of Bobbie and Grier Powers.)

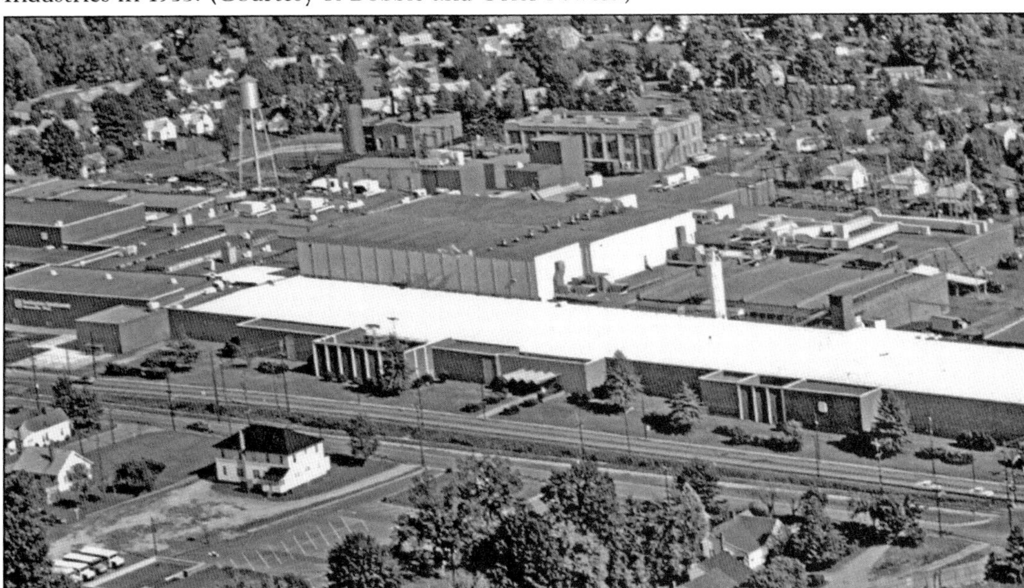

Mooresville Mills became part of Burlington Industries in 1955. Burlington mounted a $15-million renovation and upgrade of the machinery and plant structure. The mill was modernized with air-conditioning, and windows were covered with "decorative" brick. "The front," the main office, was demolished and new offices were built inside the mill building. (Courtesy of Burlington Industries.)

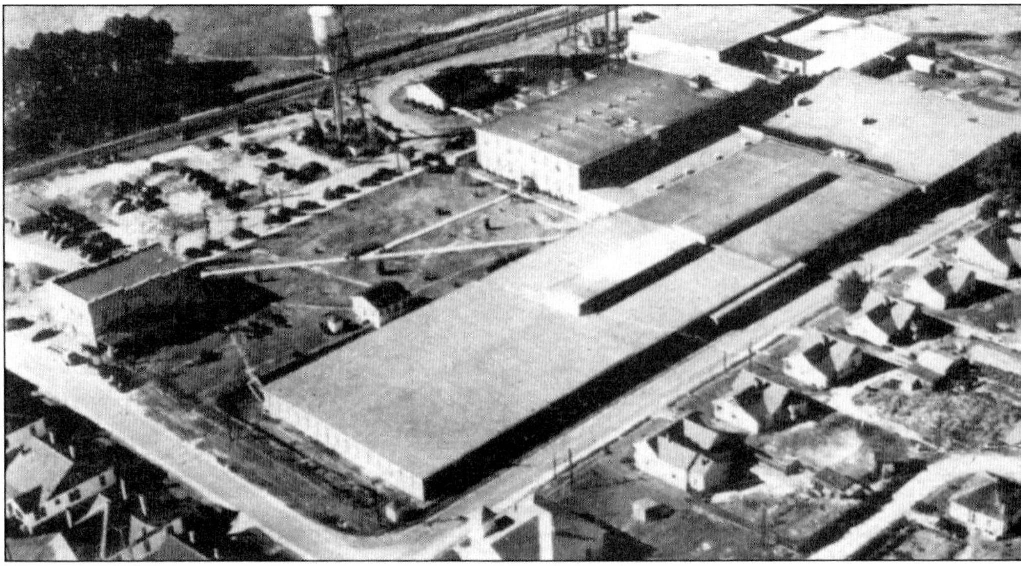

Espy Brawley organized the Dixie Cotton Mill in 1906 and began manufacturing yarns. The name was changed to Cascade Mills and by 1913 had 65 employees. Though a successful producer of quality yarn, the mill closed in 1931 as a result of the Great Depression. Burlington Industries purchased the mill and began operations in 1934 after re-equipping the plant. By 1934, the plant had an annual payroll of $182,000. A village of employee houses grew up around the mill, establishing the Cascade community. The mill and its employees supported the community in its effort to honor veterans with an award-winning float in the victory parade.

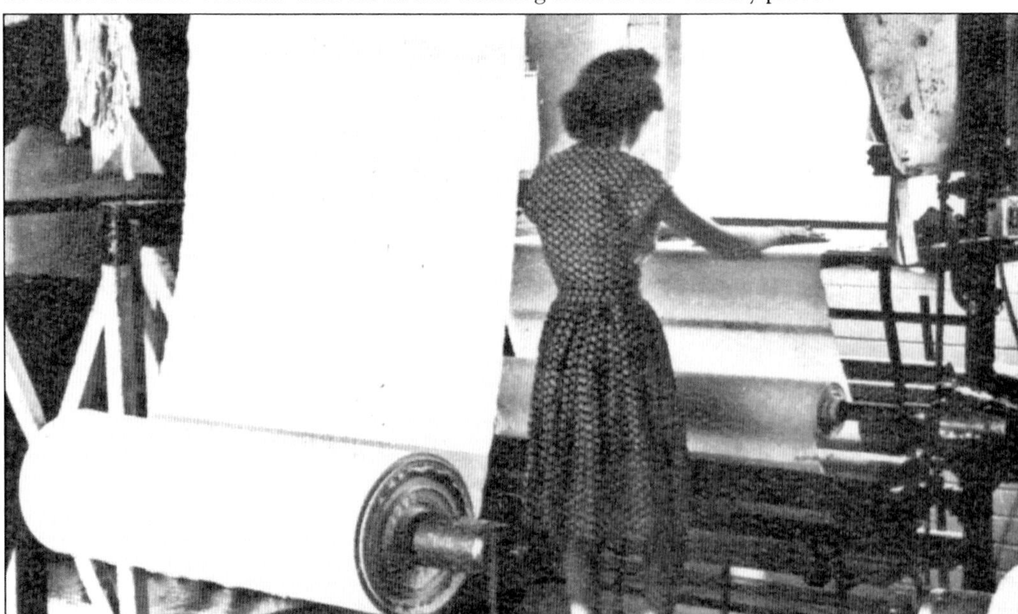

An early issue of the employee newsletter describes the changes made by Burlington Mills. The name was changed to Cascade Rayon Mills, a plant engaged in the weaving of rayon fabric and the throwing of rayon yarns use to make underwear and dress goods. Demand for synthetic products led to expansion and improvement in machinery and the size of the plant. Burlington increased the size of the plant four times since the purchase in 1933.

Three

The Best Way to Anywhere

Mooresville residents were proud of their town. A wide variety of businesses, industry, and services were available to citizens and visitors. Life was good and likely to get better for the growing community. Issac Harris led the bold move to get the railroad line to come through Mooresville instead of Statesville on its way to Mocksville and Winston-Salem. He and other leaders knew that the additional line meant more business for Mooresville merchants and more access for travelers. Meeting in Mocksville, the railroad offered each town time to present the reasons for building the railroad. After the oratory, officials were ready to award the line, on the condition that a cash deposit was made. Statesville representatives were not prepared with cash. Mooresville's Issac Harris was there with more cash than oratory, making a deposit of several thousand dollars to the railroad representatives. From then on, train traffic in Mooresville could take a branch line at Barber Junction to points northeast through Mocksville and Winston-Salem. Leaders worked to find ways to attract business and people to Mooresville. As early as 1903, the first mile of good road in the county was built leading out from Mooresville. Local citizens were the original "boosters" and supported the extension of roadways throughout the region. According to D. P. Waters, land values were enhanced by more than $1.5 million, aside from the advantages of increased comfort, safety, and economy. Citizens were interested in more than "getting there." Town infrastructure was important, and leaders paid attention to the needs for streets, water, electricity, entertainment, and recreation.

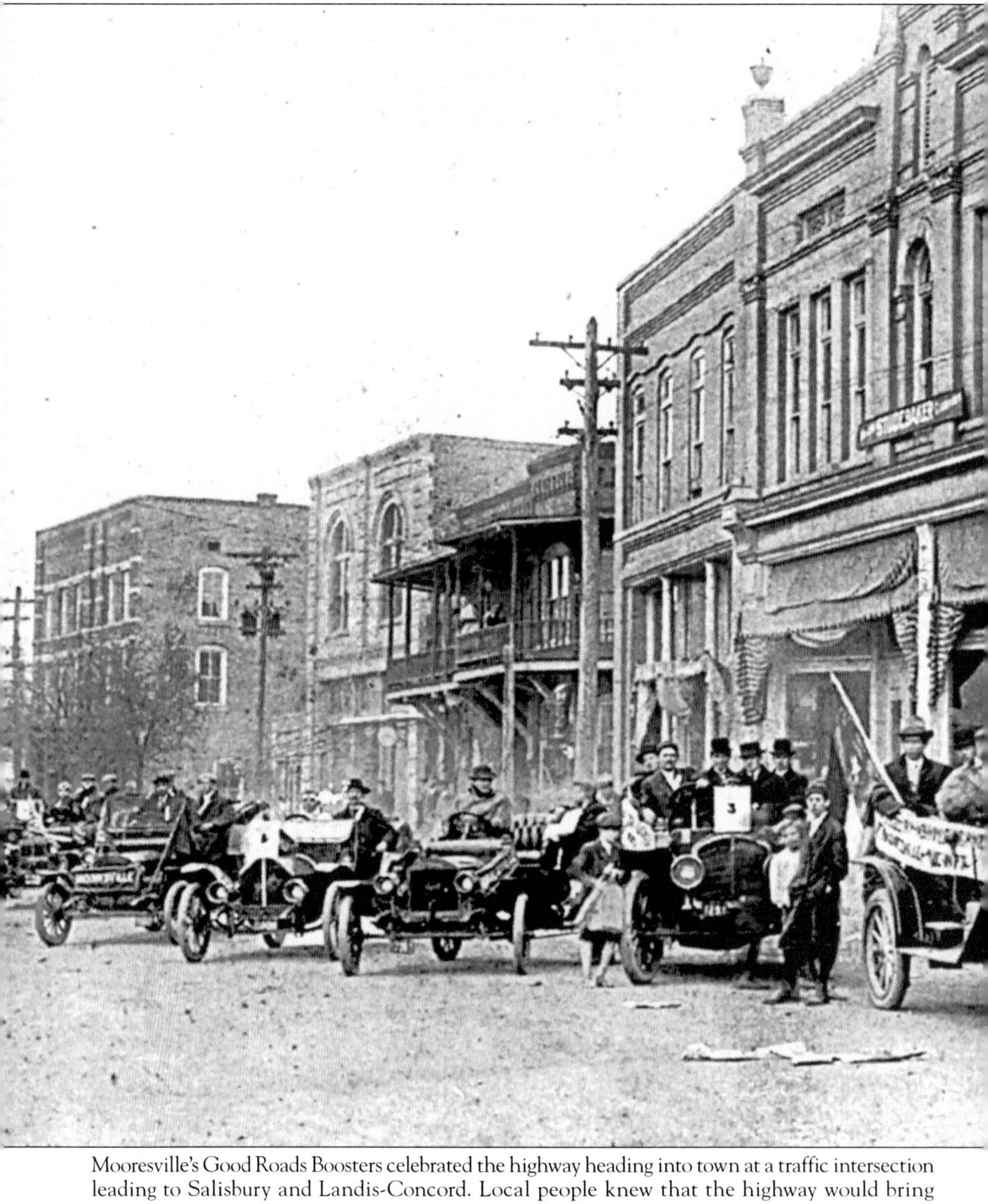

Mooresville's Good Roads Boosters celebrated the highway heading into town at a traffic intersection leading to Salisbury and Landis-Concord. Local people knew that the highway would bring

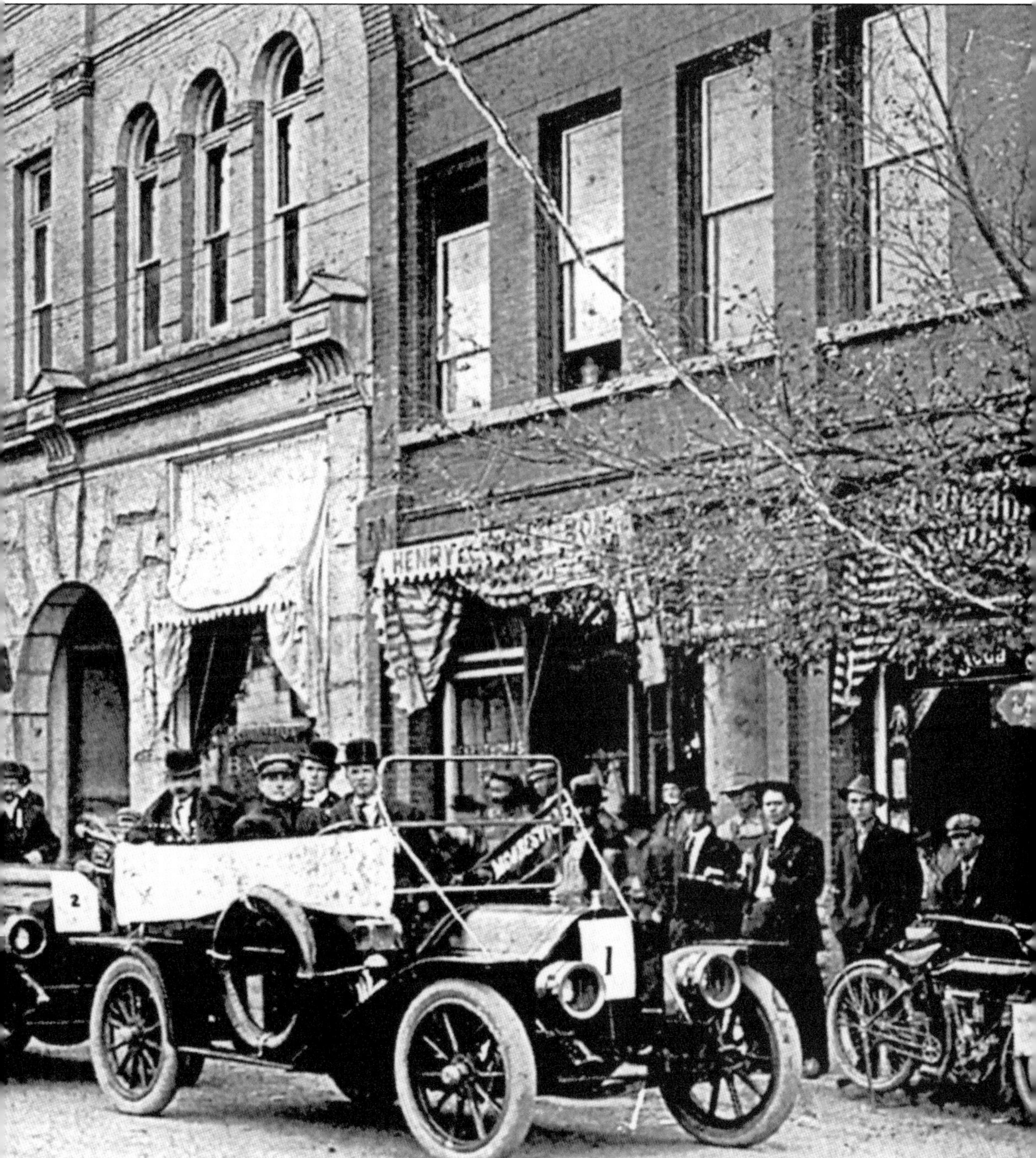

customers, visitors, and prosperity to Mooresville. It would also provide a way for local people and goods to visit other locations.

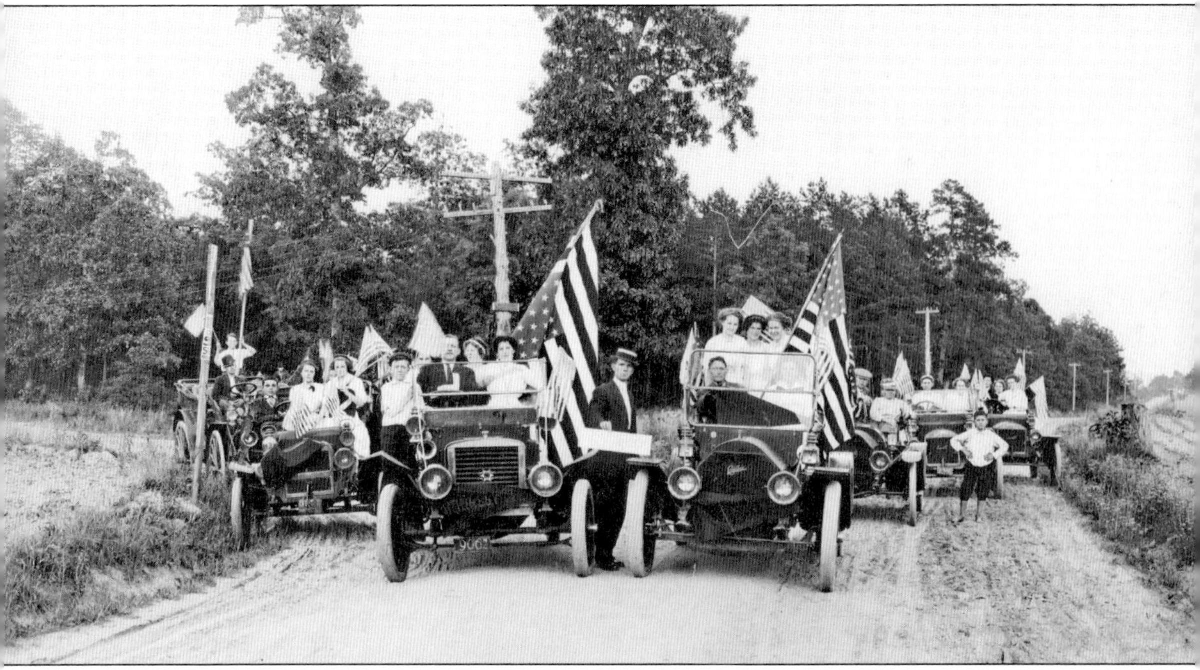

Mooresville Good Roads Boosters, promoting the "Best Way to Anywhere is by Mooresville," stopped briefly in downtown Mooresville on their journey along the Salisbury-to-Asheville highway. The locals were part of a goodwill tour on behalf of the good roads campaign. The motorcade made it as far as Hickory, when it turned around and headed for home. It took the cars and motorcycles more than three hours to get from the Catawba River bridge back to town. Among the notables are Gene Edmiston, Sam McNeely, W. P. Carpenter, Harry Deaton, Grey Sloop, Frank Freeze, George Jones, Watt Melchor, E. H. Miller, W. M. Neel, Ross Johnston, John Kennette, Ernest Mills, and Branch McNeely.

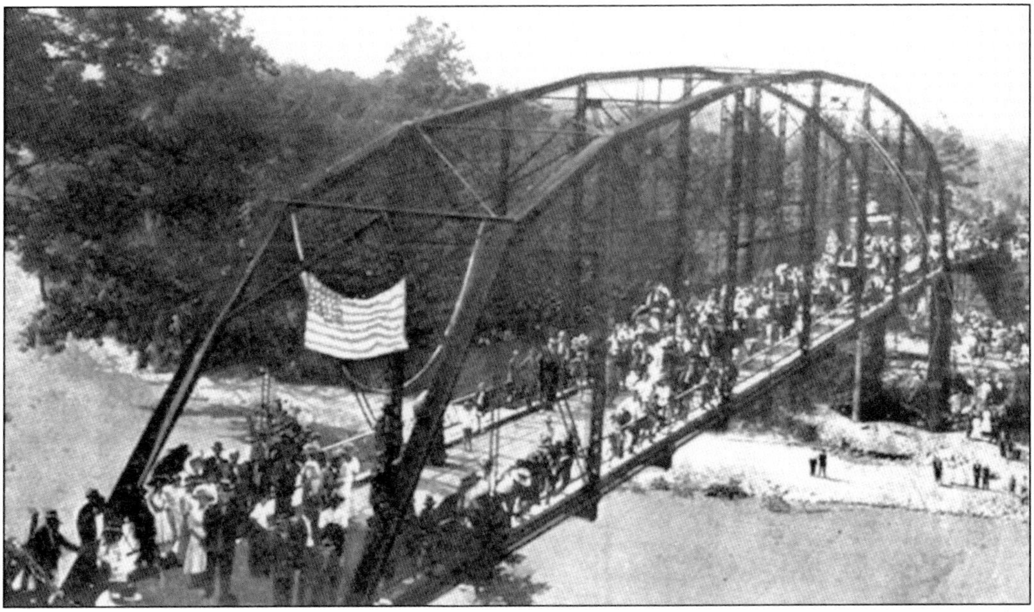

Eight miles west of Mooresville was the heaviest steel road bridge in the state. Spanning the Catawba River, the structure was the idea of Buretta Augustus Troutman and James W. Brown of Mooresville. It is due to the construction of this bridge and the enthusiasm of Mooresville's highway boosters that the route through Mooresville was chosen for the central highway. (Courtesy of Pearl Troutman Alexander.)

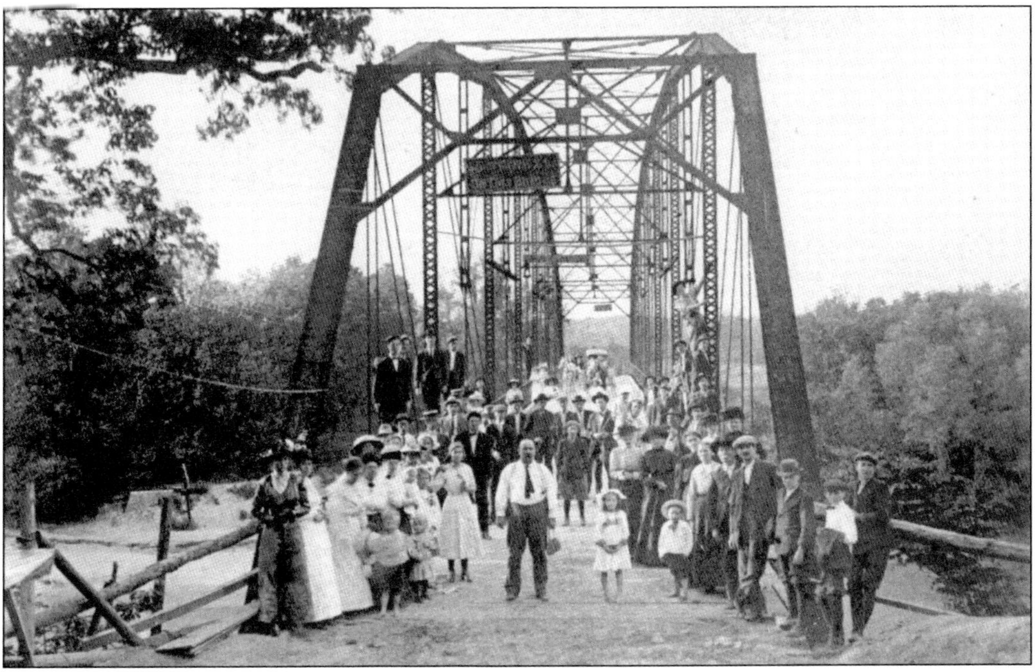

The toll bridge across the Catawba River, also known as the Mooresville Bridge, was constructed at a cost of $13,000 in 1907. Completed in 1910 and rising 44.5 feet above the high-water mark, the bridge was the only Catawba River crossing other than Buffalo Shoals. A 1910 motorcade had a picnic and good roads meeting at the site. (Courtesy of Pearl Troutman Alexander.)

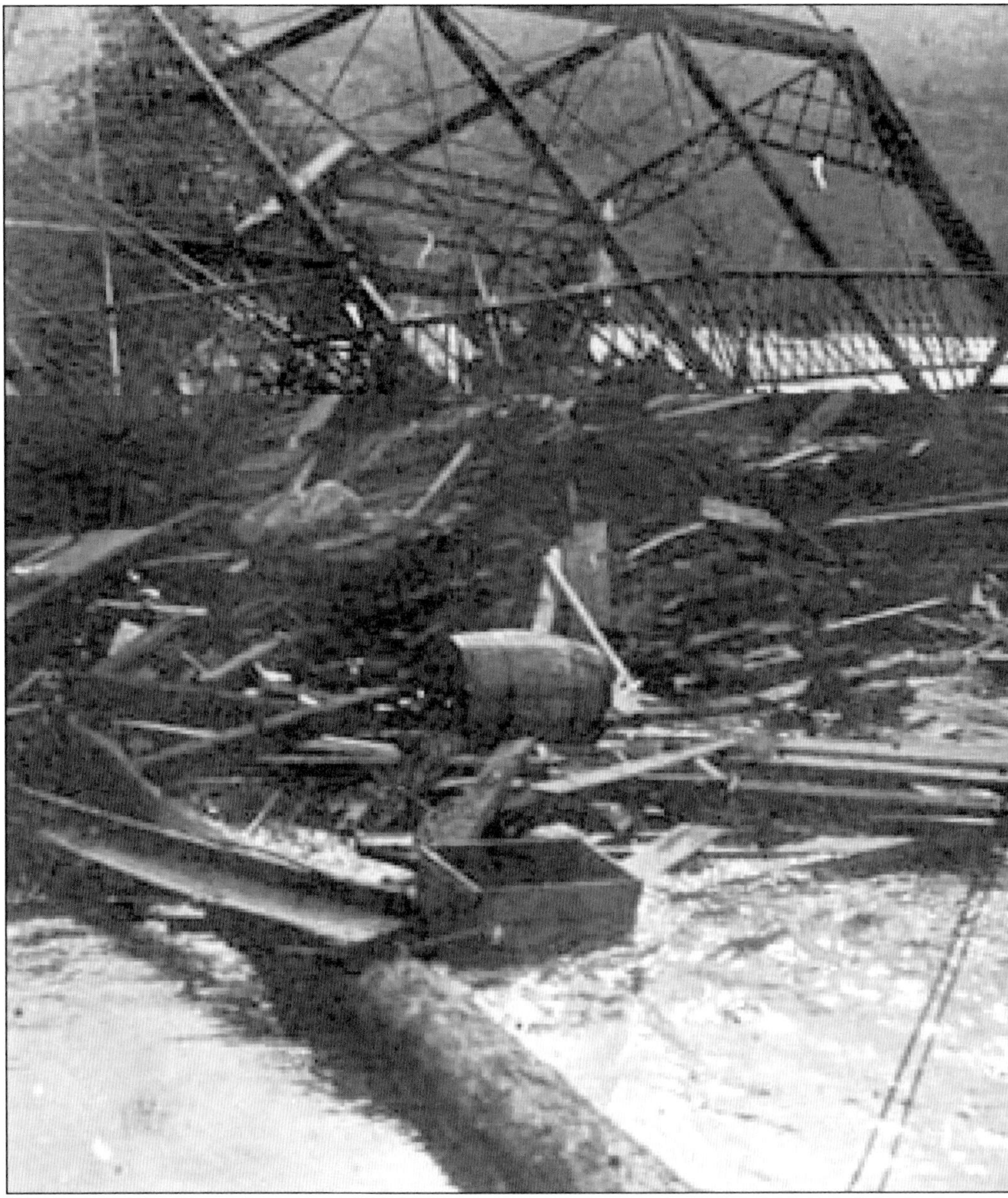

Troutman and Brown watched as their bridge was washed away in the flood of 1916. A house and debris hit the structure and destroyed it totally. The bridge destruction was a calamity for citizens and farmers in Catawba, Lincoln, and Gaston Counties, cutting the lines to markets at both the Mooresville and Buffalo Shoals crossings. Bill Kale, a merchant at Buffalo Shoals, reported that he saw houses and barns floating down the river with livestock on the roofs. The effects of the flood included the loss of electricity in Mooresville. Limited power was available for pumping water, and the mills, creamery, ice plant, and newspaper presses were idle. Troutman and Brown did not rebuild the structure. (Courtesy of Pearl Troutman Alexander.)

Four

THE QUEEN OF IREDELL

In 1937, Tom McKnight, editor of the *Rounder*, rejuvenated the slogan "Queen of Iredell" to describe the town of Mooresville. He wrote, "The descendents of the Scotch-Irish who settled this area do not confuse rhetorical slogans with tangible progress." According to McKnight, "Mooresville is a charmingly social, vigorously industrial and soundly built community which is making steady progress and where living conditions are of the best kind." The town was indeed a leader in Iredell County, working for good roads, modern homes, and dynamic business and industry. Emerging from the Great Depression, Mooresville had three large lumber mills, and the Farmers' Warehouse and Oil Mills had a wide array of shops, stores, and businesses. The Mooresville Cooperative Creamery was one of the largest in the area, shipping products to 30 states. The Mooresville Furniture Company covered an entire block, and the adjacent iron works and flour mill operated day and night. The Mooresville Cotton Mills employed 2,000 people and was the second largest manufacturer of towels in the world. The Moor Quality towels were made in one of the few textile plants in the country that built its product from the raw cotton to the finished merchandise. Life was "pleasant, comfortable and interesting." With the doctors of Lowrance Hospital providing first-rate health care and 12 churches providing religious programs, Mooresville was growing and becoming prosperous. Civic groups like the Rotary, Kiwanis, American Legion, and a Bachelor's Club provided ways for citizens to become active in all aspects of community life. Local government was active with police and fire departments, a modern water works, and a network of hard-surfaced streets totaling 22 miles. Hard work among citizens brought the community to the status McKnight described. A caring citizenry worked with town leaders to modernize the community.

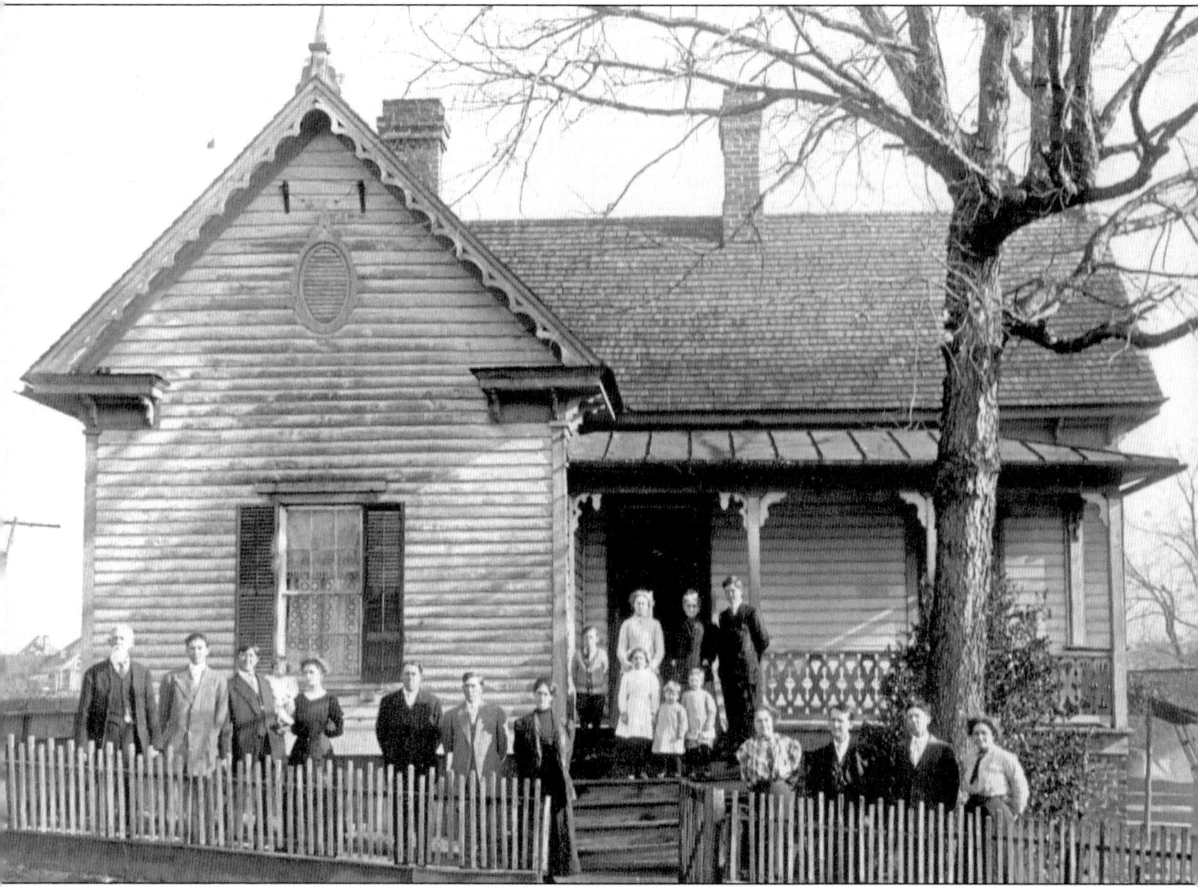

The Seminole Water Works was established with a deep well and a windmill. The project was established with the purpose of providing water to the Seminole Hill area along Academy Street, Iredell Avenue, and West Center Avenue. The board of commissioners gave their approval to lay water pipes on Academy Street in 1907. Editor Tom McKnight recounts the story: "Mort McKnight, Gus Kipka, Moses White, J. L. Honeycutt and S. S. Denny drilled a deep well, erected a large tank and windmill and laid water pipes to their homes." (Courtesy of Kay Kipka Jones.)

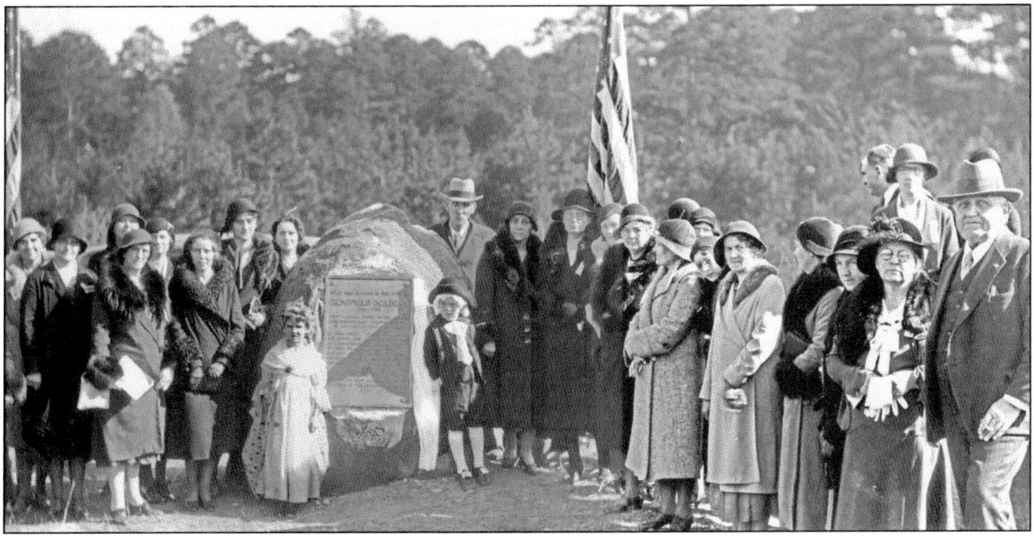

The Mary Slocomb Chapter of the Daughters of the American Revolution (DAR) unveiled a tablet to mark the site of the first classical school in the area, Crowfield Academy. It started in 1760 within the bounds of Centre Presbyterian Church and was know for the preparation of men for higher education at Princeton University and leadership positions in government. The bronze marker was set in a boulder at the site two miles south of Mooresville. Kate Templeton presented the marker, along with Mrs. Zebulon V. Turlington (Mary). Participating in the ceremony were Louisa Templeton and Frank A. Rankin. Land for the marker was donated by the Houston family and the granite boulder is from the T. J. Williams farm. (Courtesy of Emily Sigmon Kerley.)

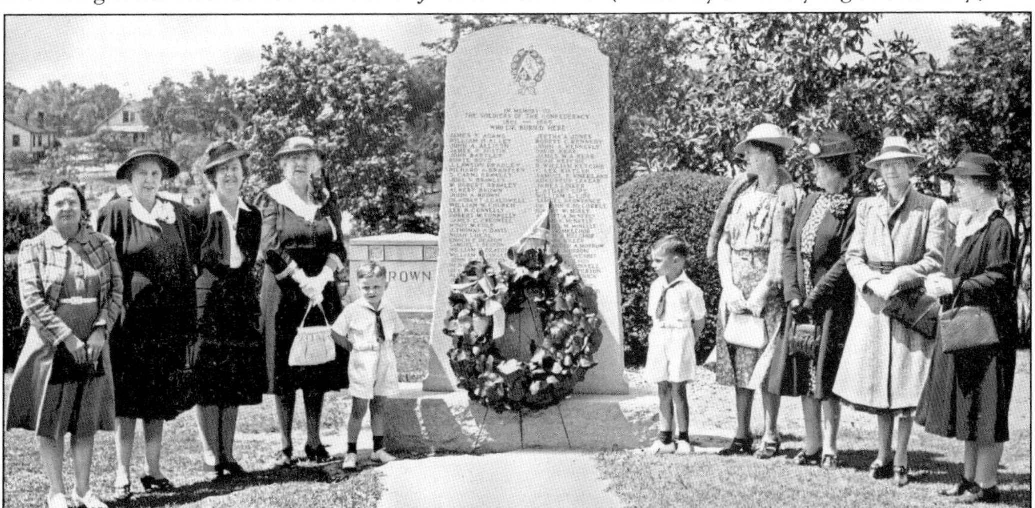

The United Daughters of the Confederacy Battle of Bentonville Chapter sponsored the construction of a marker to honor 89 Confederate soldiers buried in the Willow Valley cemetery. Dedicated on May 10, 1941, as part of the Memorial Day celebration, the marker was a 17-year project for the UDC. Dedicating the marker are, from left to right, Florence Johnston, Mary Belle McNeely, Frances Smith Craven, Minnie Lee Turner, Harding Rogers Jr., Clayton Davidson Jr., Mamie Houston, Gertrude Norman, Lila Turner, and Elizabeth Boyd. In addition to the veterans, the ceremony honored Carrie Leazar, Julia Stirewalt, and Blanche M. Deaton, former UDC presidents buried in Willow Valley. (Courtesy of UDC Battle of Bentonville Chapter.)

MEETING OF SECOND DISTRICT N. C. N. S.

Daughters of the American Revolution

Sunday School Building, Presbyterian Church
Mooresville, N. C.

OCTOBER 9 — 10:00 O'CLOCK, A. M.

SONG .... America

INVOCATION .... Dr. R. A. White

FLAG SALUTE AND AMERICA'S CREED .... Mrs. H. O. Steele

SALUTE TO THE FLAG

I pledge my allegiance to the Flag of the United States, and the republic for which it stands, one nation, indivisible with liberty and justice for all.

AMERICA'S CREED

I believe in the United States of America as a government of the people, by the people, for the people, whose just powers are derived from the consent of the governed; a democracy in a republic; a sovereign state; a perfect union, one and inseparable; established upon those principles of freedom, equality, justice, and humanity, for which American patriots sacrificed their lives and fortunes.

I, therefore, believe it my duty to my country to love it; to support its constitution; to obey its laws; to respect its flag; and to defend it against all enemies.

GREETINGS, Battle of Bentonville Chapter U. D. C. .... Mrs. D. E. Turner

GREETINGS, American Legion Auxiliary .... Mrs. J. W. Williamson

WELCOME, Regent Mary Slocum Chapter D. A. R., Miss Kate Templeton

RESPONSE .... Mrs. F. B. Ingold

INTRODUCTION OF OFFICERS AND GUESTS .... District Chairman

APPOINTMENT OF COMMITTEES .... District Chairman

KINGS MOUNTAIN CELEBRATION .... Mrs. Ralph Van Landingham

ADDRESS .... State Regent, Mrs. C. R. Whitaker

REPORTS OF STATE CHAIRMAN.

REPORTS OF CHAPTER REGENTS.

LUNCH.

The DAR presented informative programs for the community and all who wished to honor the American flag and learn more about the meaning of the Constitution. Working with churches, schools, and civic groups, the Mary Slocomb Chapter led a wide variety of activities and events for the community. (Courtesy of Emily Sigmon Kerley.)

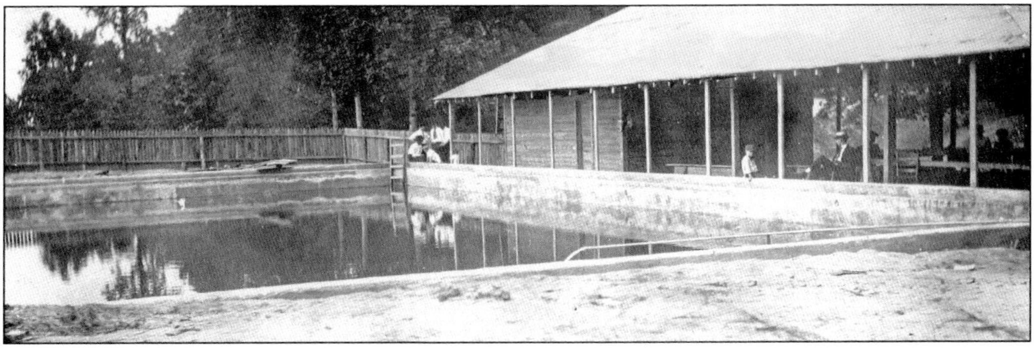

In 1920, a group of businessmen led by B. A. Troutman formed the Stewart Park and Development Company as a recreational facility. Located on West Park Avenue and Oak Street, the park boasted a concrete swimming pool, picnic areas in shaded groves, and ample visitors parking. A grand opening was held, and the community was invited to visit the park for a picnic. According to the *Mooresville Enterprise*, baseball grounds, dressing rooms for the pool, a covered pavilion, and a tennis court were added by 1921. The board of directors included B. A. Troutman, W. C. Johnston, A. L. Starr, and J. A. Stewart. The major feature of the park was the concrete "bathing pool," with sanitary water supplied by driven wells and the Town of Mooresville. (Courtesy of Pearl Alexander.)

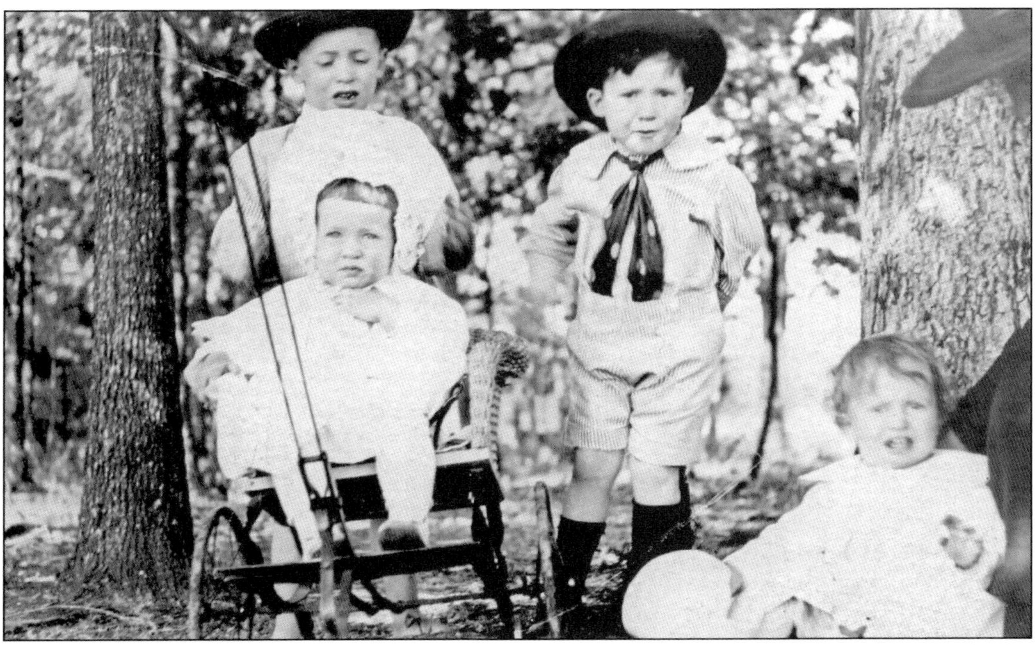

Children of all ages enjoyed Stewart Park activities, none more than those in the Charles Troutman family. From left to right and front to back, Pearl, Carolyn, Charlie, and James made the trip many times from their Main Street home for picnics, ball games, and fun in the shaded walkways. (Courtesy of Pearl Alexander.)

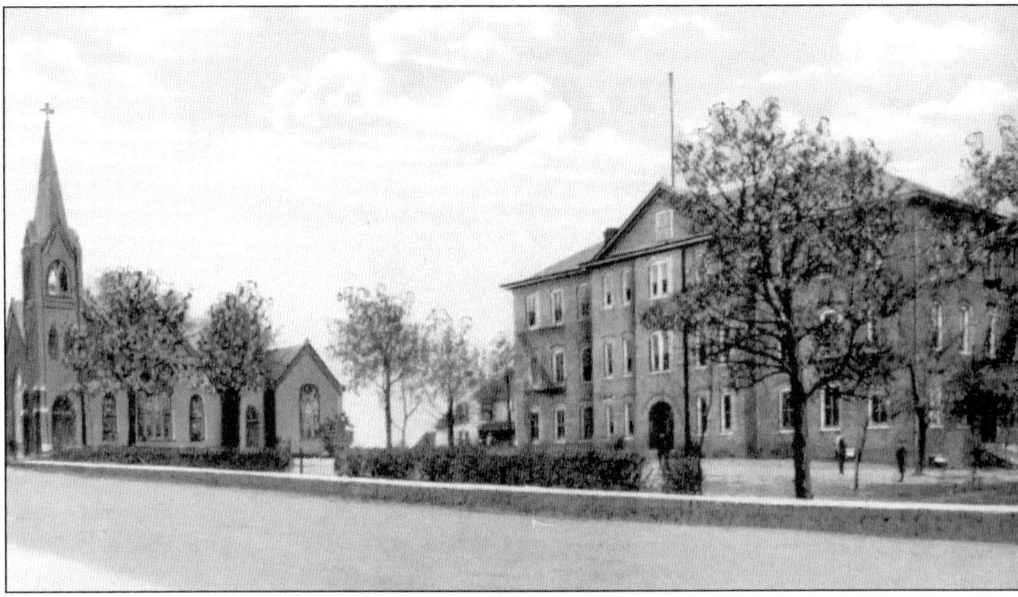

Original residents, regardless of their religion, attended services in the North Bend School and other locations. Each denomination had its own minister. Citizens in Mooresville were actively interested in providing places for education and worship to ensure the success of the community. (Postcard courtesy of Bobbie and Grier Powers.)

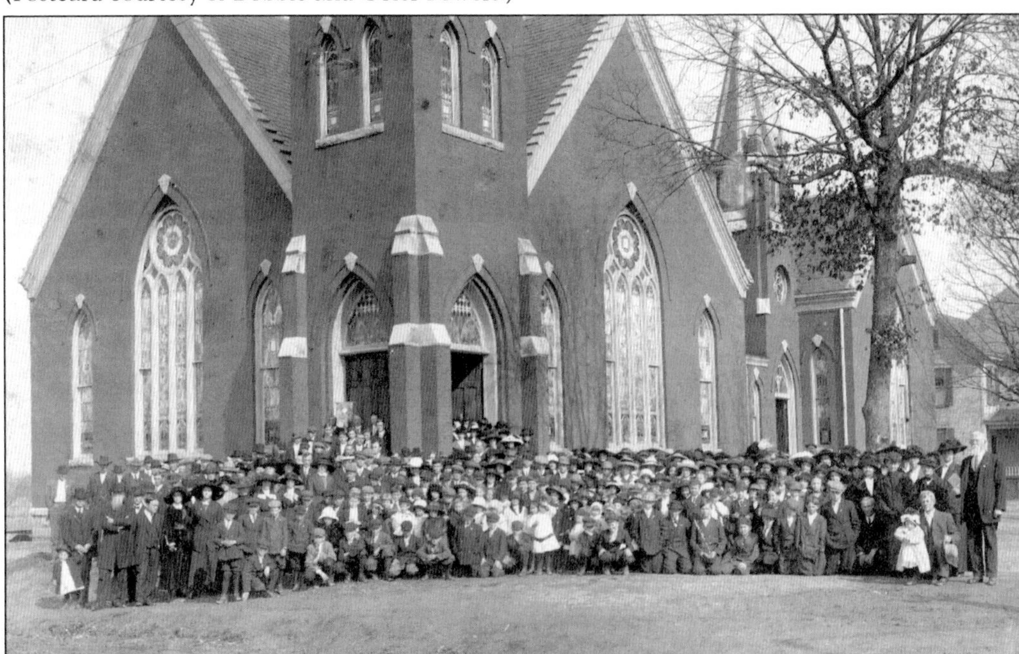

The pastor of the South Iredell Methodist Circuit, Rev. T. L. Triplett, organized 30 members of Central Methodist Church in 1877. John Moore donated land for a church on the corner of West Moore Avenue and North Academy Street. Even though the congregation was small, they managed to erect a church building. The Masonic Lodge helped to build the church and used the second floor as a meeting room. (Postcard courtesy of Bobbie and Grier Powers.)

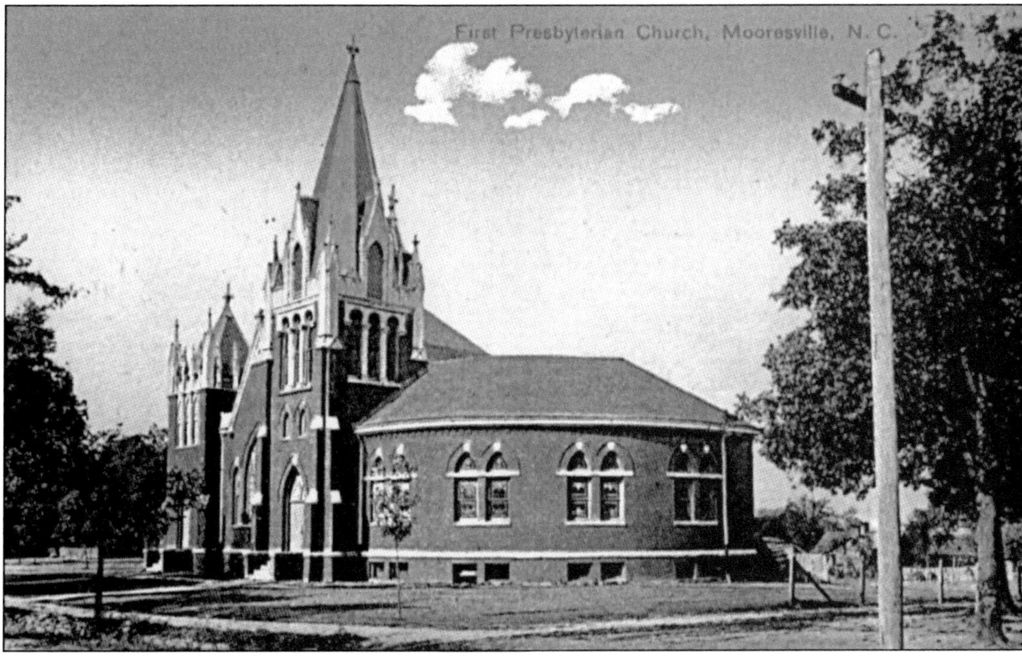

Presbyterians were the first to organize their own church within the corporate limits of town when 19 members of Prospect Presbyterian Church struck out on their own. In 1876, Rev. P. T. Penick was called as minister to both the Prospect and First Presbyterian congregations. Before the First Presbyterian building was under construction, the congregation met in the Mooresville Academy. They built a church on the corner of Church Street and McLelland Avenue, across from Willow Valley Cemetery. In 1899, they moved to a new building on the corner of McLelland Avenue and Academy Street.

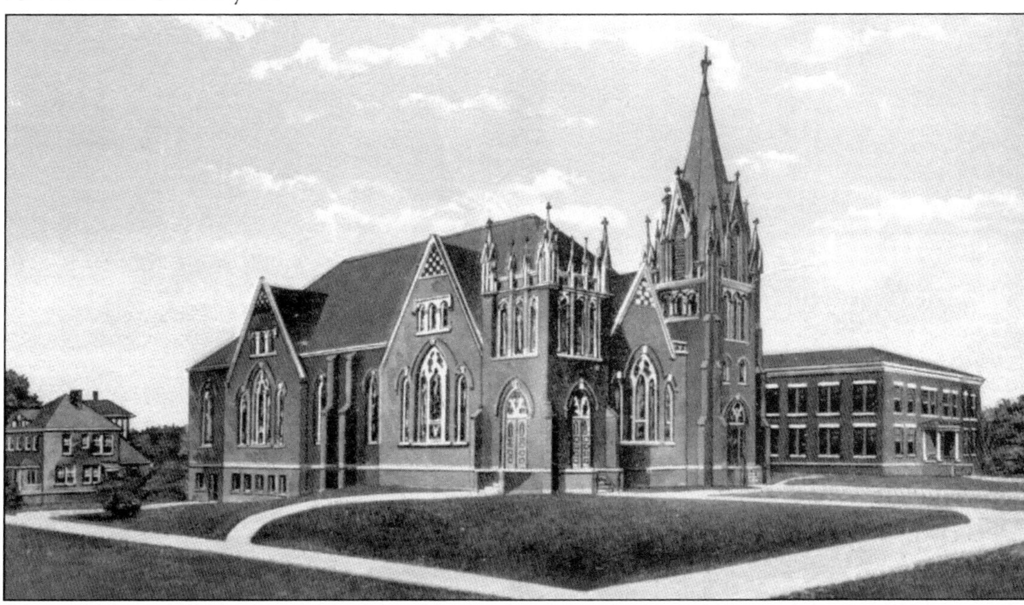

A manse and Sunday school building were added in 1922 to meet the needs of the growing congregation. Space in the Sunday school building was available to local civic groups, like the Daughters of the American Revolution, for programs and other events.

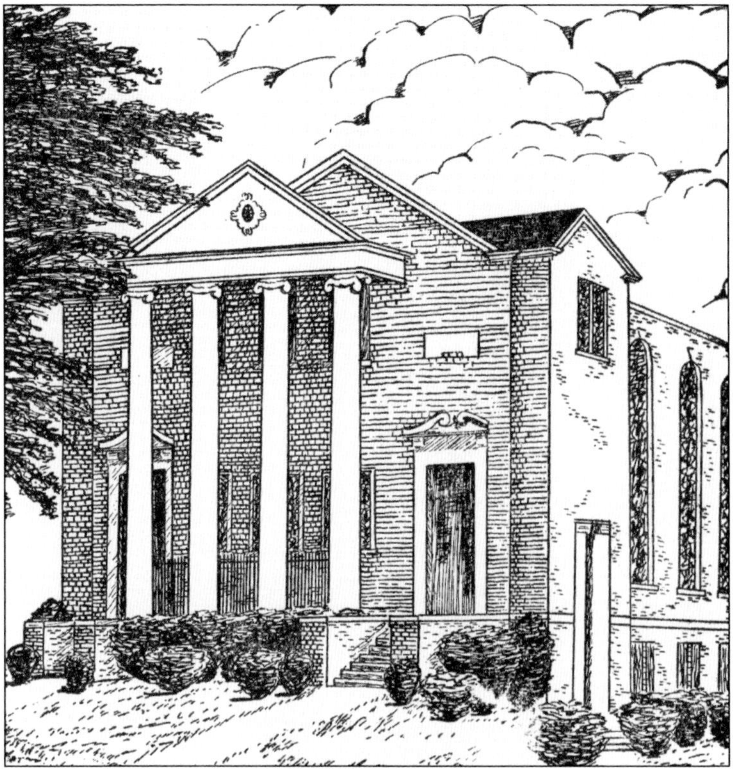

In 1882, a small group of Baptists met under a large tree on what now is the Mooresville Golf Course to organize a church in Mooresville. With only seven charter members, they used a building on the corner of South Academy Street and Kelly Street until 1902. They purchased a site on Church Street from the Presbyterians to establish a permanent location. The original frame building burned in 1933, and the growing congregation started a new building project for a sanctuary and educational building.

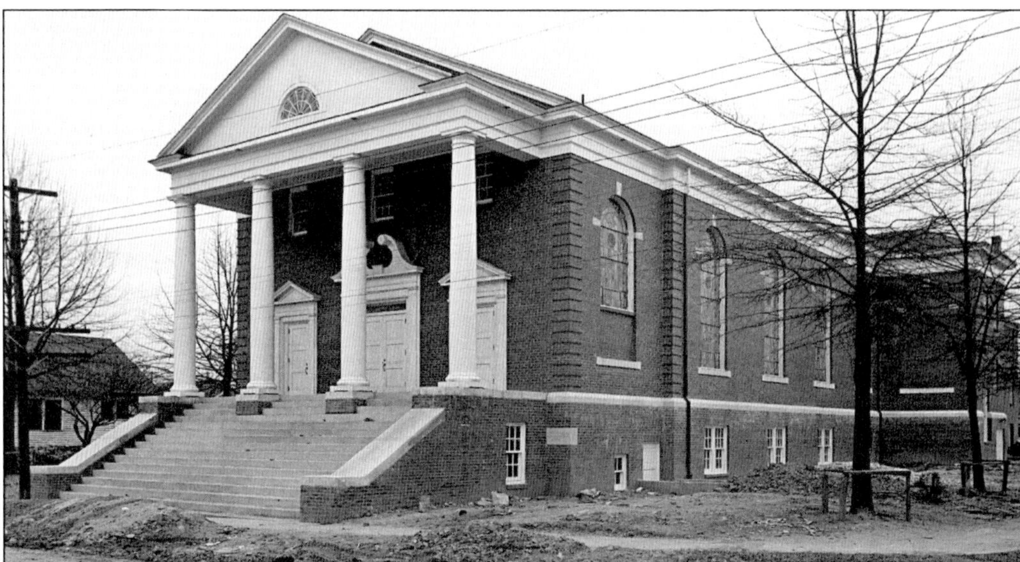

Southside Baptist Church was formed with 89 members of the First Baptist Church who were looking for a new place to worship. They found a meeting place known as the Band Hall at the end of Church Street. When the congregation began to outgrow the building, they purchased a lot on South Academy Street from J. Y. Templeton. They applied for membership in the South Yadkin Association in 1915 so that they could be recognized as an organized church. (Courtesy of Lorene Rash.)

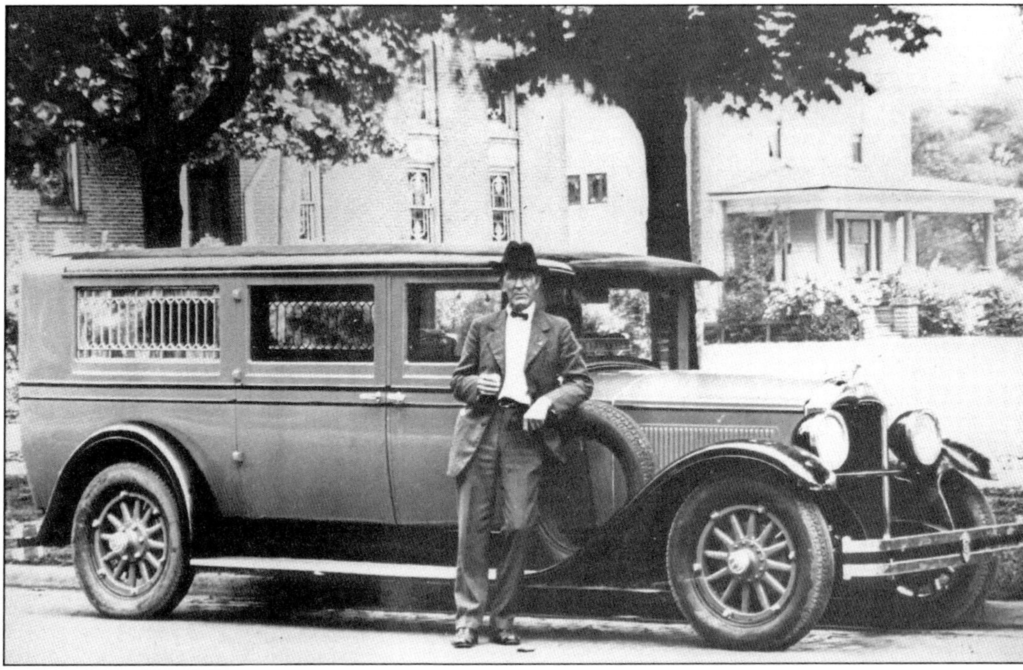

J. P. Cavin purchased Nesbit, Pressley and Company in 1914 and reorganized as People's Home Furnishing Company. The firm was the first to start an installment plan to buy furniture, pianos, organs, and sewing machines. Cavin graduated from the Renouard School of Embalming in 1917 and became Mooresville's first licensed embalmer. His Cavin Funeral Home was a family business, incorporated in 1925. (Courtesy of Bob Cavin.)

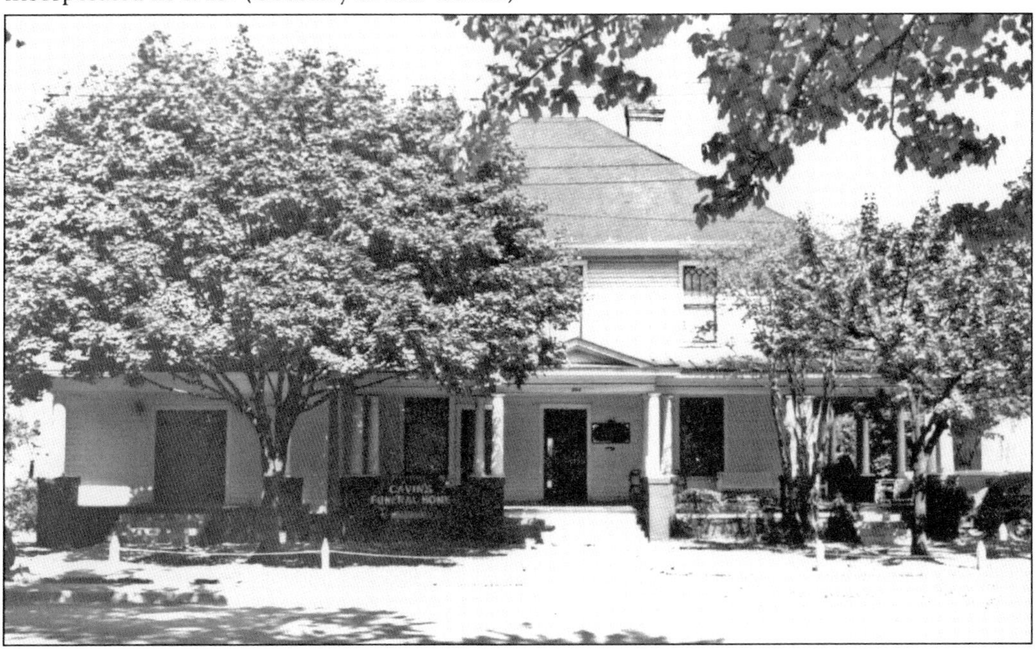

After Cavin Sr. died in 1935, the business moved from the corner of West Moore Avenue and Broad Street to a large home on Main Street. Clara Starrette Cavin and Joel Brawley operated the business until Cavin's sons could take over. (Courtesy of Mike Cook.)

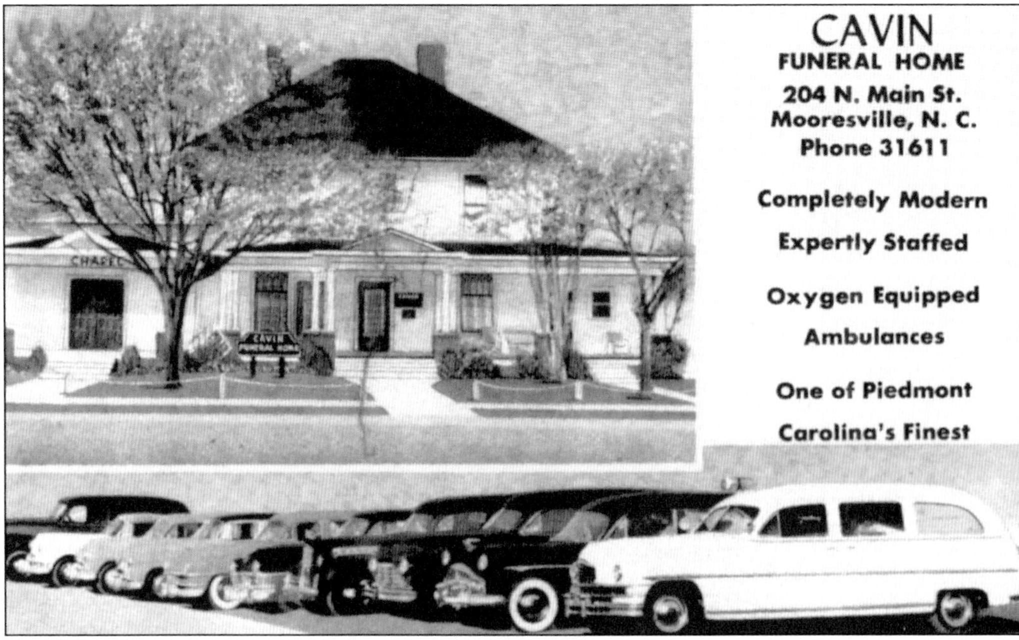

When John Cavin Jr. was killed in an automobile accident, his father established a lasting memorial by starting the first ambulance service in the area. Bob Cavin, John Jr.'s brother, remembered that his father felt that an ambulance might have saved his John Jr.'s life. (Courtesy of Mike Cook.)

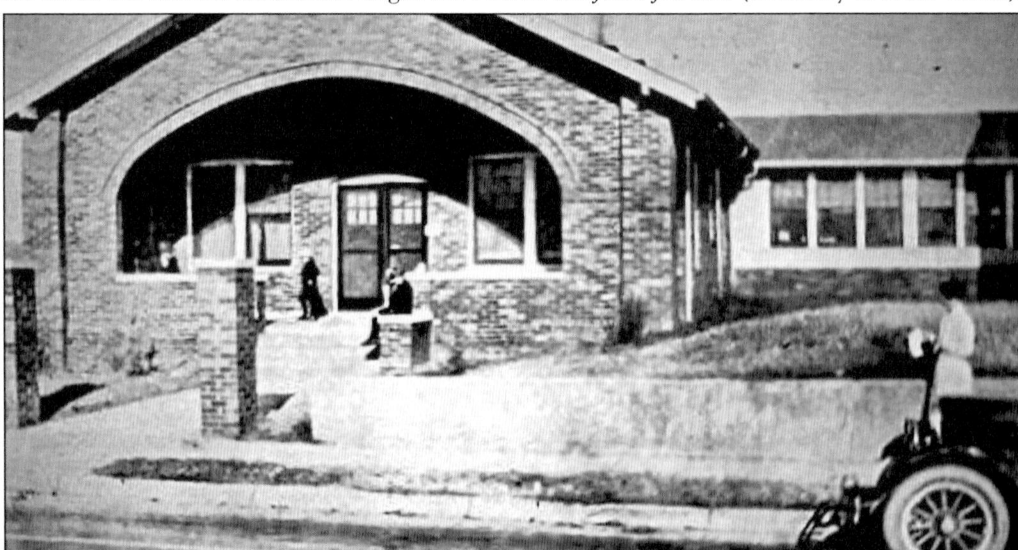

According to records prepared by Mrs. A. B. Sloan, the illness of Samuel Lowrance made Lowrance Hospital a reality. He met with Dr. Davies McLelland and Dr. George Taylor and made an offer of a building, land, and money to support a hospital. He asked them to help him build a hospital for Mooresville. Five doctors—A. E. Bell, Marvin Lackey, Allen Sloan, McLelland, and Taylor—formed a stock company to open a facility on West Center Avenue. Even though stockholders supported the hospital, a gift of $10,000 from S. Clay Williams was needed to emerge from the Great Depression on a solid footing. In 1929, the hospital converted to a nonprofit organization to take advantage of funding from the Duke Endowment.

Dr. Davies McLelland led the corporation and set about to develop a plan to raise the $12,000 needed for equipment and materials. They sold shares for $25. The facility was opened on April 20, 1926, to the public. The original home and the new brick addition soon filled with patients. Nurses had quarters in the upstairs of the Lowrance home, and doctors had space for offices.

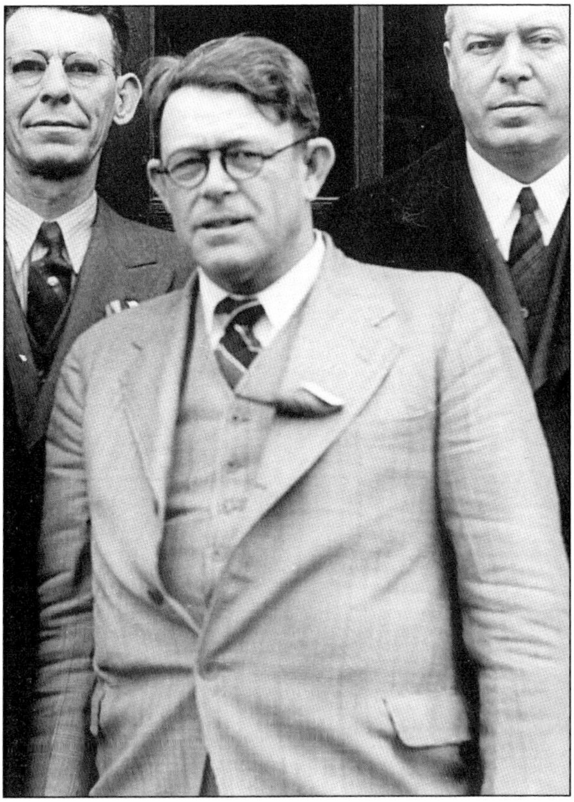

The Lowrance School of Nursing was established next door to the hospital. It was directed by Barbara Dellinger, Jesse Cashion, and Louise Harkey. Norma Furchess, longtime head of the nursing school, joined the staff in 1926. In 1938, a nurses' home was constructed on the site. Furchess Hall trained hundreds of nurses to work in hospitals, doctors' offices, and health centers throughout the region. (Courtesy of Penny Setzer Christie.)

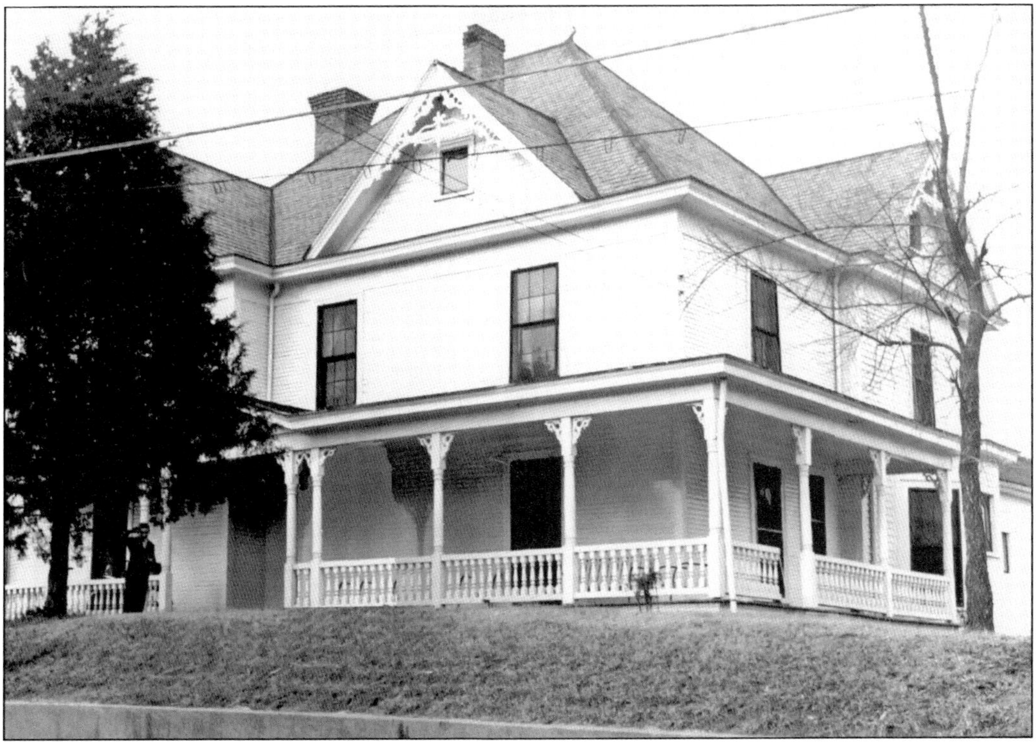

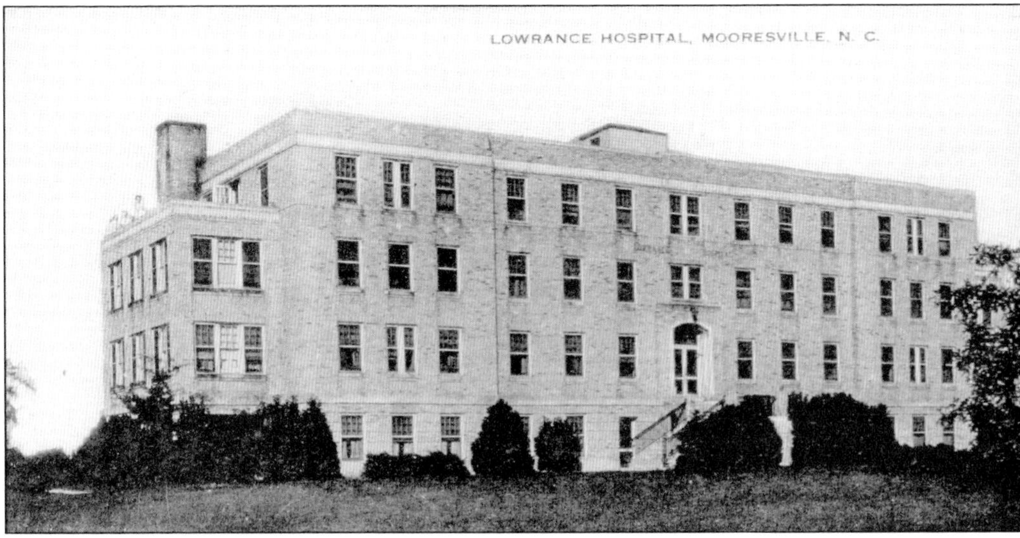

Plans for a larger building started in 1929. The town made $30,000 available to support the project in the beginning stages. George C. Goodman offered a lot in the Eastern Heights section bounded by Carpenter Avenue, Evergreen Street, and Statesville Avenue. Goodman sold the remainder of the block for $4,000 so that the hospital could face East Center Avenue. The Duke Endowment contributed $62,000 to build the four-story structure. Dr. Creighton Wrenn and Dr. W. W. Painter joined the staff in the 1936 and 1940 respectively. The hospital continued to grow and provide much-needed services to Mooresville and the surrounding area.

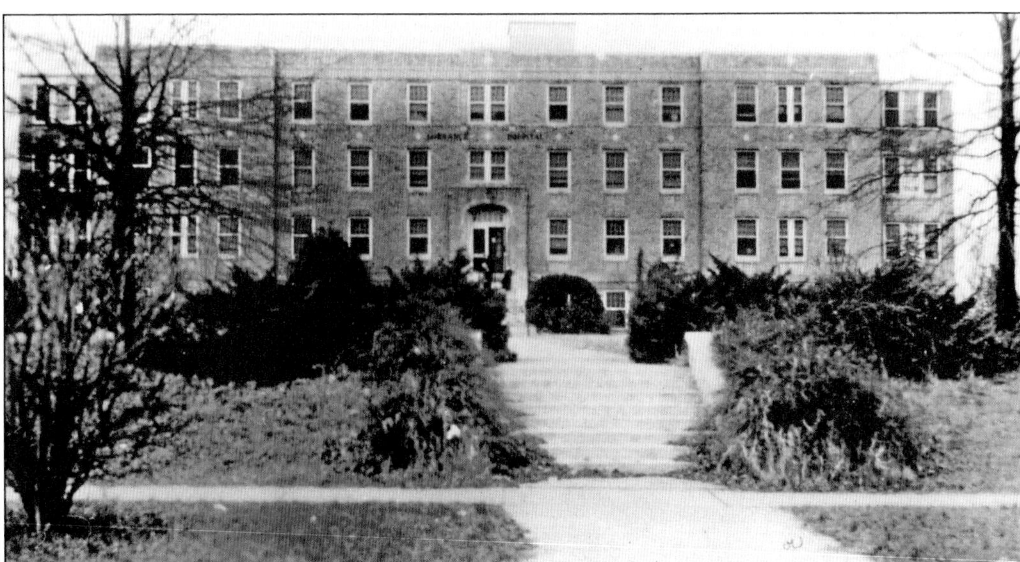

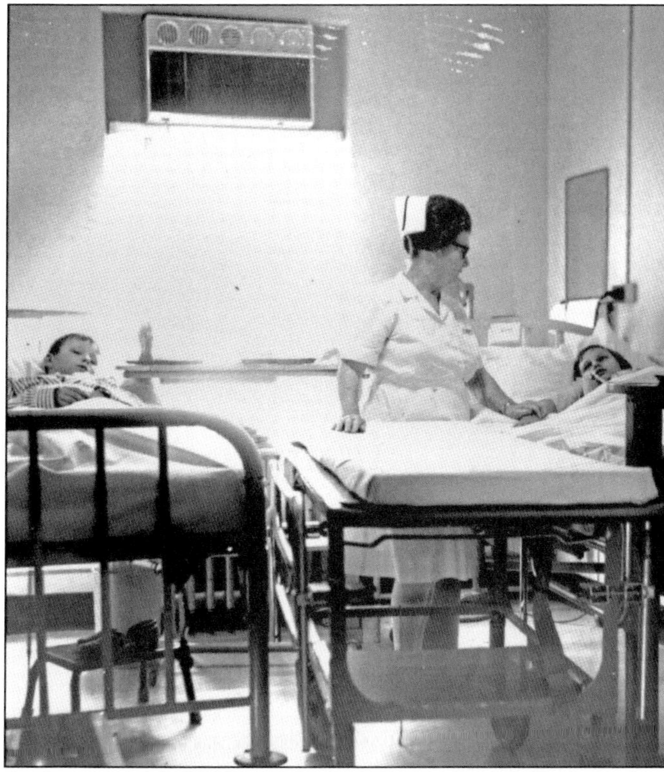

The community supported the construction of this needed facility with funds to furnish individual rooms. Some of the contributors are John Mack and Son, Clara Starrette Cavin, S. Clay and LuTelle Sherrill Williams, UDC Battle of Bentonville Chapter, Sallie Harris, Emma Harris Sherrill, Rotary and Kiwanis clubs, Belk's, and People's Home Furnishings. The new hospital included a kitchen, dining room, classroom, operating room, and an emergency department with X-ray room and other equipment. Patients receive the finest care with the latest equipment. The first patient there was Pattie Sue Phipps, who occupied room four on the second floor. (Courtesy of Lake Norman Regional Medical Center.)

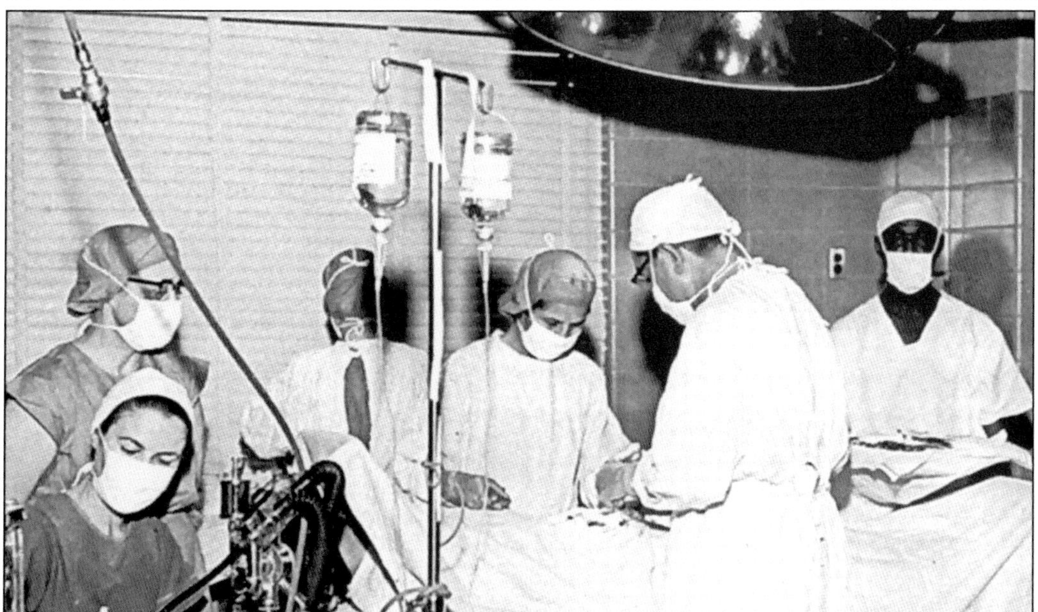

Dr. Creighton Wrenn and a team of doctors and nurses provided life-saving surgery in the new Lowrance Hospital facilities. Over the years, lives were saved with skills and procedures not available to the community before the organization of the hospital. Thanks to the efforts of citizens from all walks of life, health-care professionals were able to work in modern facilities. (Courtesy of Lake Norman Regional Medical Center.)

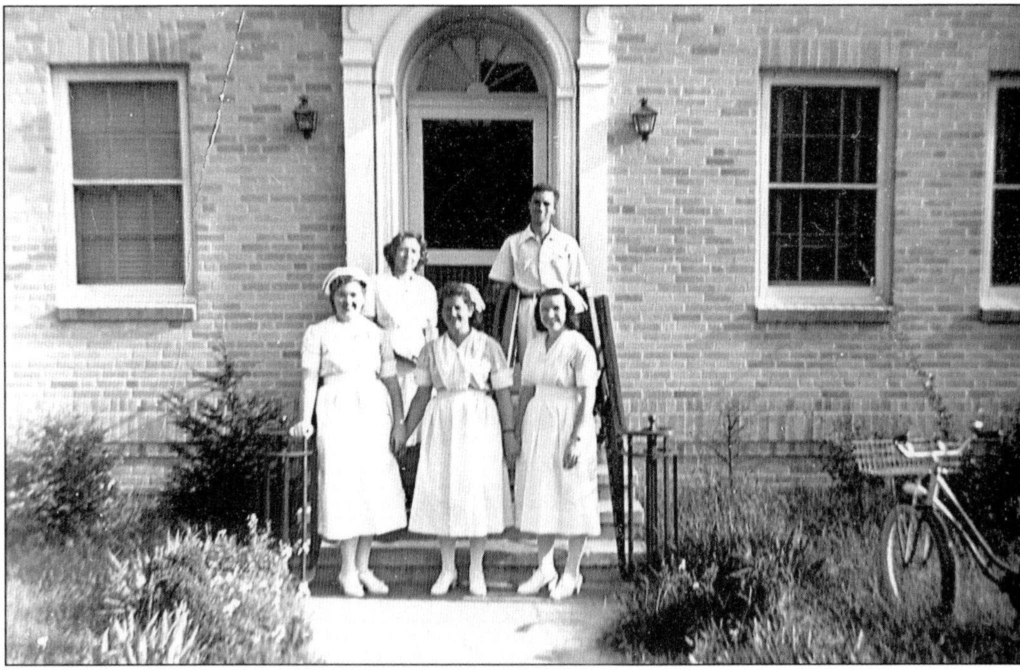

The nursing school was regarded as one of the best in the region and trained hundreds of nurses over the years. From left to right, Josephine Linn, Benizer Lytle, Ruby Davis, Faye Little, and Gladys Anderson were among the 1940 graduates. (Courtesy of Penny Setzer Christie.)

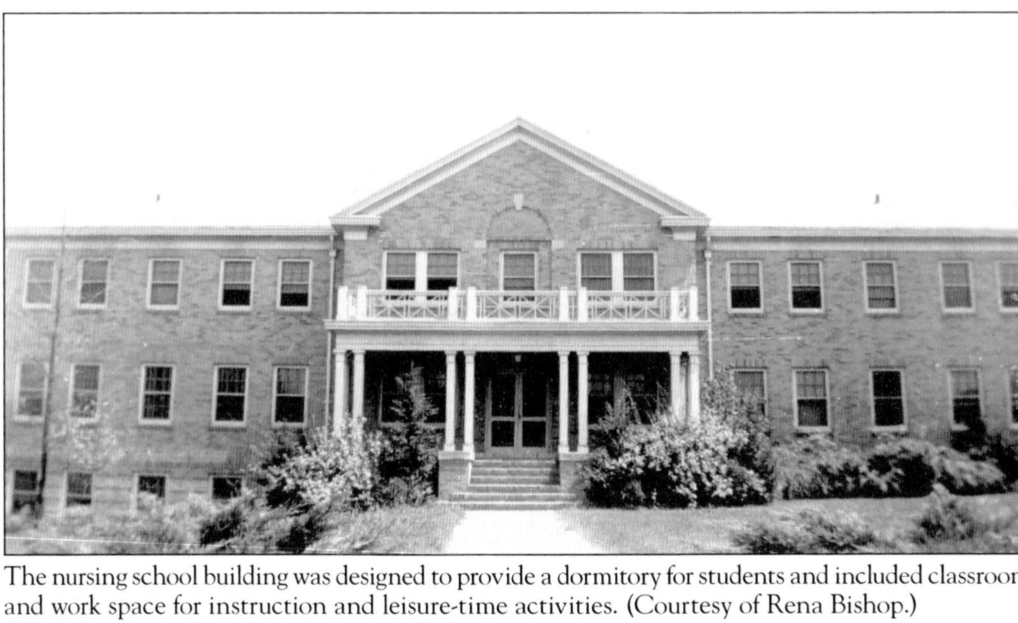

The nursing school building was designed to provide a dormitory for students and included classroom and work space for instruction and leisure-time activities. (Courtesy of Rena Bishop.)

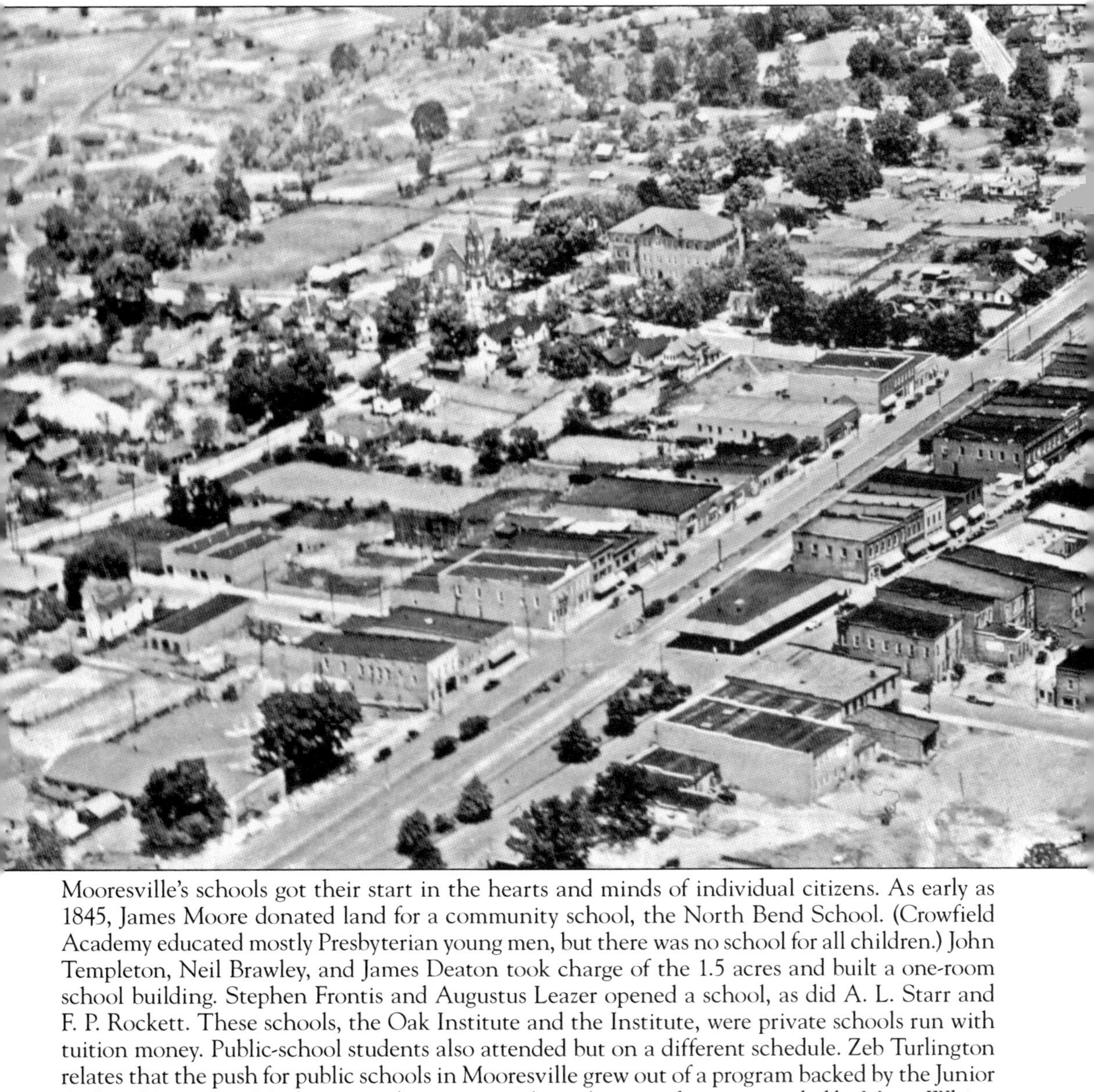

Mooresville's schools got their start in the hearts and minds of individual citizens. As early as 1845, James Moore donated land for a community school, the North Bend School. (Crowfield Academy educated mostly Presbyterian young men, but there was no school for all children.) John Templeton, Neil Brawley, and James Deaton took charge of the 1.5 acres and built a one-room school building. Stephen Frontis and Augustus Leazer opened a school, as did A. L. Starr and F. P. Rockett. These schools, the Oak Institute and the Institute, were private schools run with tuition money. Public-school students also attended but on a different schedule. Zeb Turlington relates that the push for public schools in Mooresville grew out of a program backed by the Junior Order of American Mechanics and an active and vocal group of proponents led by Moses White, B. A. Troutman, J. P. Mills, T. B. Smith, and W. C. Johnston. With a grant of land by John F. Moore and a bill in the North Carolina Legislature, the Mooresville Graded School District was established in 1905. It took two elections to pass a $20,000 bond issue to build a school on the site of the old Mooresville Academy. The cornerstone was laid on June 29, 1907. A. C. Kerley was superintendent and C. L. Carr was principal. This aerial photograph from the 1920s shows the academy as it looked in the early days of the school district.

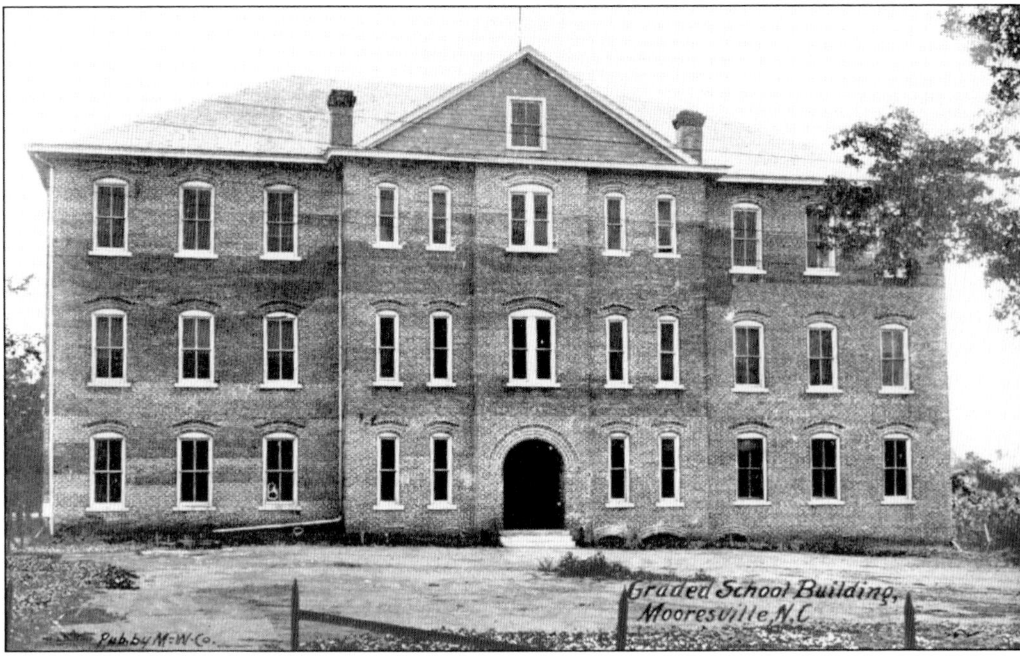

The Mooresville Academy was founded in 1874 as a result of Moore's civic pride. He believed that every community needed schools and churches, and he donated land for their construction. According to records, the land at the corner of Moore Avenue and Academy Street was deeded to the school committee and the Grange, which became defunct. The private school was supported by student fees.

MOORESVILLE ACADEMY,

A first-class Preparatory School for Boys and Girls, will begin its twenty-sixth annual session September 2, 1901. Experienced teachers. Thorough instruction. Mild, but firm, discipline. For further information apply to C. T. CARR, A. B., PRINCIPAL.

MISS CAMILLE McCORKLE,
MISS LULA GREY, } ASSISTANTS.

The academy began its 26th session in 1901, advertising for students in the *Mooresville Enterprise*. The academy intended to be "a first class school for boys and girls. Those who wish to enter college will receive such a course of instruction that will prepare them to pursue their studies successfully in the higher institutions of the state. Those not wishing to take a collegiate course will receive such training as will fit them for the ordinary vocations of life."

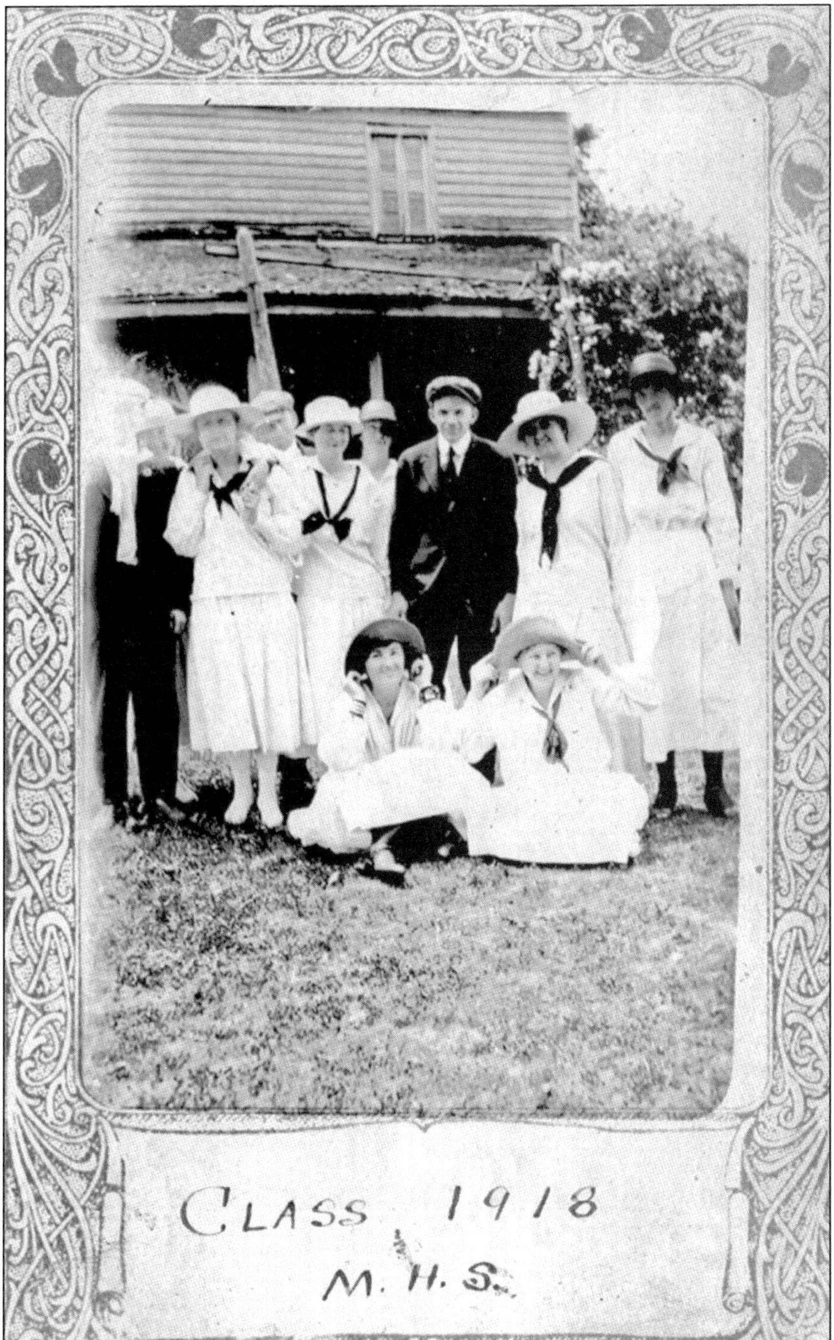

Dr. S. W. Stevenson, the man who laid out the streets of Mooresville, was a great supporter of public education. In 1907, he wrote, "The most valuable asset of any community is its young blood, the children. May every citizen of Mooresville rise above prejudice, above avarice, above narrowness, above ignorance and lend a cheerful helping hand to develop and train our young blood." The Mooresville High School class of 1918 took advantage of the high-quality education available from the Mooresville Graded School District.

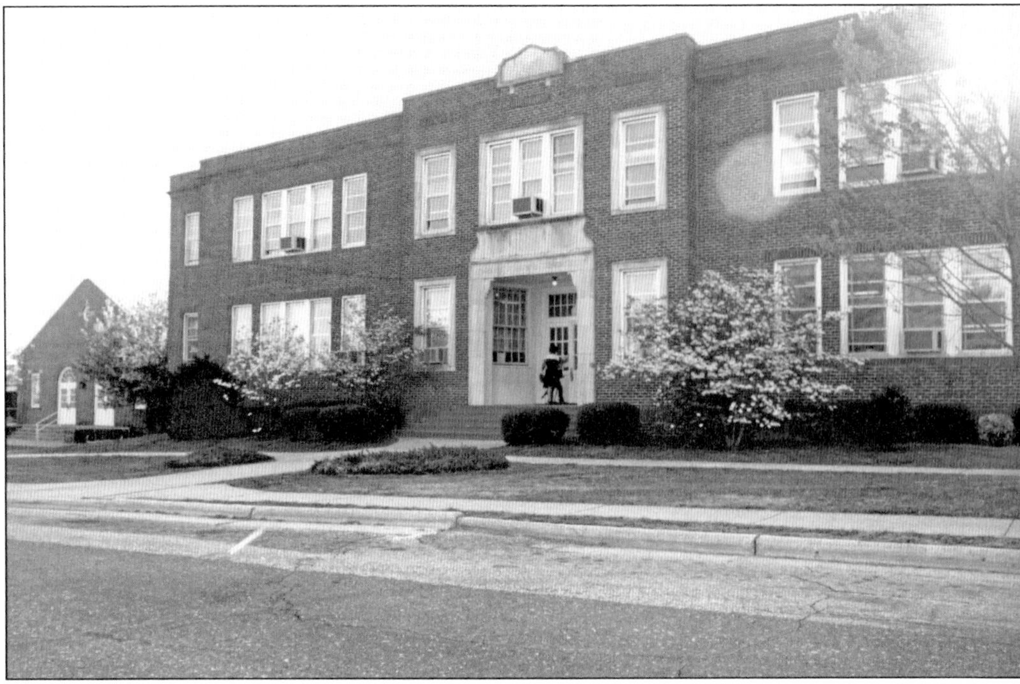

The second school in the district was North School, located on the corner of Oak Street and McNeely Avenue. The building was purchased in 1911 to be used by students in grades one through four. Designed as a residence, the building was used until 1925, when a new school building was built across the street. Named Park View School for its proximity to Stewart Park, the building included 11 classrooms, offices, and a basement.

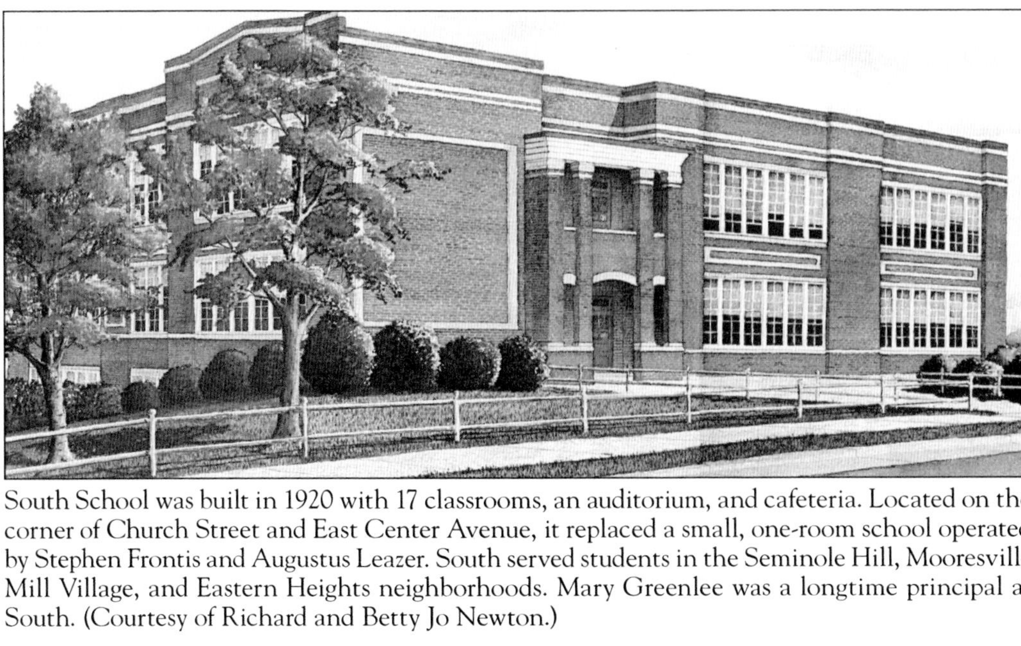

South School was built in 1920 with 17 classrooms, an auditorium, and cafeteria. Located on the corner of Church Street and East Center Avenue, it replaced a small, one-room school operated by Stephen Frontis and Augustus Leazer. South served students in the Seminole Hill, Mooresville Mill Village, and Eastern Heights neighborhoods. Mary Greenlee was a longtime principal at South. (Courtesy of Richard and Betty Jo Newton.)

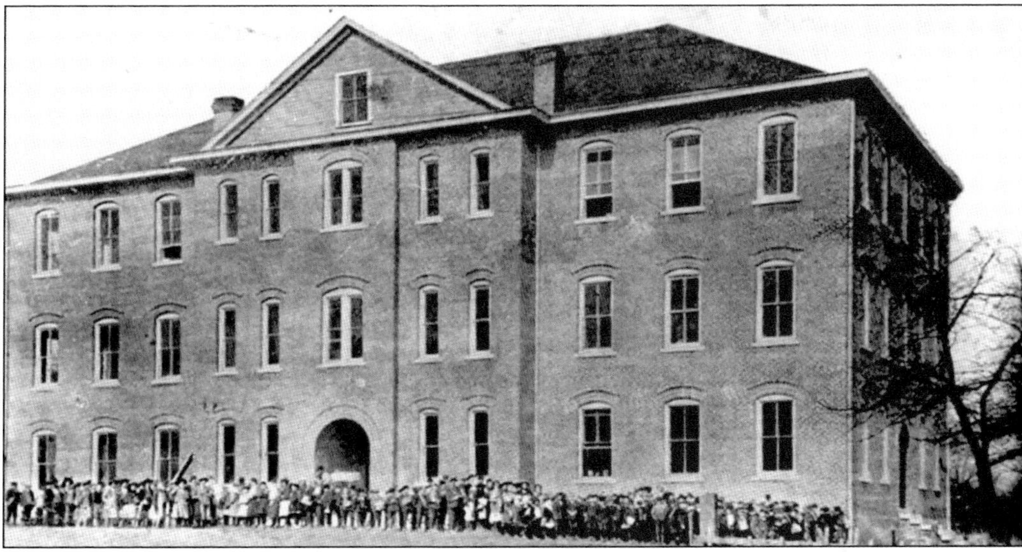

With the construction of elementary schools for the district, the academy building was used for high school students. The building was adequate for classrooms, a library, and laboratory as the number of students grew with the population of the town. In 1932, flames starting in the attic over the third floor destroyed the interior of the building. The school board met and called in the services of the state school building inspector, who declared the interior of the building a total loss. The brick walls were able to be saved and used as the foundation of the new building.

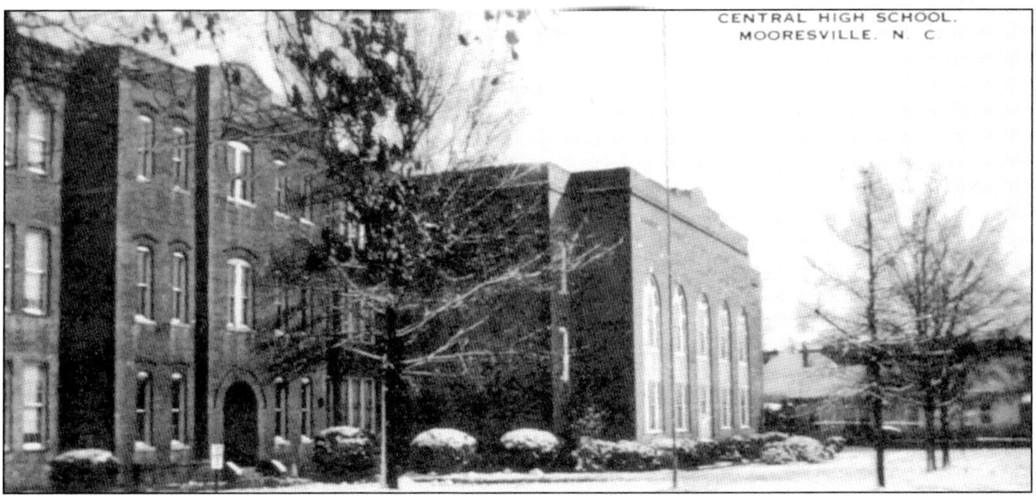

Work on the new began almost immediately. High school students continued their classes at Park View, and elementary students attended South School on a staggered schedule. The new school was built with modern conveniences and up-to-date laboratory spaces and equipment. In addition, a large auditorium was added to the building to be used for school as well as community functions and activities. The new Central High School of 1935 was a complete and modern facility, with gymnasium, auditorium, cafeteria, and athletic field on the campus at the corner of West Moore Avenue and Academy Street. Land was purchased in the Eastern Heights section in 1948 for a new high school. Construction was delayed due to a lack of funds, but the building was completed to house junior high students until 1958, when high school students moved into the building. The Mooresville High School class of 1959 was the first to graduate from the new building. Junior high students relocated to the old Central High School building.

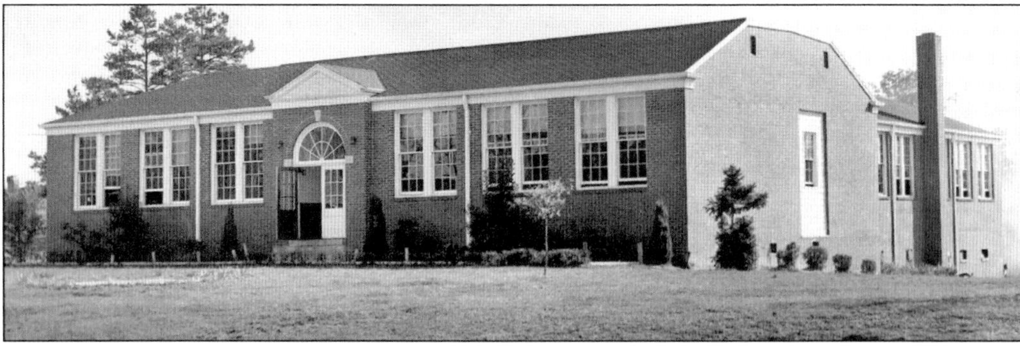

In 1941, Dunbar School was built on McLelland Avenue. The brick building replaced a two-story frame building located near the junction. The school was named for Paul Laurence Dunbar, the first African American poet to gain national prominence. Dr. Naurice F. Woods served as principal for 35 years. In 1972, the school was renamed in Woods's honor and served elementary students until the technology program began to use the building. (Courtesy of Sylvia Smith.)

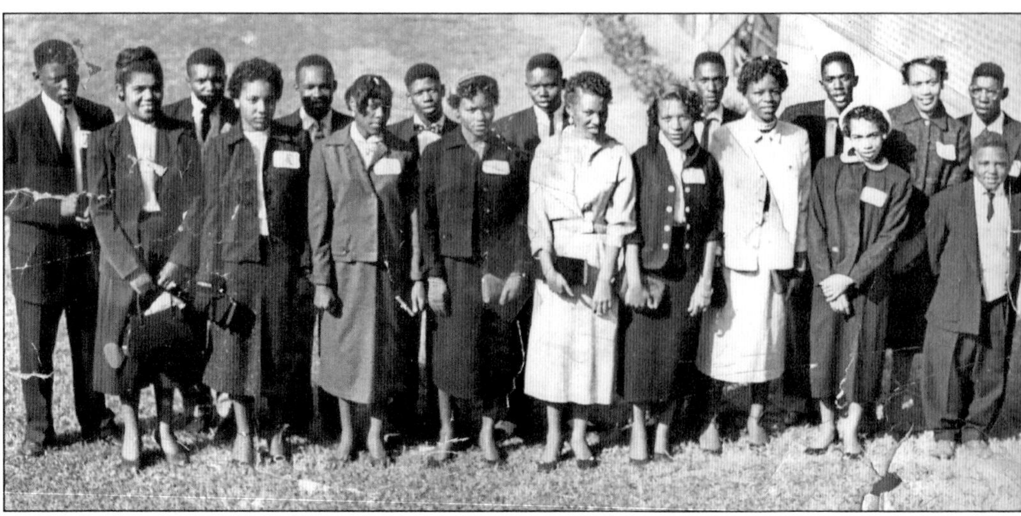

Dunbar High School's class of 1956 set records on the sports field and in the classroom, posting high grades and achievement. (Courtesy of Mary Gabriel.)

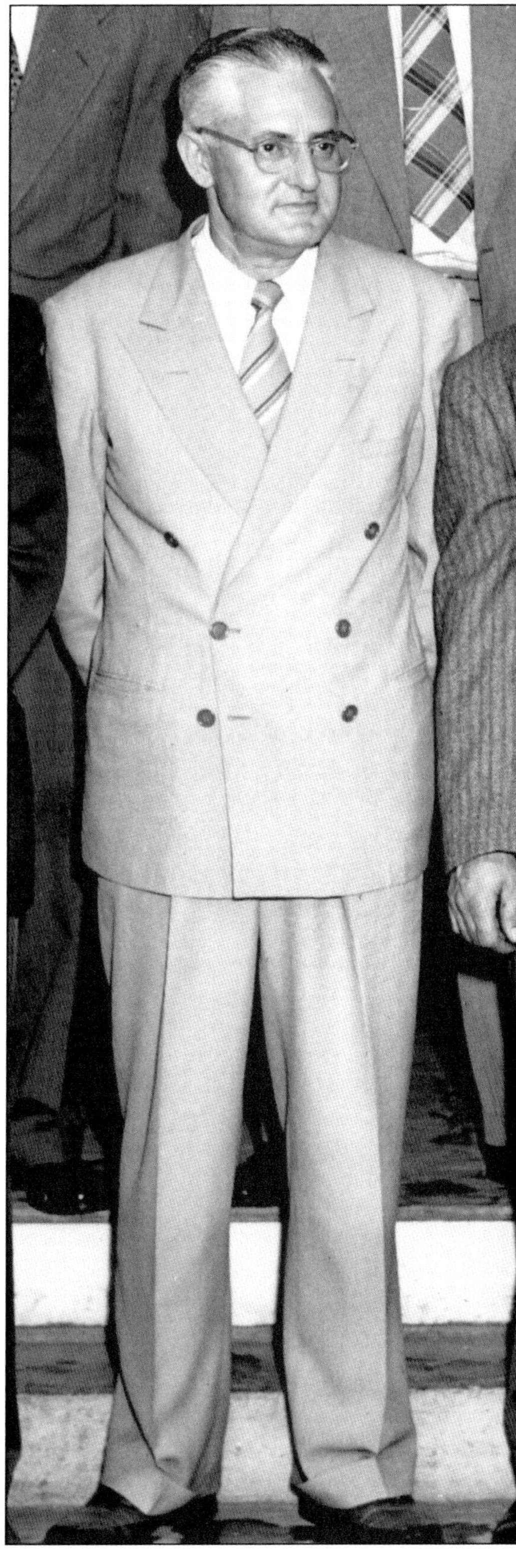

Avery C. Craven came to Mooresville in 1926 and set about to make its Belk Department Store one of the most successful in the Belk organization. His leadership was evident in Mooresville chamber programs such as the Mooresville Plan to develop the downtown business district into a pedestrian-friendly shopping area. Craven's honesty and integrity helped guide the town board of commissioners during his tenure. (Courtesy of Mooresville–South Iredell Chamber of Commerce.)

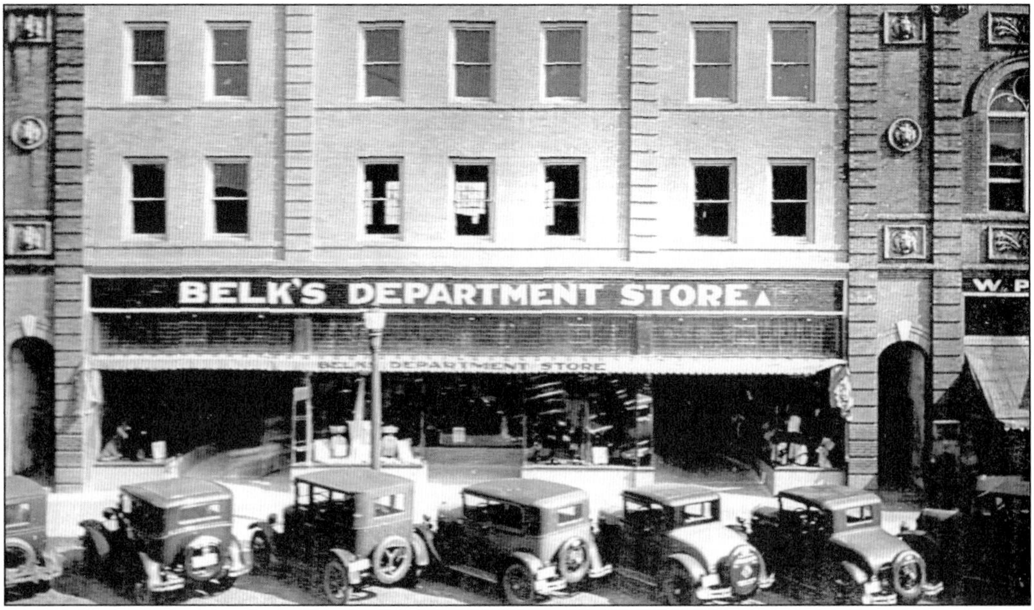

Belk's Department Store opened for business on Main Street on March 24, 1924, purchasing the inventory of W. M. Freeze and Company. Joe Gudger, the first manager, expanded the store's floor space and inventory by purchasing the Hub, an adjacent store. Avery C. Craven became manager in 1926 and guided the purchase of a building in the next block. The building was remodeled and opened on August 30, 1929, with a great opening day sale and values for Belk customers. Belk's became famous for offering quality merchandise at reasonable prices. (Courtesy of Francella Craven Kerr.)

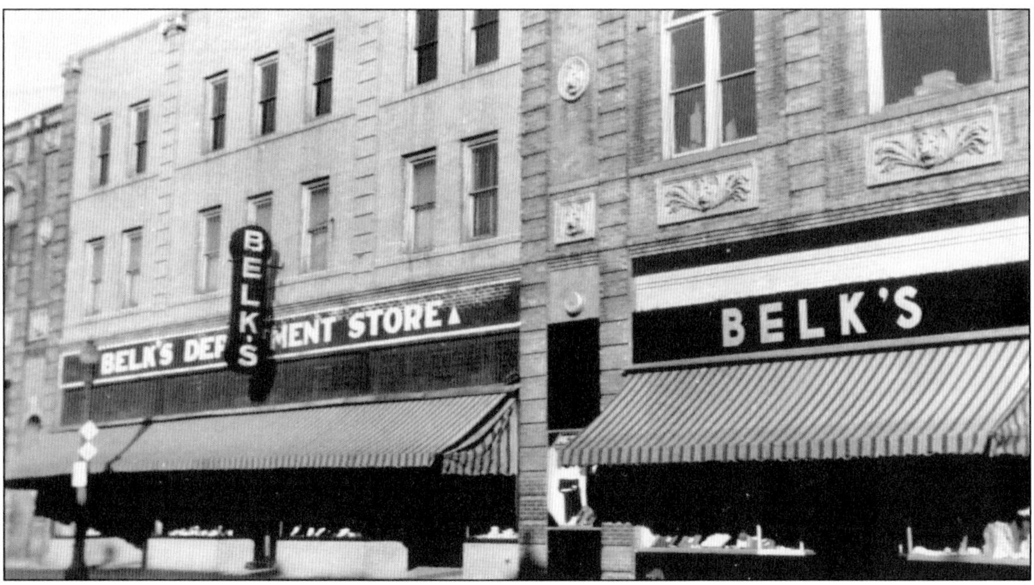

Additional floor space was purchased from the Carpenter and Whitley-Wilkinson stores, and remodeling added a second floor, mezzanine, and back parking spaces. Belk's became the premier department store in Mooresville, offering value on the extensive variety of goods available. At one time, a customer could buy a lawnmower, socks, and piece goods in one shopping trip to Belk's. (Courtesy of Mooresville–South Iredell Chamber of Commerce.)

Robert Kerr (left) and Frank Harris (right) were among the many leaders of the Belk store in Mooresville. Marketing to locals was based on the personal involvement of all employees. Customers were called by name and given a high level of service and value on the wide range of merchandise available in the town's largest department store. Shopping downtown usually meant a trip to Belk's for clothing, shoes, housewares, and toys. Mooresville's busy streets welcomed hundreds of shoppers to the largest store in town. (Courtesy of Ray D. Boone.)

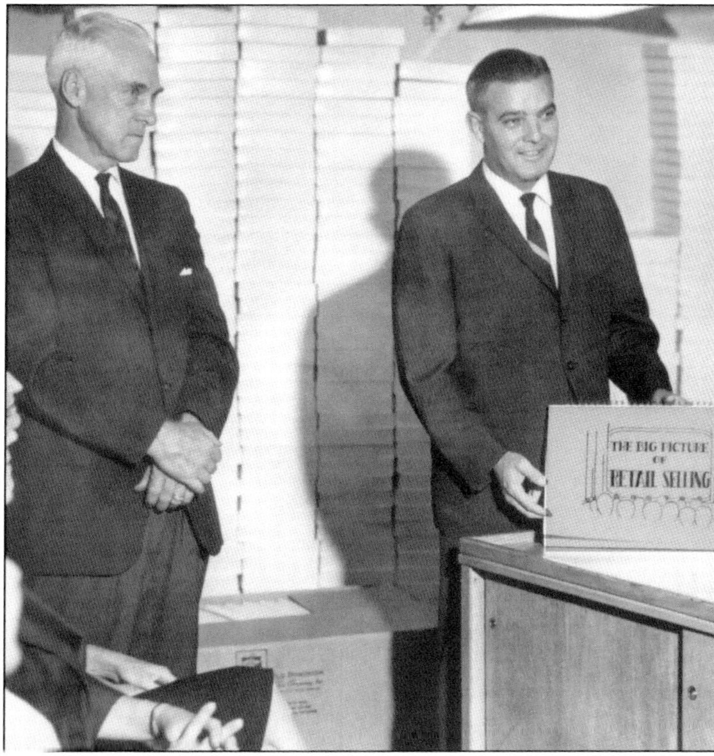

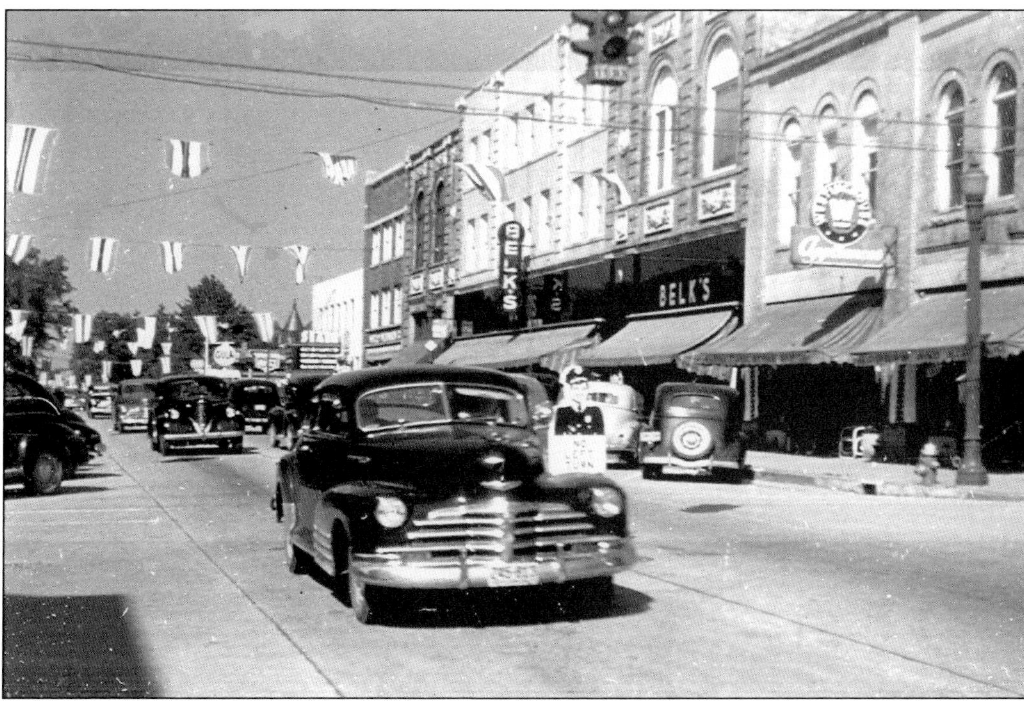

Downtown Mooresville became a shopping destination and an excellent place to open a business in the 1940s. Stores included Raylass, Belks, Piedmont Bank, Mills Bootery, Morrow Brothers Furniture, and Western Auto, just to name a few. (Courtesy of Ray D. Boone.)

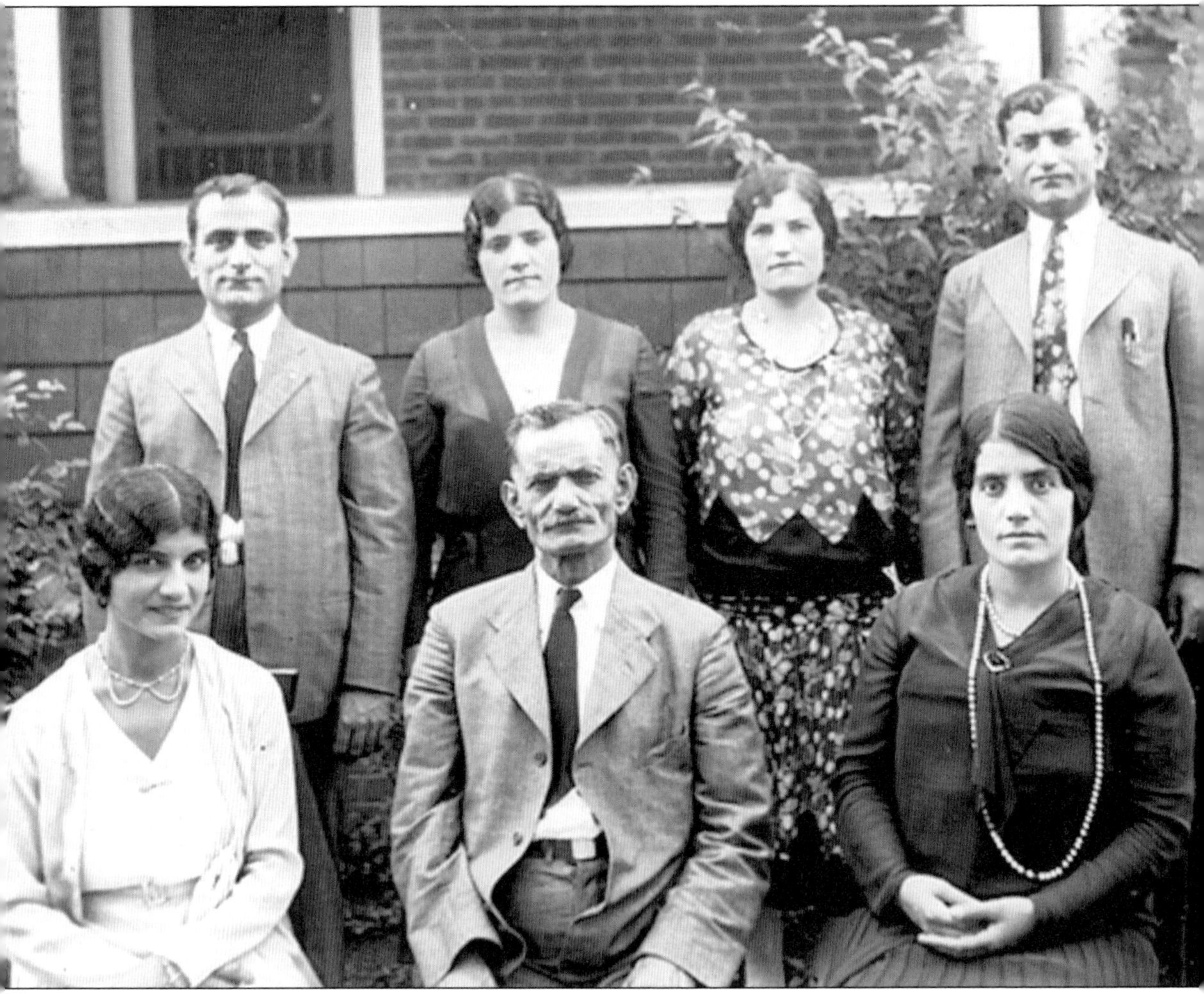

Mooresville merchant John Mack decided to leave his home in Lebanon for a better life in America. Friends and relatives already living in the United States told of grand opportunities for hardworking businessmen. Leaving his home as Hannah Mahcool Fakoury, he came to America through Ellis Island, where a clerk misunderstood the pronunciation and registered him as John Mack. His original destination was Marion, South Carolina, but the confusion of train schedules took him to North Carolina, finally to Charlotte and then to Mooresville to make a home for his family. After a return to Lebanon and the unfortunate death of his wife, Naceem, the Mack family made their home in the United States as merchants and community builders. John Mack and Son opened for business on December 24, 1912. Even though the store was open and successful, Mack continued house-to-house selling until the 1920s. Pictured are, from left to right, (first row) Bahia, John Mack, and Sophia; (second row) Charles, Lucille, Nora, and Side. (Courtesy of Mitchell Mack.)

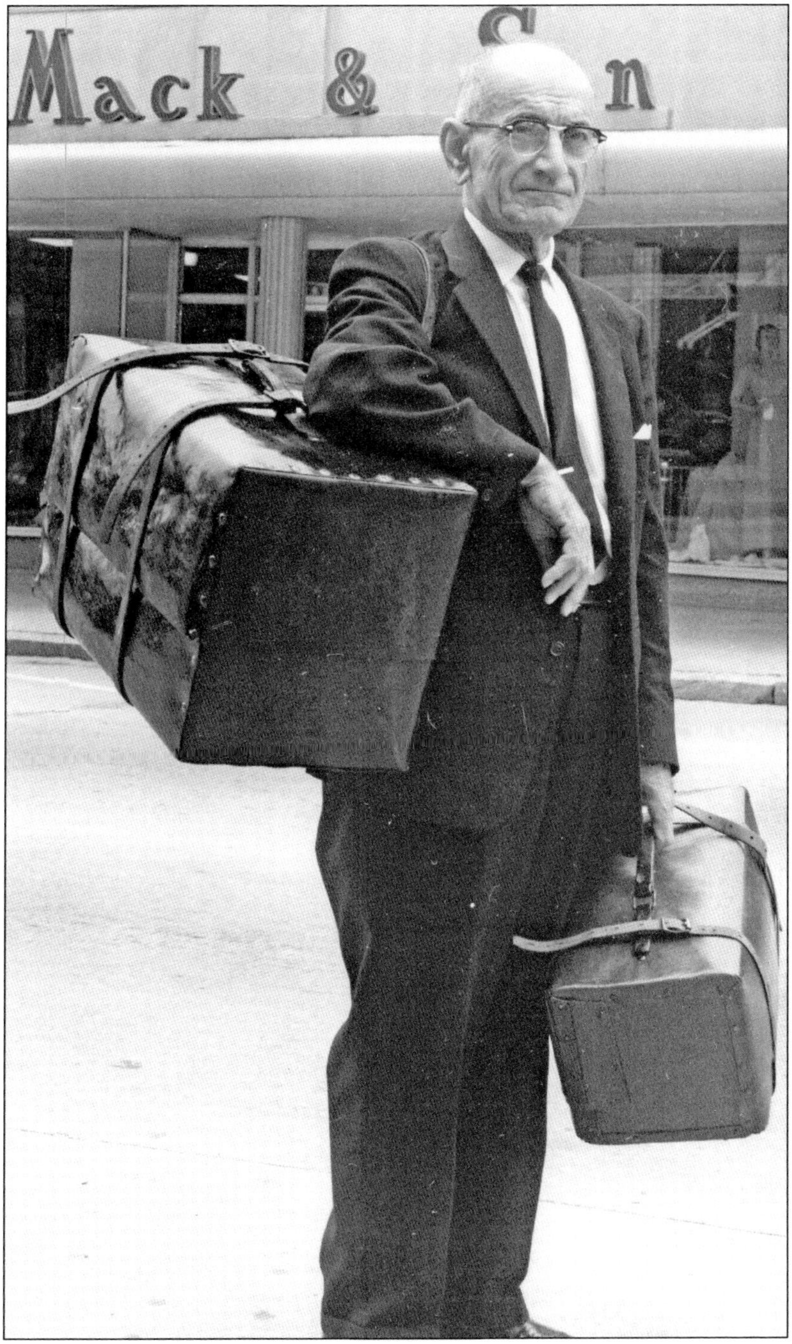

Side Mack came to America in 1908 to join his father, brother Charlie, and sister Nora to work in the Charlotte store. Traveling over a 50-mile radius on foot and later by horse to sell goods, he and his father met hundreds of people and made many friends, including many in the growing town of Mooresville. Side Mack made his home in Mooresville, marrying Tabetta Ikall and raising a family of four children. A leading merchant and community leader, Side Mack was involved in Rotary and Boy Scouts, earning the coveted Silver Beaver award for his dedication and contributions. (Courtesy of Mitchell Mack.)

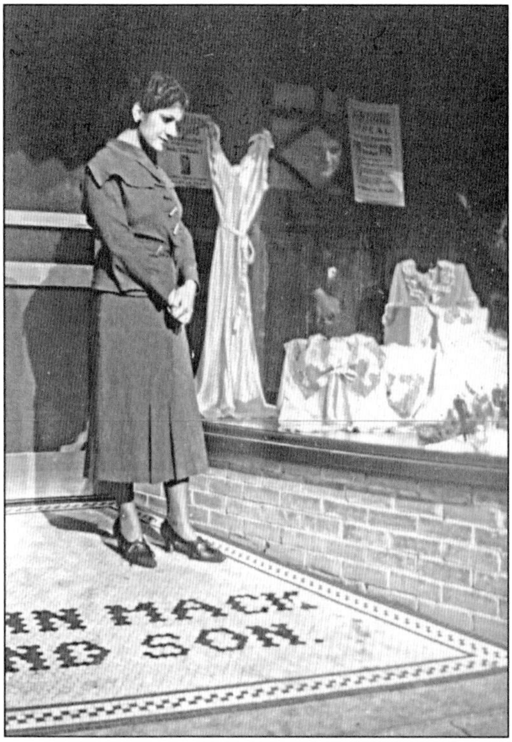

Bahia Mack (Weaver) worked with her father and brother and managed the women's department of the store on Main Street. She offered a wide variety of clothing and accessories for women and young ladies. She left the family business to start her own store featuring a beauty shop, jewelry, and fashions. (Courtesy of Mitchell Mack.)

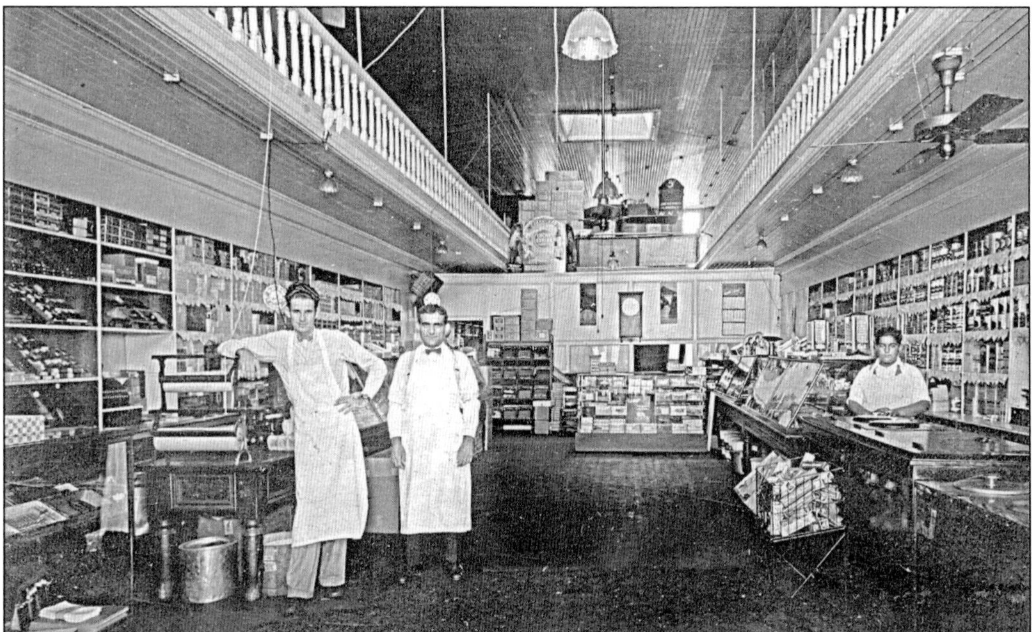

Charles Mack, center, was a multi-talented merchant with skills ranging from candy and ice cream making to merchandising essentials like foods and tobacco. Charles Mack and Sons got its start in the confectionery business and his recipe was the foundation of the Mooresville Ice Cream Company. From its store on East Center Avenue, Mack provided a wide variety of goods to individual and wholesale business customers. (Courtesy of Mitchell Mack.)

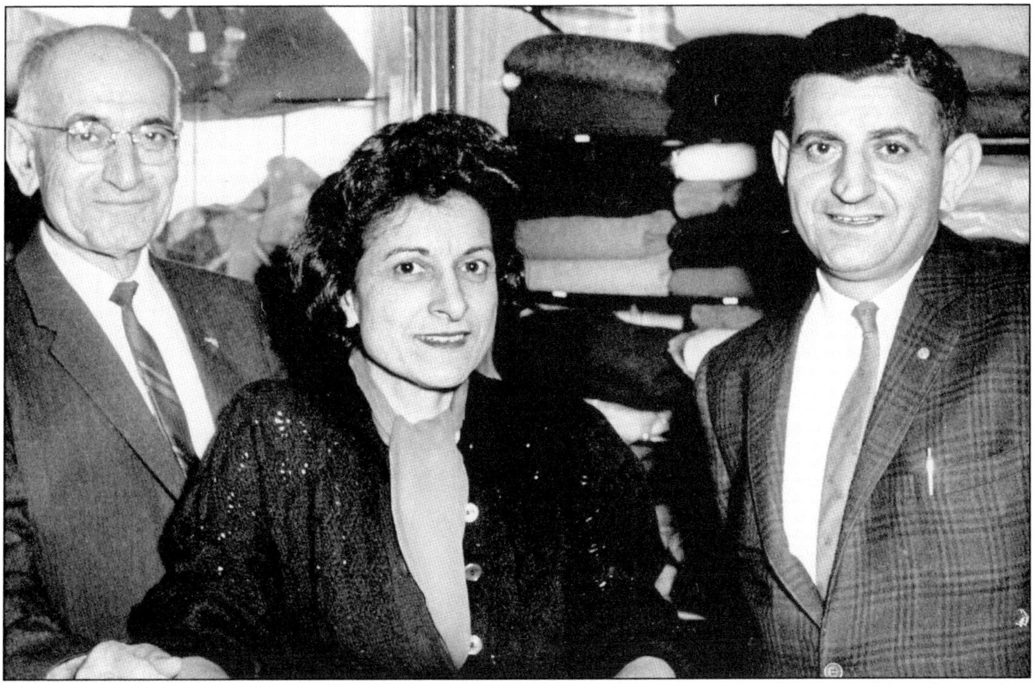

Madeline and Mitchell Mack were a dynamic merchandising team. They offered high-quality fashions for men and women and always provided service with the sale. Operating the store with their father, Side, each learned the trade from a master salesman. (Courtesy of Mitchell Mack.)

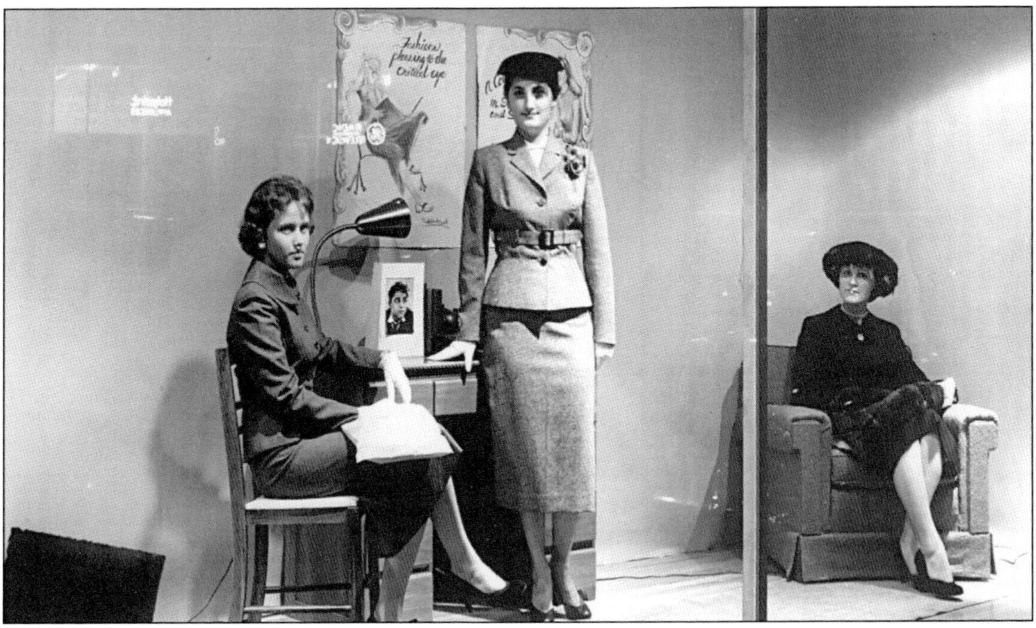

Bahia and Madeline Mack were innovative merchandisers. They featured the only live mannequins in window displays in town. Madeline's fashion and decorative drawings and artwork became part of each display, regardless of the season. She used her talent to design and construct all of the visual merchandising materials used inside the store and in the window displays. Joan Morrow (left) and Dolores Mack (middle) were favorite models. (Courtesy of Mitchell Mack.)

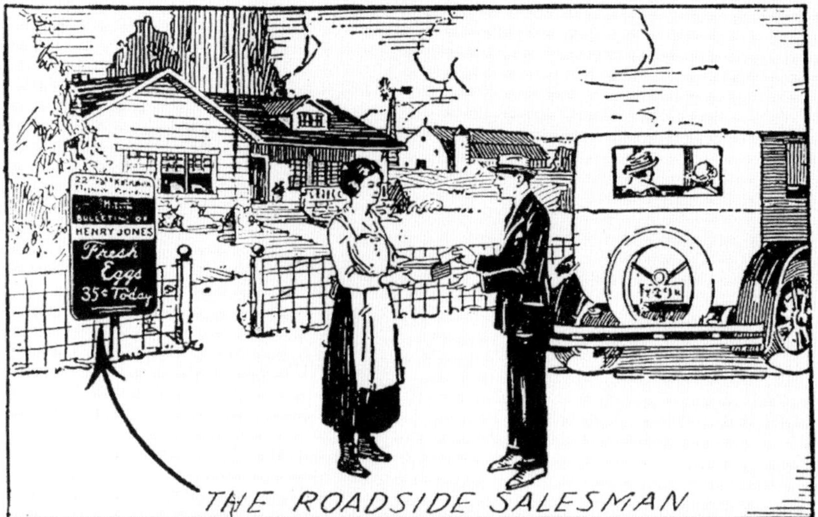

It is easy to sell eggs, poultry, berries, fruit, potatoes, horses, cows, hogs, sheep, hay, grain, or farm tools and hundreds of other things if you have one of our Roadside salesman in front of your house.

Don't let your wife sstand out in the hot sun waiting for motorists to come along—write what you have to sell in chalk on the Roadsside salesman and the motorist will stop an come into your yard. No peddling from doo rto door—no loading and unloading your produce and taking a chance of getting a low price in town. Put the Roadside salesman in front of your housse where a motorist can see it, or on a post in the front yard, or on the fence or the gate.

It is a rust-proof black board device which will last five years. It is only the work of a minute to write your message on it. It will make you money —work for you by day, rain or shine, winter or summer—it is always on the job—not only good for selling, but if you want to buy something write your wants on the black board.

Use it to stop the mail man for money orders—use it to stop the oil man for gasoline or oil. You can use it every day for something.

We are offering you this wonderful Roadside salesman, 26 guage, Keystone Copper-bearing Steel, with three colors baked on, at a ridiculouly low price of 85 cents, owing to the fact that our ad appears on part of the surface. A Roadside salesman like this if you bought it yourself would cost many dollars. Drop in the store at your first opportunity and get one of these before they are gone. Your name and the distance you are from town will be painted on your Roadside salesman. It's your name plate—informs people who you are and where you are!

John Mack & Son

John and Side Mack never forgot the importance of personal selling and offered a "roadside salesman" outdoor signboard for every house in a 1925 advertisement in the *Mooresville Enterprise*. There is no record of the number of sales of the unique item.

A U.S. post office opened on Main Street in August 1871 with William Wilson as postmaster. Z. W. Dusenberry delivered mail on Star Route 5213. According to the *Mooresville News Leader*, James A. Farley said, "The records of the department do not indicate the mode of transportation or the frequency of service, but it is reasonable to assume the mail was carried on horseback or by horse-drawn vehicle. The salary of the first postmaster was $12 per year in 1871. By 1873 the salary rose to $68." In 1920, the post office moved to a building on the corner of Moore Avenue and North Main Street. (Courtesy of the Edward Kipka family.)

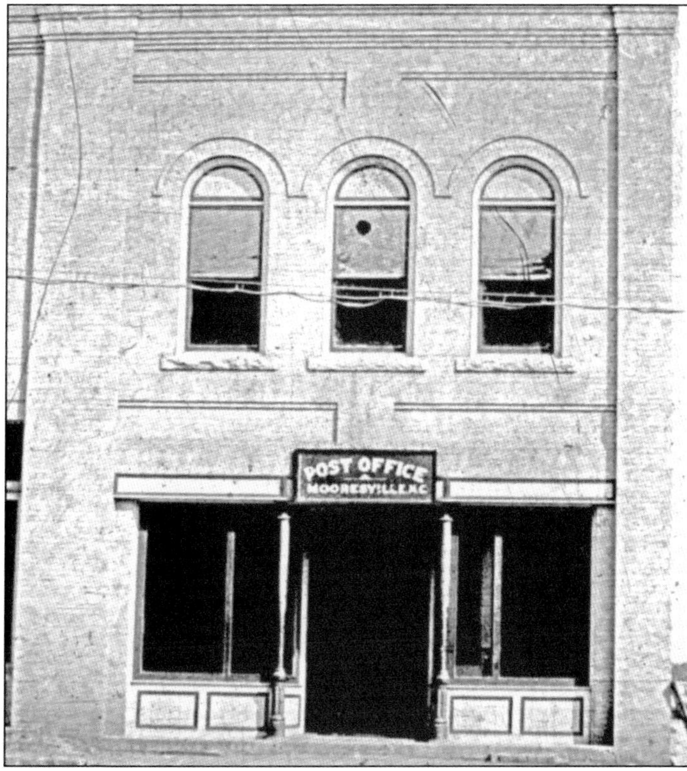

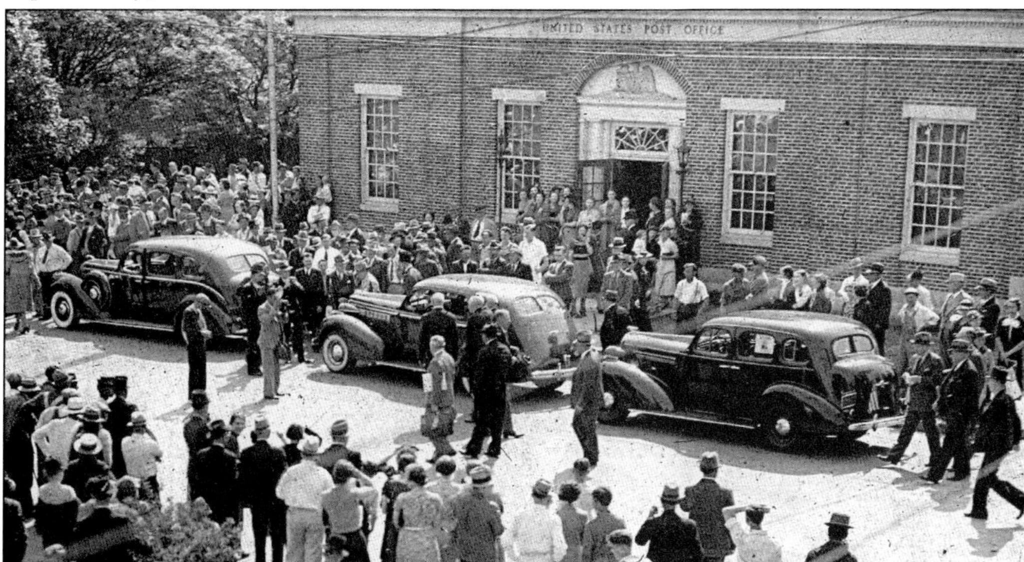

In 1937, the first federally owned building was constructed by the Treasury Department under the authority of the Emergency Construction Program Act of 1935 as part of the national recovery from the Great Depression. The property on the corner of Main Street and East Iredell Avenue was purchased from W. C. Johnston for $10,000. Designed by the Treasury Department's supervising architect, the Mooresville Post Office was one of more than 1,100 postal facilities built with Depression-era funding. (Courtesy of the Edward Kipka family, Frank Freeze, photographer.)

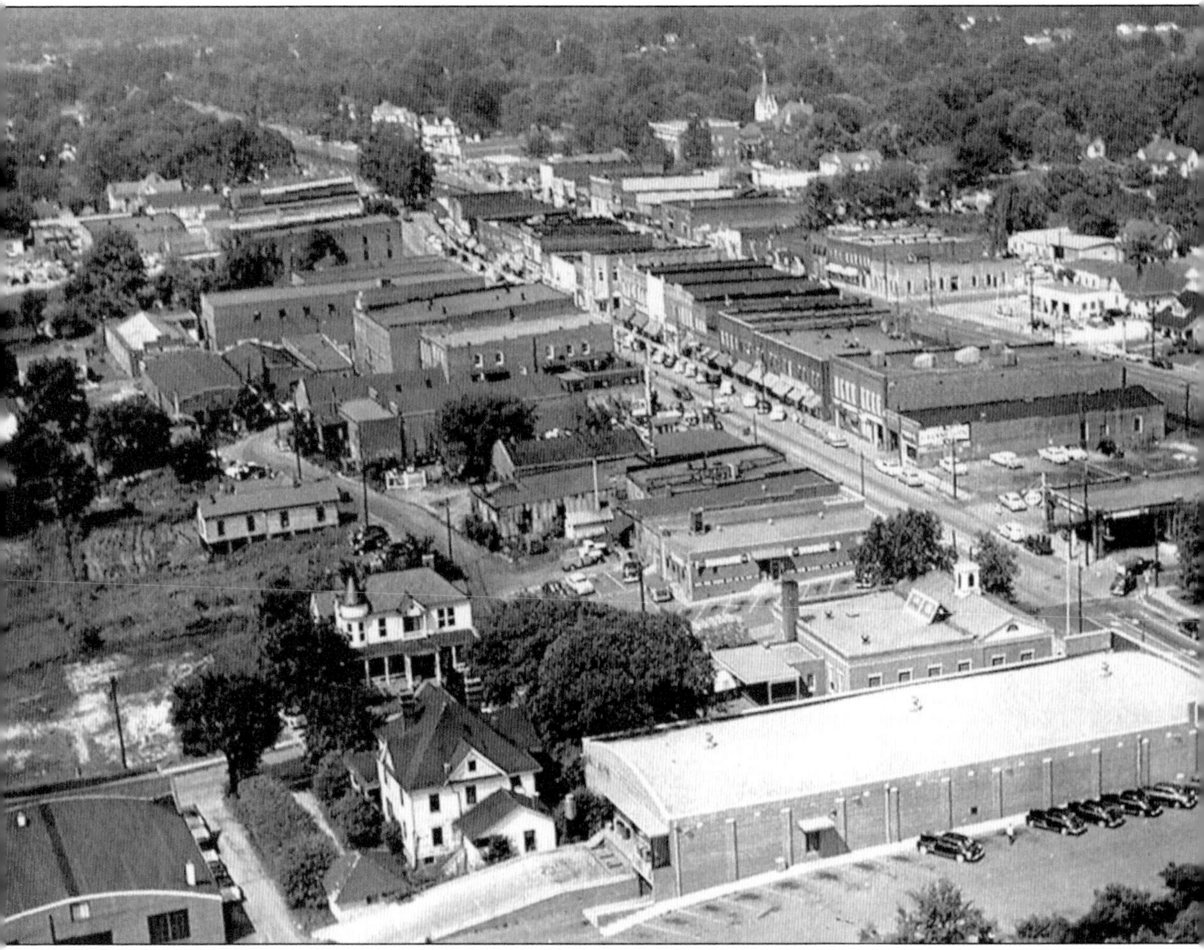

Situated on a busy corner near the center of activity, the new post office was within walking distance of most businesses. It became an informal meeting place for the more than 400 box holders as they visited the facility to pick up mail and take advantage of the services offered.

DEDICATION CEREMONIES

MOORESVILLE, NORTH CAROLINA

TUESDAY, APRIL 26, 1938

9:30 o'clock A. M.
NORTH MAIN STREET

Concert at Post Office Building 8:30 to 9:30 A. M.
By Kannapolis Band

PRESIDING:
Con C. Johnston, Representative in N. C. Legislature

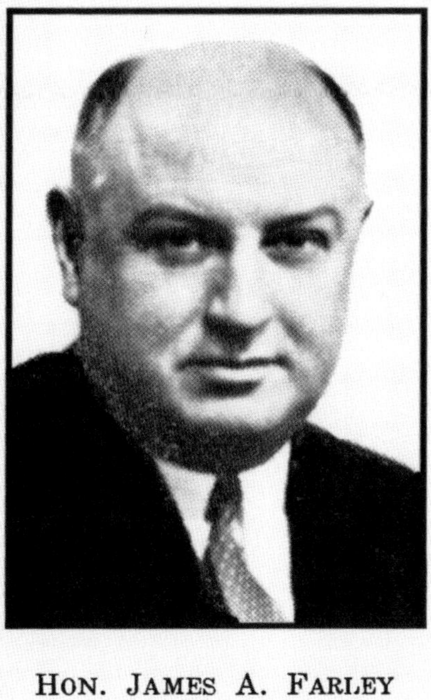

HON. JAMES A. FARLEY
Postmaster General
United States of
America

INVOCATION
Rev. R. A. White, D. D.
Pastor First Presbyterian Church

NORTH CAROLINA STATE SONG
Mooresville Public School Children
Miss Selma Johnson, Director

JOHN M. KENNETTE
Postmaster

INTRODUCTION OF HONORED GUESTS
(Time Permitting)

HON. ROBERT L. DOUGHTON
Representative in Congress, Ninth District

HON. JAMES A. FARLEY
Postmaster General of the United States

BENEDICTION
Rev. Arthur Kale
Pastor First Methodist Church

Postmaster General James A. Farley joined a long list of dignitaries and postmaster John Kennette opening this state-of-the-art facility. According to newspaper reports, "several thousand" people crowded North Main Street for the event. Limousines carrying dignitaries crowded Main Street, and crowds gathered around the speakers' stand and in the street.

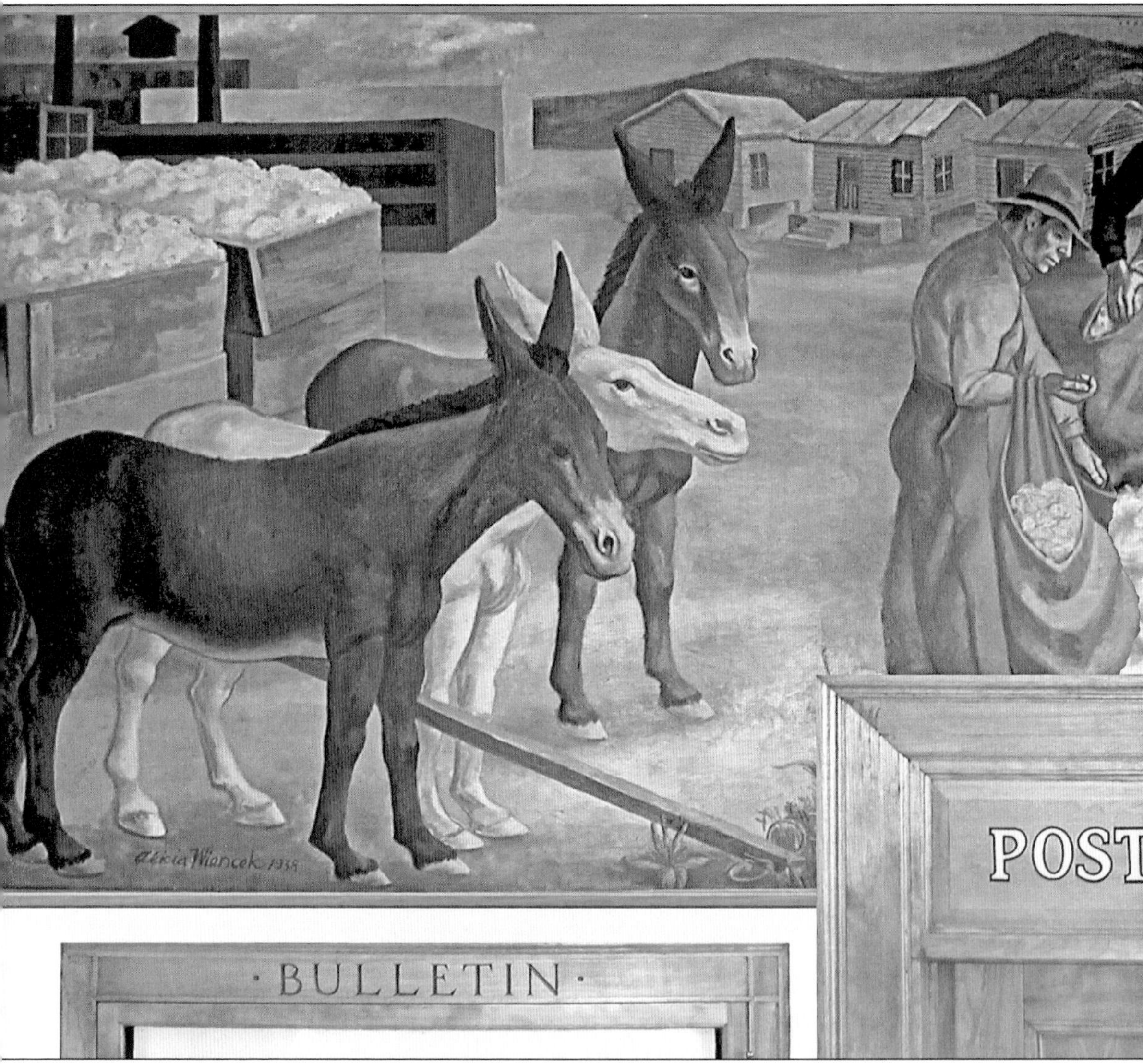

In 1934, Pres. Franklin D. Roosevelt, at the urging of artist George Biddle, sought to provide relief from the Great Depression to artists through the Federal Art Project of the Works Progress Administration (WPA). The Treasury Department's Section of Painting and Sculpture, established in 1934, was responsible for the construction and decoration of federal buildings, small-town post offices in particular. Artists were usually selected through competitions judged by a committee of local citizens. Artists who won were urged to visit the towns and meet with people to discuss

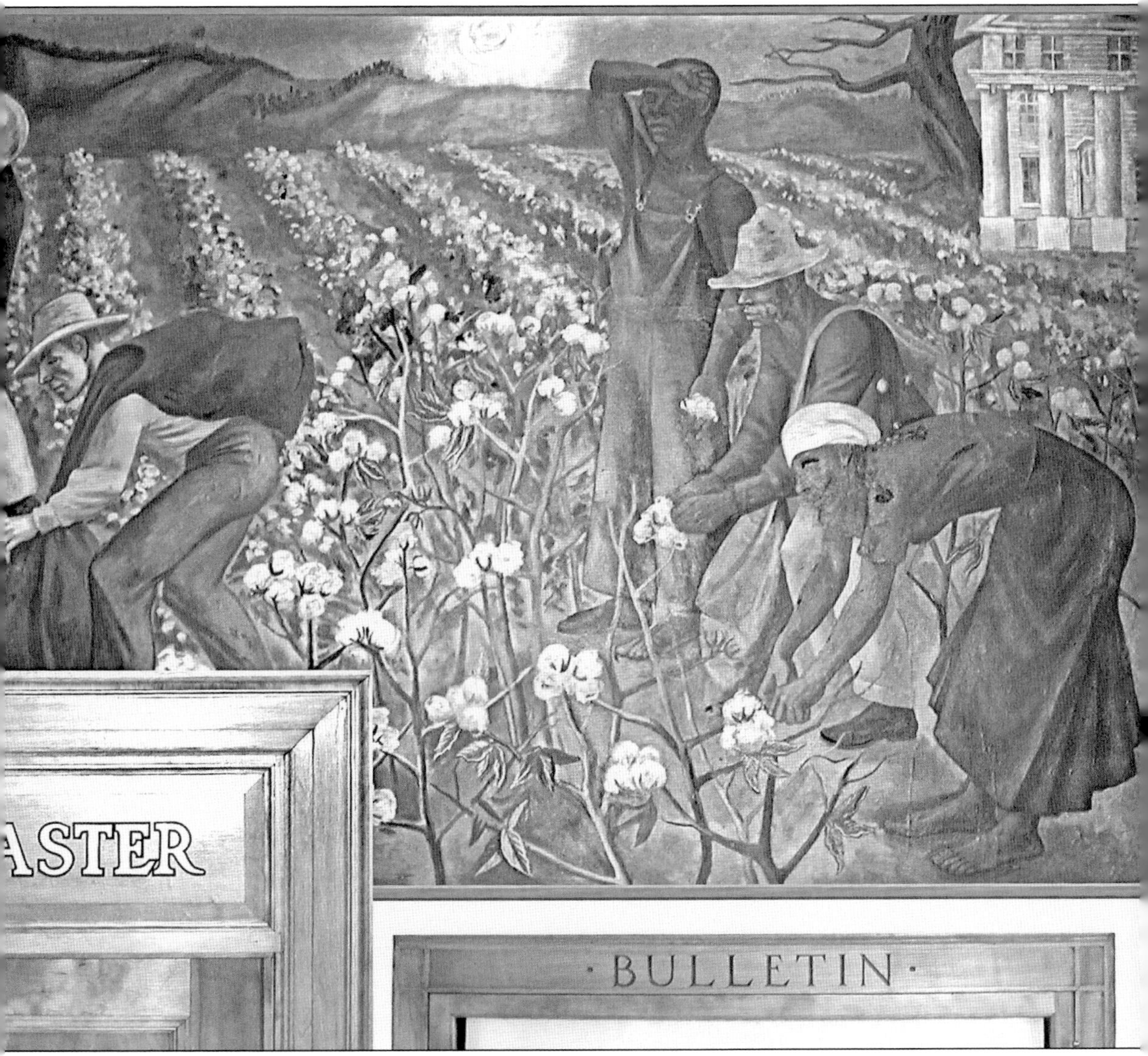

possible themes for the work. Alicia Weincek was chosen to produce the mural in Mooresville. She met with many local citizens and settled on a design depicting the cotton industry. The oil-on-canvas mural is permanently attached to the wall above the "postmaster" office door, now the office of the Mooresville Graded School District. The mural has been maintained since 1938 and is in near-original condition. (Photograph by Cindy Jacobs.)

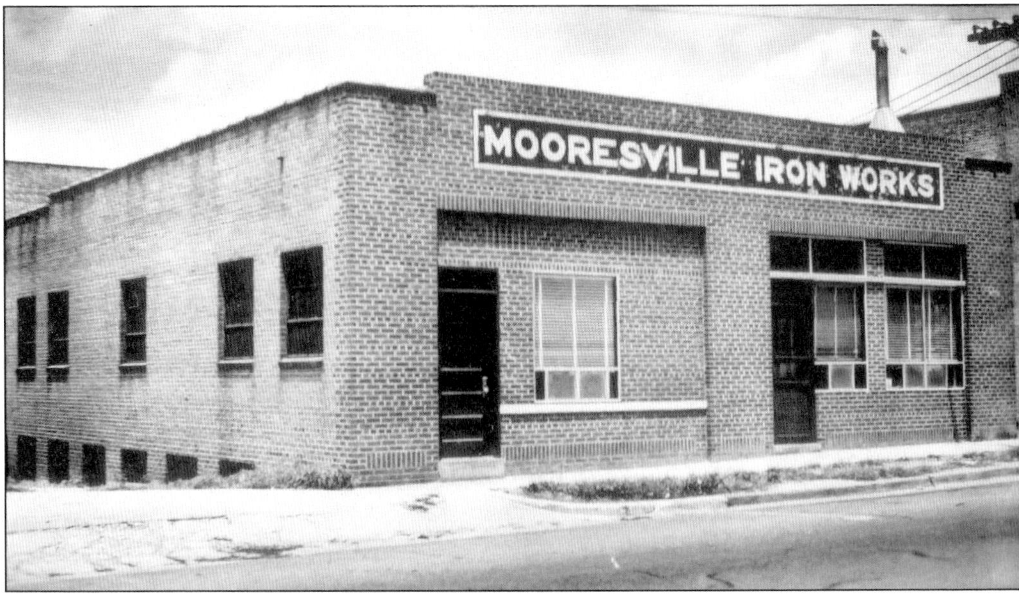

Metal working in Mooresville got its start with the Troutman family operation on North Main Street c. 1900. In 1922, B. A. Troutman and Ben S. Houston began operations as the Mooresville Foundry and Machine Shop. The operation produced a wide variety of farm implements, machinery, and machine replacement parts. On September 1, 1936, Robert J. Holthouser and R. J. Higgenbotham rented the Mooresville Foundry and Machine Shop from B. A. Troutman. Their partnership, Mooresville Iron Works, operated a complete pattern shop, foundry, and machine shop to manufacture textile machinery and replacement parts. In 1937, the assets, land, buildings, and machinery were purchased from Troutman. Holthouser became the sole owner in 1942. (Courtesy of Robert J. Holthouser Jr.)

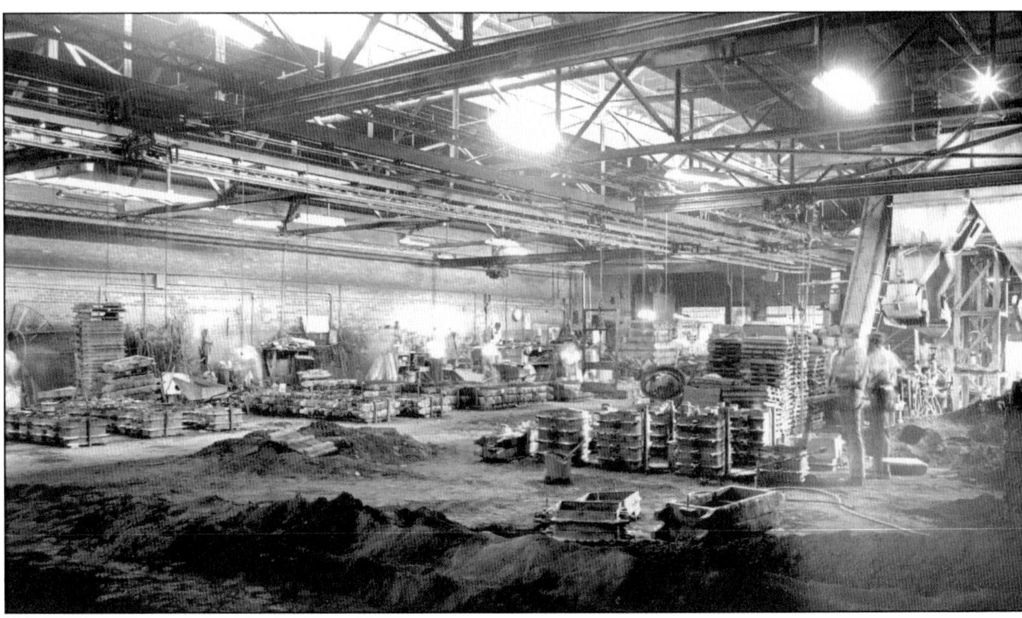

Five

The Community at Heart

It's the people who make a community. John Moore could have continued to run his store and his siding without inviting others to join the great adventure of building a town. He could have been a prosperous farmer and merchant. He knew, though, that it is not the buildings and the fields that make a family successful and happy; it is the association with others and the opportunities for involvement that are the real keys to success. Mooresville's pioneer citizens subscribed to the community-in-action theory, always working together to make a better life for all. Civic and social clubs like the Pythians, Daughters of the American Revolution, United Daughters of the Confederacy, Civic League, Kiwanis, Rotary, Lions, and Scouts enabled people to enjoy their leisure time with friends and colleagues. Their activities, beyond the social, inevitably turned to civic improvement. A wide variety of skills, knowledge, and insights came into play as ideas for recreation, entertainment, and community services were discussed and plans for projects evolved into action. The strength of the Mooresville community can be seen in the success of the Lowrance Hospital, the Mooresville Public Library, the War Memorial Community Center, the Recreation Commission, Mooresville Graded School District, American Legion, Veterans of Foreign Wars, and other organizations and services. In an article in the *State Magazine*, March 15, 1937, Ben Houston wrote, "Mooresville is an excellent trading center because it has other things as well as its commercial and industrial market." He encouraged others to visit the town to inspect it "first hand" and to get to know the people who make it a success.

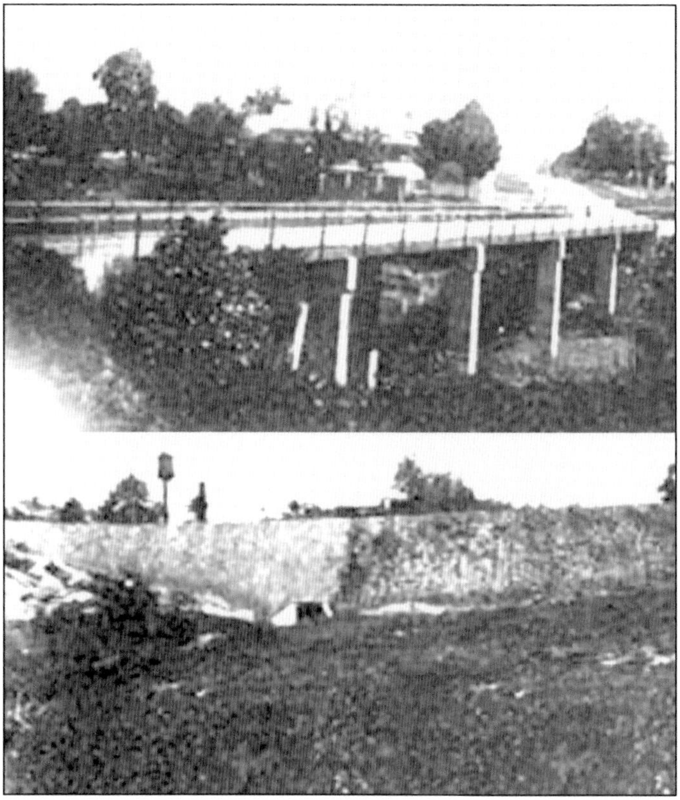

In 1905, Paschal Boyd championed the idea to extend First Street (East Center Avenue) from Church Street toward Eastern Heights. The town was expanding in the area with homes being built. A bridge was required to cross the Slippery Rock Creek. Boyd estimated the cost at $350, of which the town would contribute $150. The low-tonnage bridge was torn down in 1935 with funds from the WPA's Civilian Conservation Corps (CCC). Traffic was free to travel to the developing area as well as to the Lowrance Hospital, which was opened in 1930. This somewhat fuzzy photograph appeared in WPA materials showing the area before and after renovation. (Courtesy of the Keeter family.)

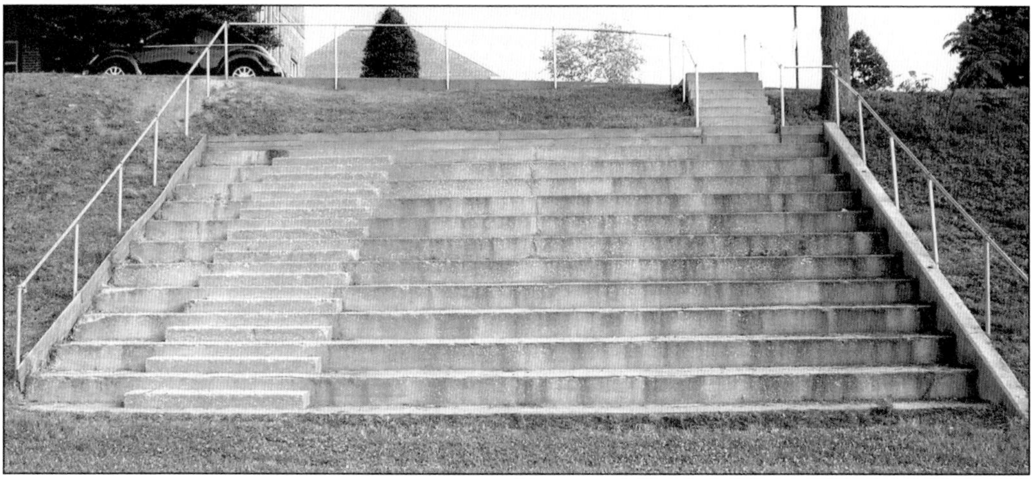

In conjunction with the bridge project, the CCC moved 26,000 cubic yards of dirt from the field to fill the road space created by the culvert over the creek. Hood Field not only expanded the South School athletic field, it provided a public field for baseball, softball, football, and pageants. In 1938, more than 600 South School students took part in a dramatic presentation of Longfellow's *Song of Hiawatha*, attracting 3,000 people, according to the May 19, 1938, *News Leader*. The extravaganza involved the construction of a multi-section stage complete with banks of spotlights. The newspaper noted that Harold Doster, Nealess Mills, Samuel Hiatt, and Fletcher Davis painted the curtain. Shown are the Hood Field bleachers as they appear today. (Photograph by Cindy Jacobs.)

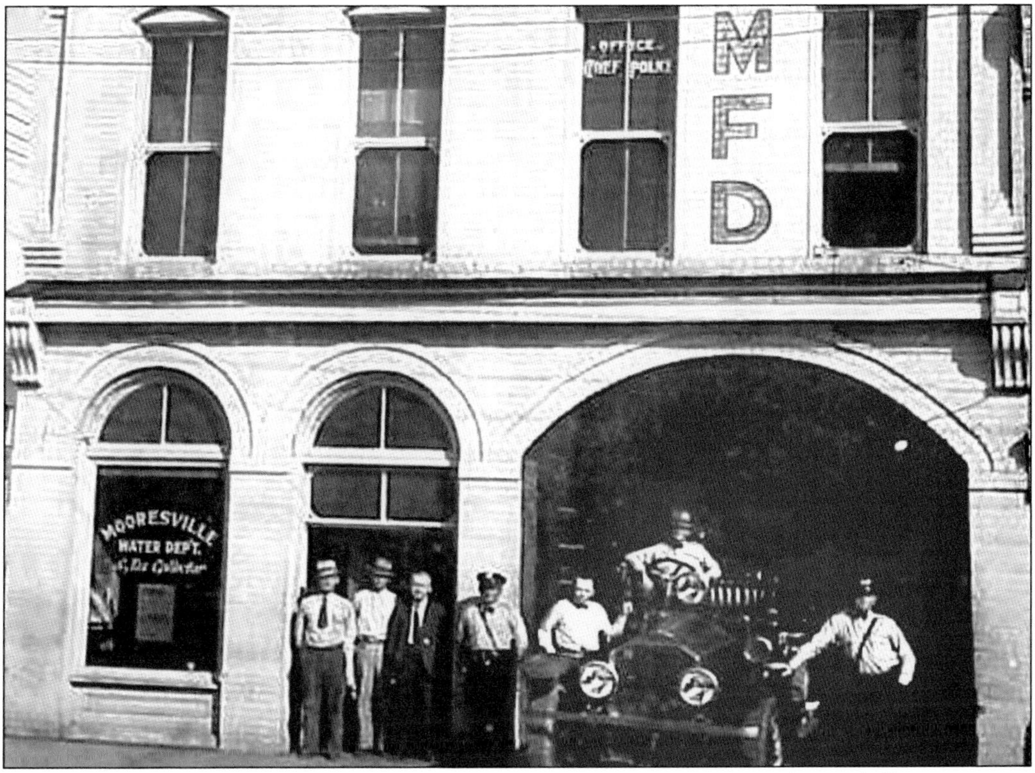

Mooresville built an office for government on Broad Street. The building housed all government functions, including the water department, tax office, fire department, police department, and office of the mayor. (Courtesy of the Edward Kipka family.)

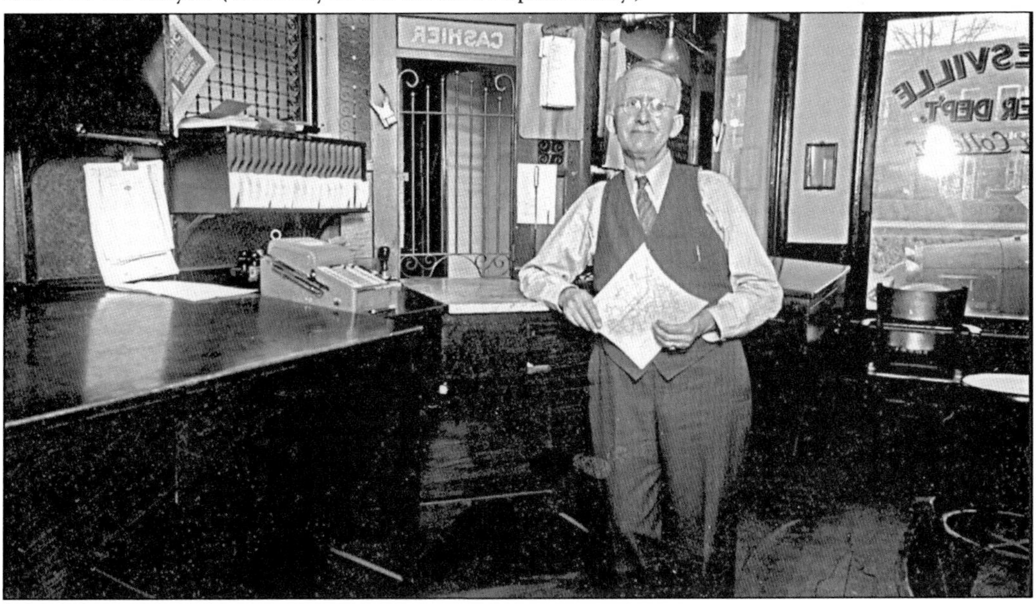

Gus Morse Kipka collected taxes and fees for water service from the town hall on Broad Street. During his tenure as clerk, he kept detailed minutes of all meetings and the actions taken by the commissioners. (Courtesy of Kay Kipka Jones.)

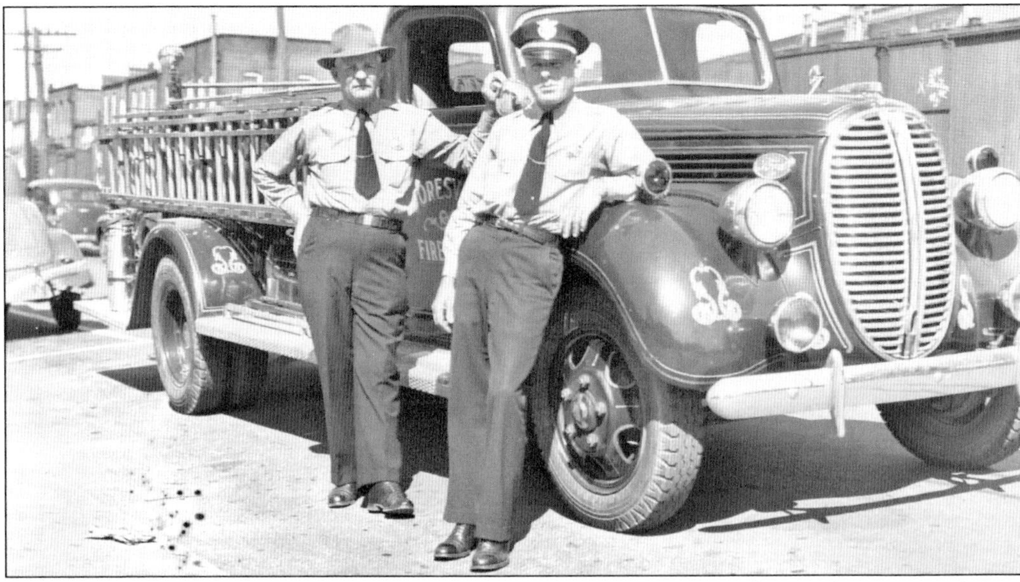

The fire department was organized with a hook and ladder, pump, and water hose in 1885. Isaac Harris loaned the town $275 to purchase the equipment. A well was dug and citizens had fire protection for the first time. J. H. McLelland served as chief of the 12-man volunteer department. Original volunteers include Pete McLelland, E. D. Turner, and Charles Troutman Sr. When the town hall was built on South Broad Street, the fire department had a home for their truck and equipment. Smith Alexander Lytle is pictured on the right. (Courtesy of Pearl Alexander and Karen Brown Smith.)

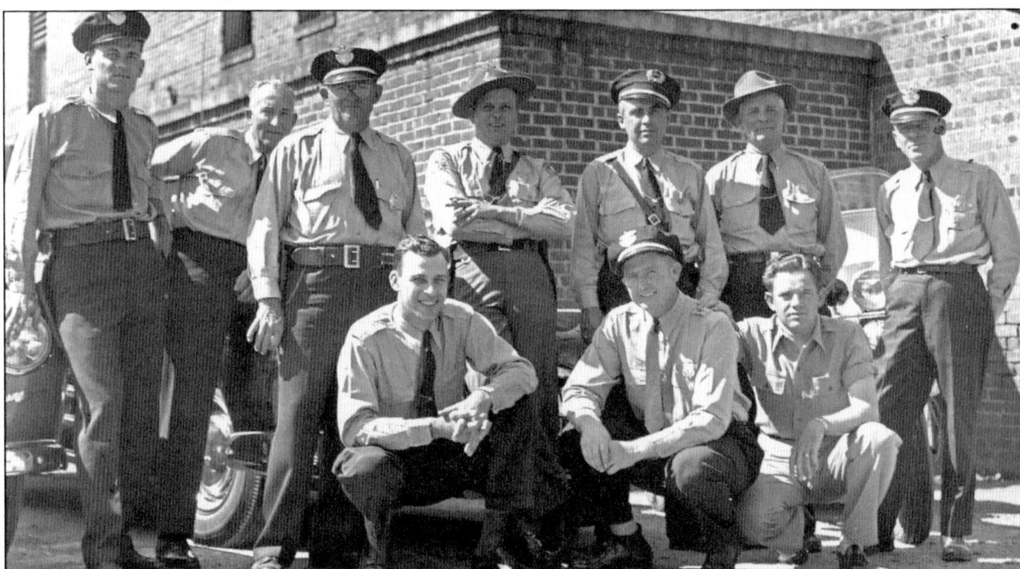

Protection from danger is a common concern for all communities. As early as 1875, commissioners appointed constables and authorized C. E. Wilkinson to build a calaboose (jail). To "preserve peace and good order," the mayor was authorized to hire additional officers and night watchmen. In the early days, policemen attended to duties such as public health, tax collection, and garbage disposal. With the construction of the town hall in 1919, the police department was given phone service in its own office rather than in the homes of the policemen.

MOORESVILLE

NORTH CAROLINA

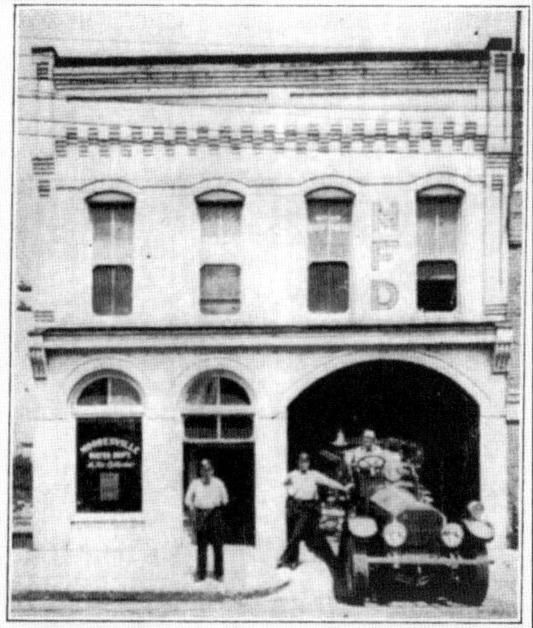

MOORESVILLE HAS MODERN FIRE EQUIPMENT

GOOD SCHOOLS GOOD WATER
UNLIMITED POWER GOOD CHURCHES

AN EXCELLENT TOWN TO VISIT
AN EXCELLENT TOWN TO STAY IN

●

One of North Carolina's BEST INDUSTRIAL TOWNS offers to the manufacturer something of more permanent value than a friendly gesture

●

FOR INFORMATION
WRITE

BEN S. HOUSTON
MAYOR

Mooresville began to market itself to business in print advertising in 1937. It promoted the ideas of safety, education, religion, and economic opportunity as reasons for business to locate in Mooresville. This promotional effort continued with publications offered by both the town and the chamber of commerce. (Courtesy of the Mooresville–South Iredell Chamber of Commerce.)

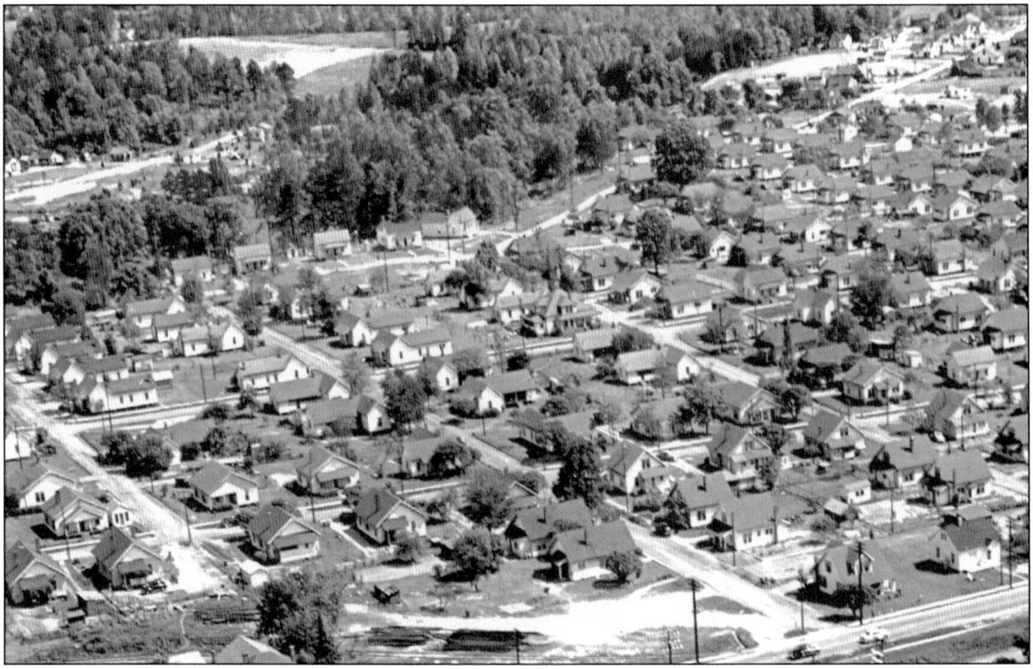

By the time the Mooresville Cotton Mill had its entire operation on South Main Street, management was seeking ways to help and support employees. One of the most significant programs involved providing adequate housing for workers. A few mill houses were built around Plant 1. The majority of the more than 400 homes were built after 1916 on East Wilson Avenue, Brawley Avenue, Mill Street, Summers Street, and other areas surrounding the mill. A mill worker could rent a home for about 50¢ per room, including water and sewer services. Rent was deducted from the payroll check. Most homes were within easy walking distance to the plant and downtown stores. (Courtesy of Burlington Industries.)

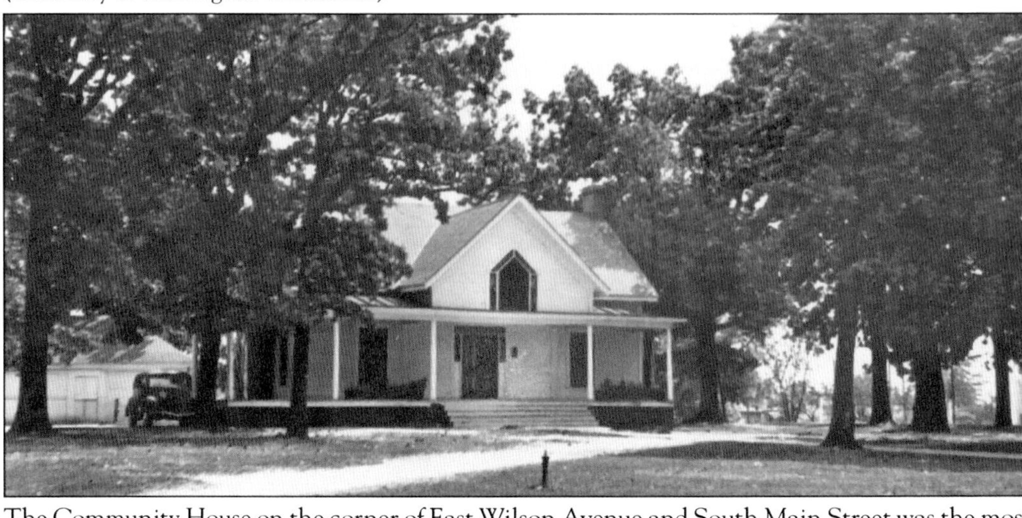

The Community House on the corner of East Wilson Avenue and South Main Street was the most complex service provided by the mill. A nursery school for the children of first-shift workers was popular and successful. More than a nursery, the house was renovated so that clubs and Scouts could meet, the mill band could practice, and all ages could enjoy indoor and outdoor activities like cards, softball, horseshoes, and tennis.

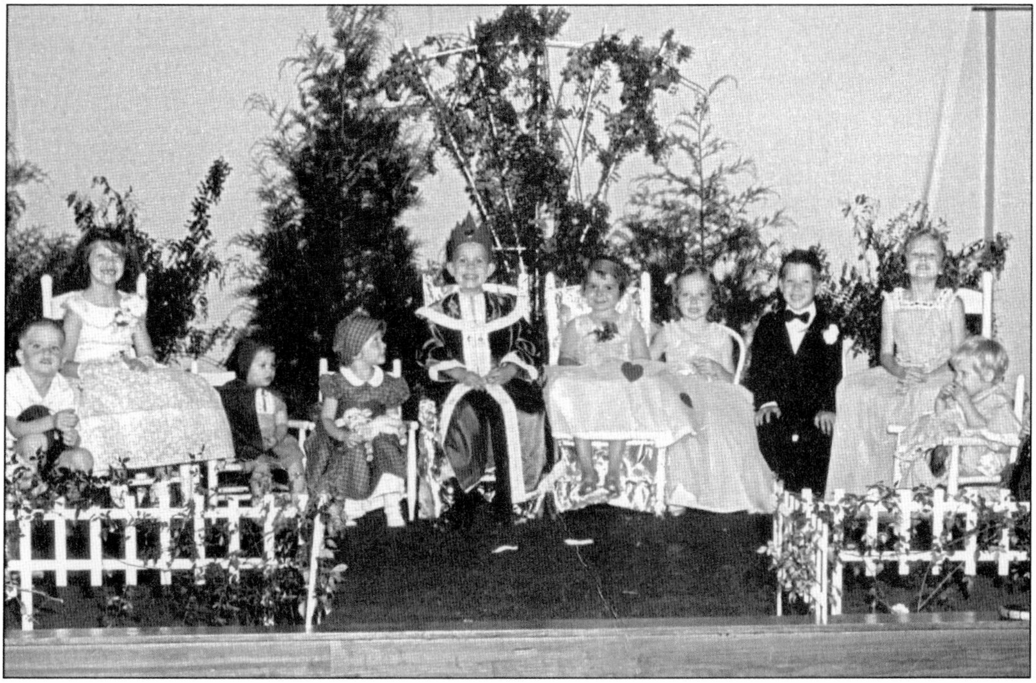

Pageants sponsored by groups like Vivian Combs' Kindergarten could make use of the facility. Parents who were mill workers got together with citizens in other lines of work to celebrate their children's accomplishments. Michael Levan and Debra Jacobs were king and queen for the day.

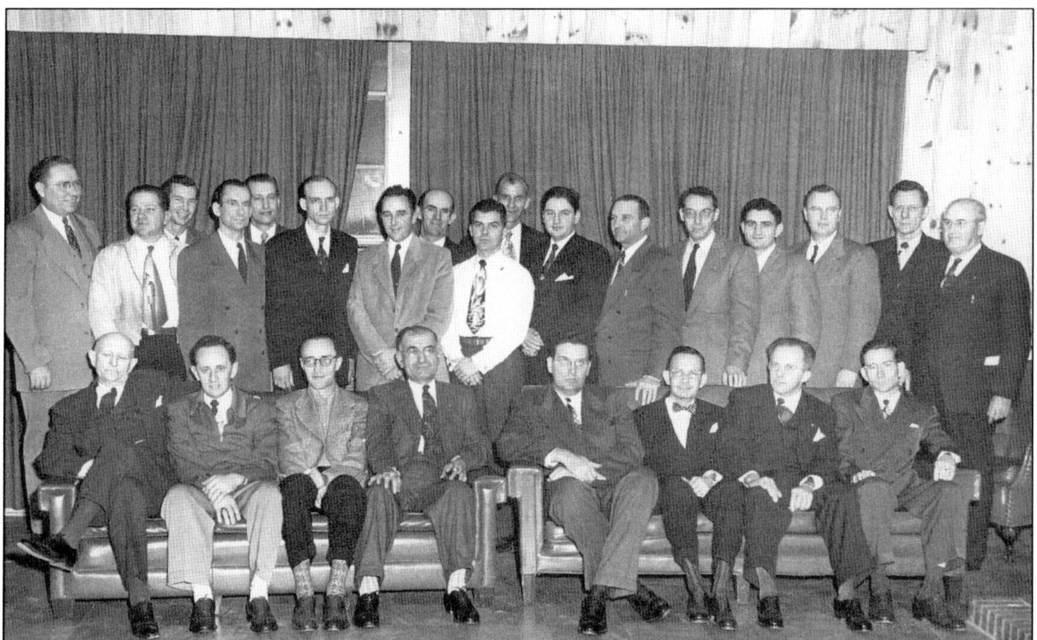

Scoutmasters, led by Side Mack (center), used the community house for troop meetings, athletic events, and instruction for merit badges. Started in Mooresville in 1912 by Zeb Turlington, Scouting grew to involve several hundred boys. Later many troop activities were held at the War Memorial.

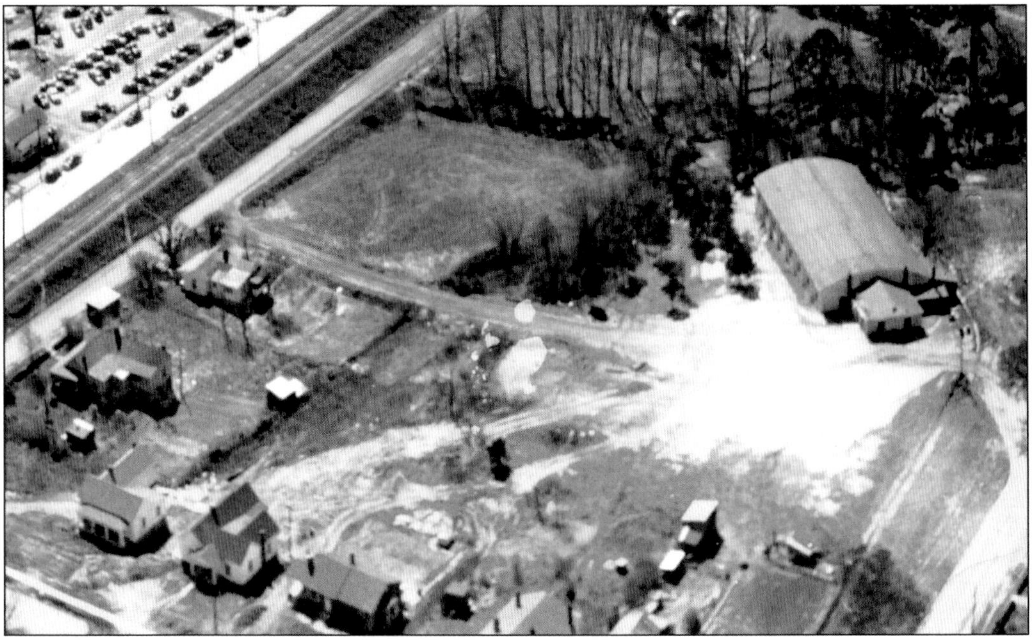

The mill provided other recreational facilities for mill workers and the community as a whole. A skating rink and bowling alley was opened on South Academy Street. While the rink was open to all, the facility was part of the mill's program to provide recreation and leisure-time activities for its employees. (Courtesy Burlington Industries.)

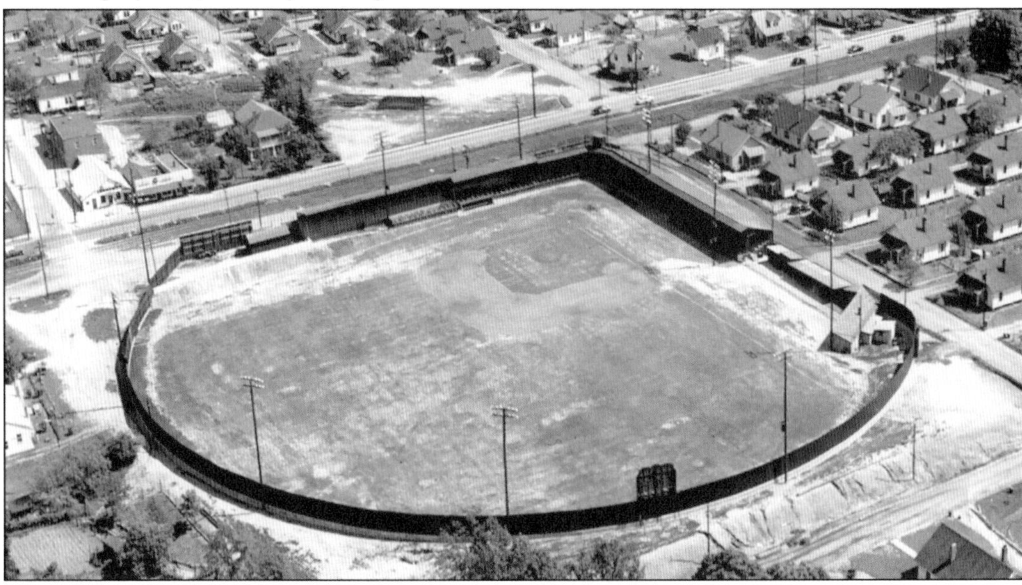

Moor Park became a larger-than-life recreational experience for the entire town. The mill sponsored a semi-professional baseball team, the Mooresville Moors. The baseball park included covered bleachers and box seating for baseball games and other events. Moors baseball was the main attraction, and the games drew large crowds supporting the hometown team. The park was built and maintained by the Mooresville Cotton Mill as a community recreation facility and was made available for the Mooresville High School band and sports teams for practice and play. (Courtesy Burlington Industries.)

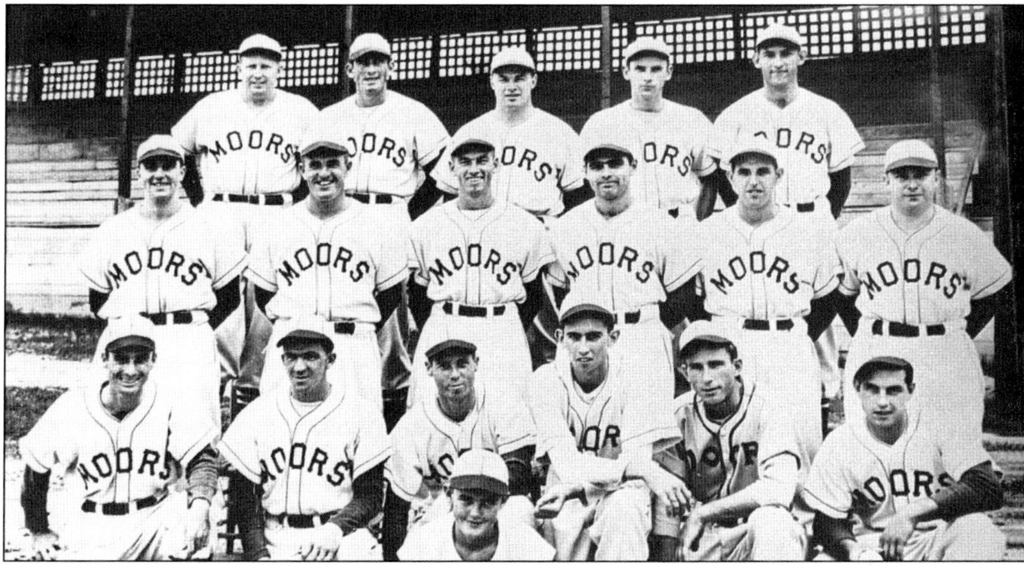

The Mooresville Moors were a phenomenon for the town. Beginning in the 1920s, the home team filled the bleachers at Moor Park each time there was a home game. The team, as early as 1925, was part of organized leagues. Many textile mills in the region sponsored teams, including Concord, Kannapolis, Forest City, and Shelby. In 1937, the Moors joined the North Carolina State League and played under the leadership of manager Jimmie Poole. To a standing-room-only hometown crowd, they won the league championship in 1937. (Courtesy of What-a-Burger.)

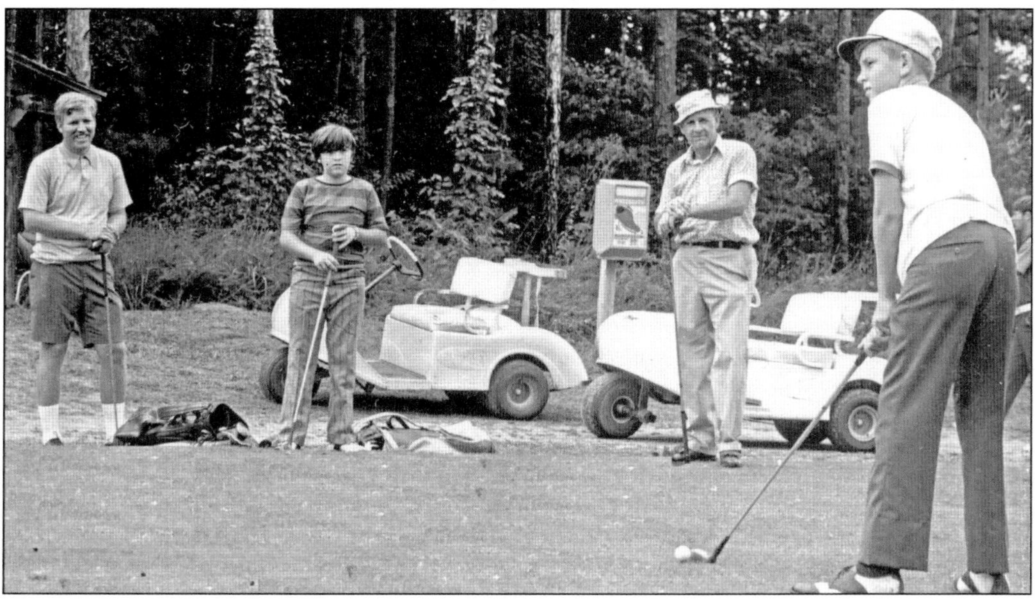

Mooresville Cotton Mills contracted with Scottish golfer Donald Ross to design and build a nine-hole golf course on property off West Wilson Avenue. A dam and reservoir on the property provided water to the mill and mill village. The golf course plan was part of the mill's recreation program for its employees and the community. Completed in 1949, the course became popular and attracted both men and women to participate in the sport. Golfers of all ages and abilities were welcome to play, and lessons were offered to young people. Mike Barnhardt took advantage of the opportunity to learn to play the game. (Courtesy of Mike Barnhardt.)

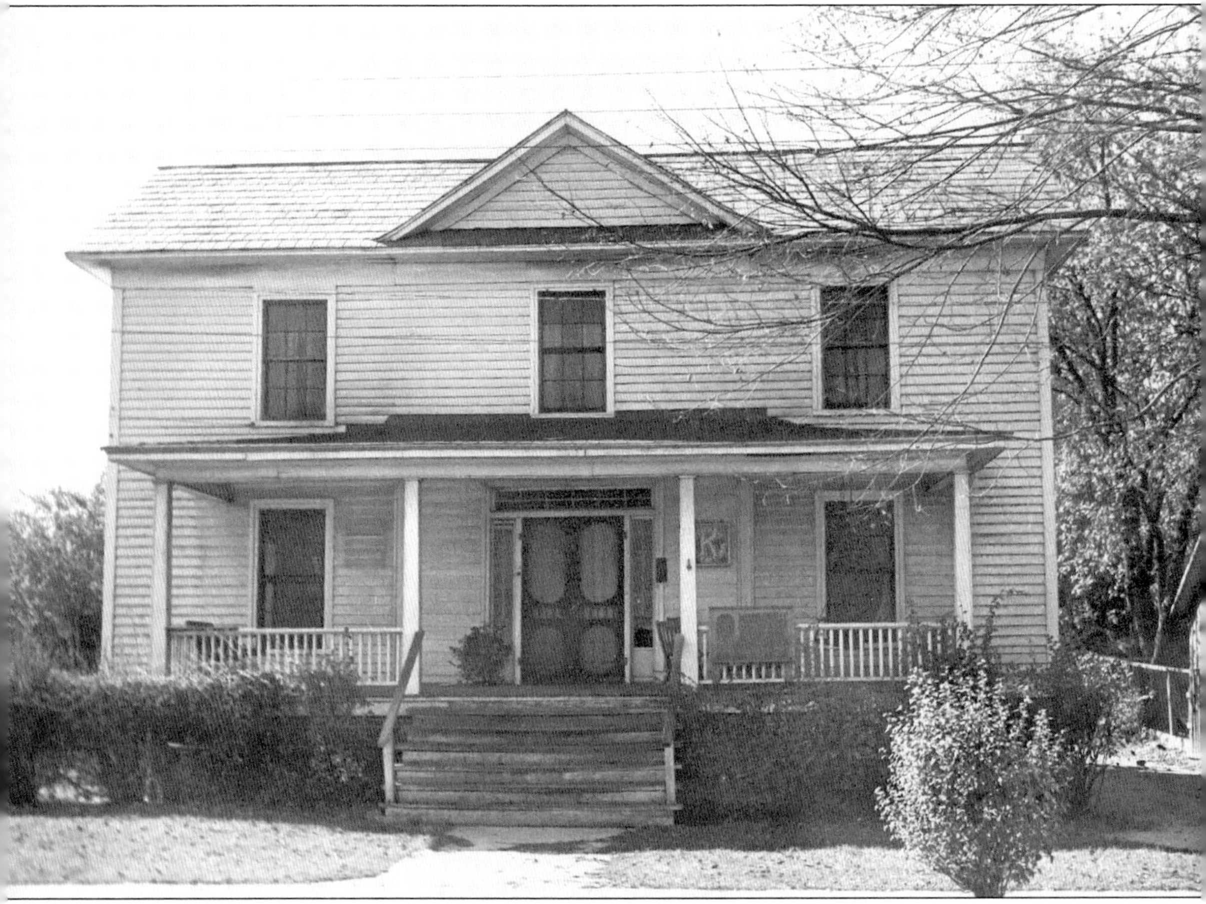

In 1922, the Civic League opened the Community House on West Center Avenue as a place for civic activities and community events. Maude Lentz, Mrs. C. F. Melchor (Lucy Culberson), and Mrs. George C. Goodman (Annie Wilfong) took leadership roles in the group dedicated to the improvement of Mooresville. They established Good Will Day; worked with the Red Cross; sponsored Clean Up, Paint Up, Fix Up Week; planted a flower garden in the area across from the depot; and campaigned for paved streets, sanitation, and a public restroom downtown. They supported good works and the betterment of the community. This organization was an important influence in the development of Mooresville, taking an active part in politics by encouraging women to vote in all elections. This group paved the way for the Civic Planning Council, Inc., to take over the reins of civic responsibility and guide the town into the future. In 1947, the league transferred ownership of the Community House and its assets to the council for its use in developing a recreation program for the community. The first task of the new group was to organize a campaign to build a memorial to war veterans in the form of a new community center. (Courtesy of the Edward Kipka family.)

AMERICAN LEGION
JUNIOR CHAMBER OF COMMERCE
JUNIOR CIVIC LEAGUE

KIWANIS CLUB
LIONS CLUB
MAYOR OF TOWN

MOORESVILLE WOMAN'S CLUB
ROTARY CLUB
VETERANS OF FOREIGN WARS

CIVIC PLANNING COUNCIL, Inc.

MOORESVILLE, NORTH CAROLINA

The Civic Planning Council was comprised of eight civic clubs and the town government. Their goals focused on providing a place for recreation and leisure-time activities. In 1947, a project evolved to build a new community center that would include meeting space, kitchen facilities, recreation space, and outdoor parks, fields, tennis courts, and a swimming pool. The center would be built as a living tribute to veterans. Led by Beth Matheson, Virginia McKnight, and James "Bub" McKnight, the council asked the town commissioners to establish a recreation commission and develop a recreation plan for Mooresville. Charles M. Graves, a parks and recreation engineer, made a "scientific study" of the existing facilities and community needs. This master plan for recreation was presented to the public and was the foundation of an ordinance passed by the board of commissioners on March 9, 1948, establishing the Mooresville Recreation Commission. The council and commissioners identified a source for funding of recreation programs in parking meter revenues. Members of the commission included the Civic Planning Council, Mooresville city manager, superintendent of schools, president of the Ministerial Association, a town commissioner, and a school staff member. These groups were charged with using the master plan to construct a community center, the War Memorial. (Courtesy of James Houston and Marvin Sigmon.)

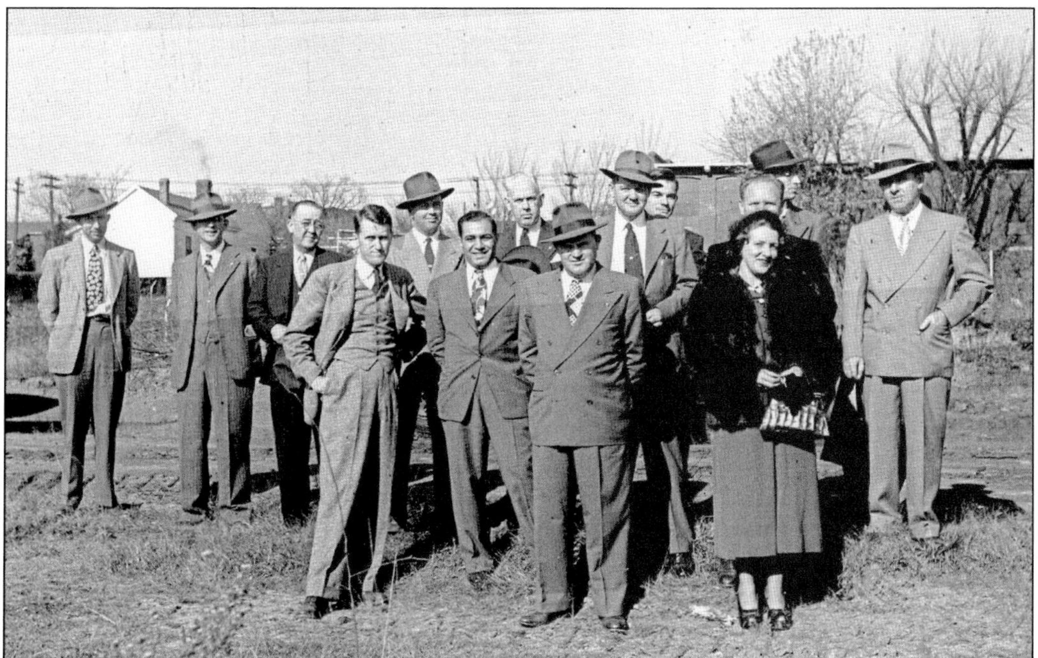

Members of the Civic Planning Council gathered at the Maple Street property to evaluate its potential as a site for the community center. (Courtesy of Marvin Sigmon.)

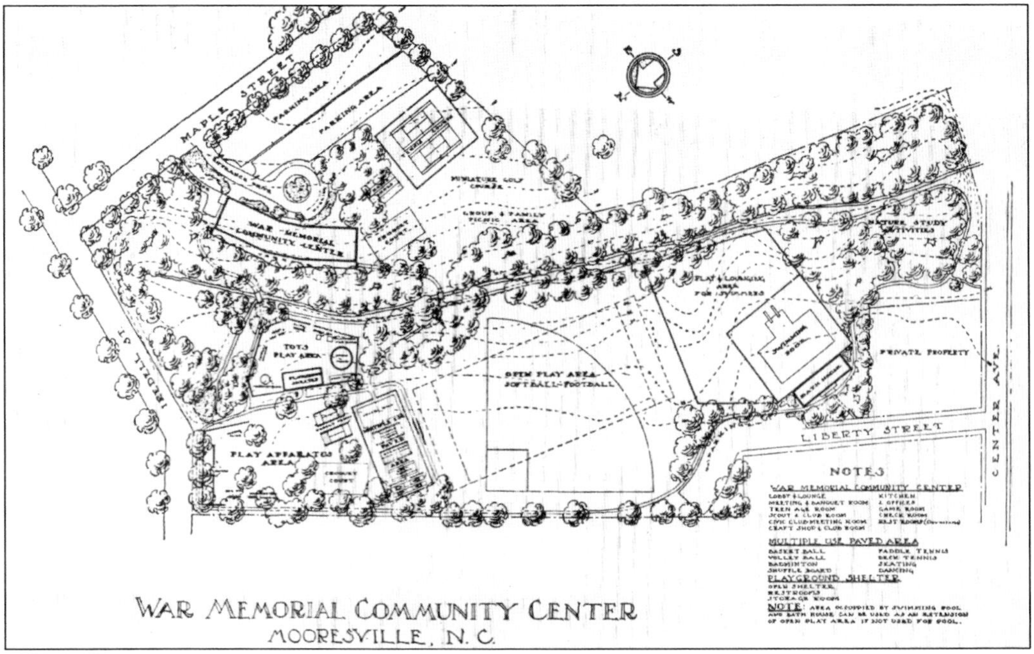

Engineering drawings and architectural renderings were prepared for the 15-plus-acre site of the proposed recreation complex. (Courtesy of Marvin Sigmon.)

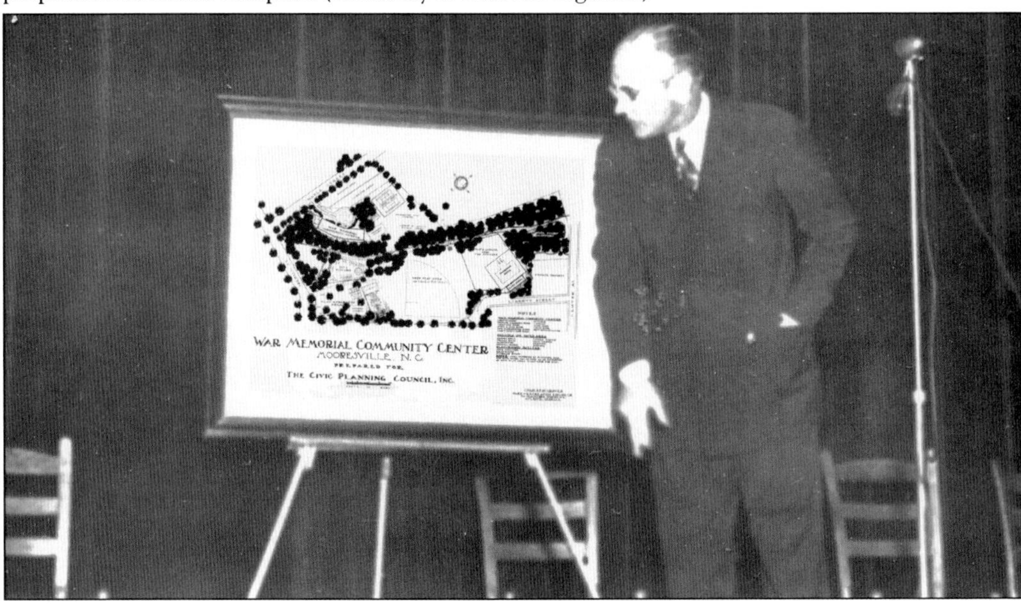

Recreation engineer Charles M. Graves developed a comprehensive recreation plan and preliminary drawings for the community center after extensive research in Mooresville. He described a building and recreation space encompassing a 15-acre tract of land bordered by East Iredell Avenue, Maple Street, and Liberty Street and spanning Slicky Rock Creek. Further consultation with Ronnie Sheffield, assistant director of the North Carolina Recreation Commission, helped guide the group to develop a detailed plan that included future community needs. The program to erect a living tribute to veterans and fallen heroes of war proceeded with precision. (Courtesy of James V. Houston.)

The living tribute envisioned by the Civic Planning Council started on the road to reality with a week-long fund-raising campaign. The community, the ultimate beneficiary of the project, was asked to give $150,000 toward the building. Each donor of $12 or more received a memorial certificate, but each and every one who donated to the project was recognized and listed in the official archives of the War Memorial. (Courtesy of James V. Houston.)

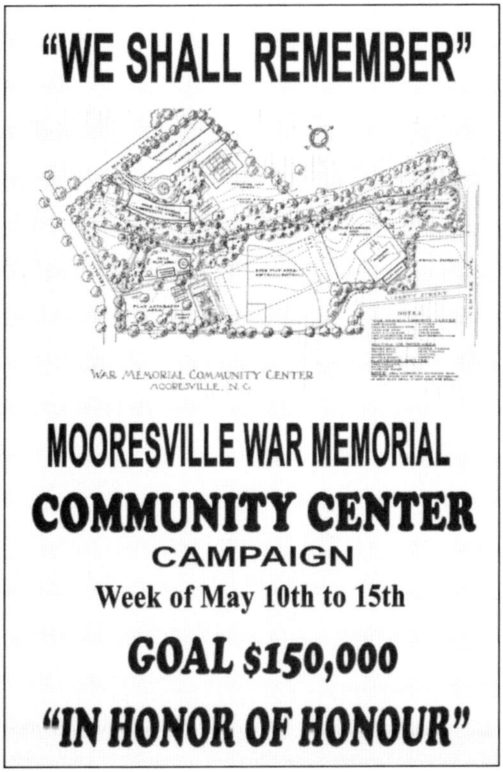

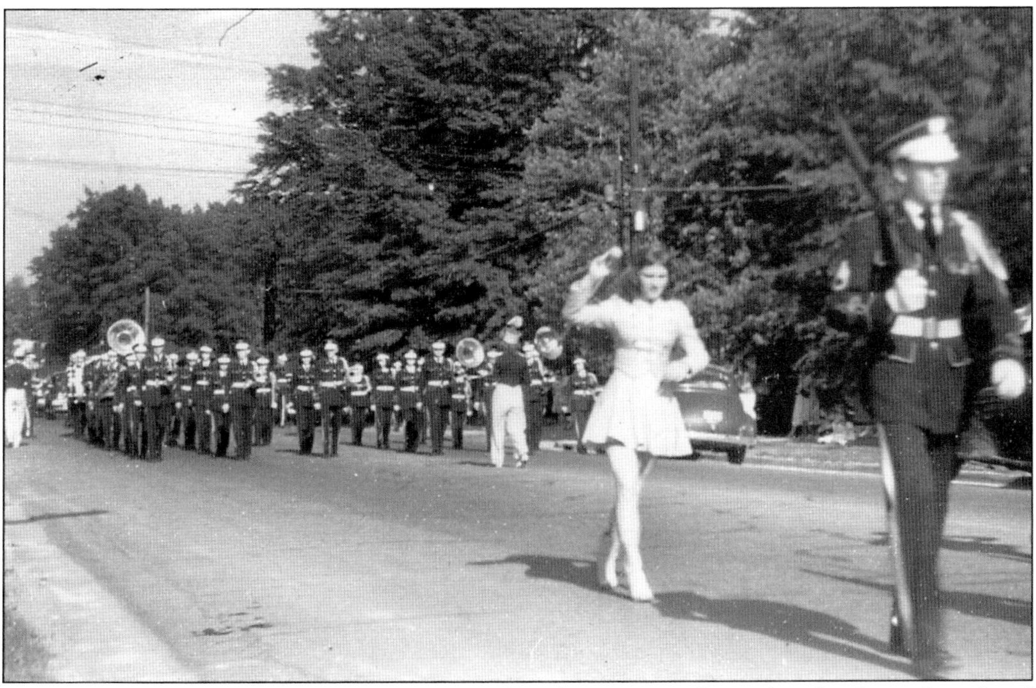

The campaign was kicked off with a parade led by the Mooresville High School marching band through town. The parade was followed by a community dinner at South School. Civic groups, business, and industry participated in the week of events. (Courtesy of Kay Kipka Jones.)

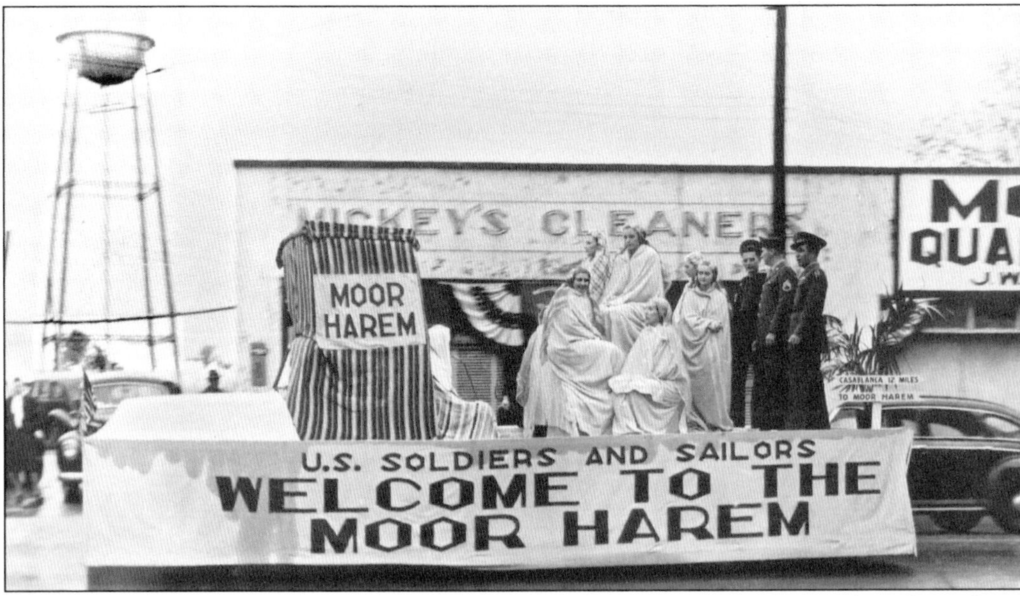

Mooresville Mills, a major benefactor of the project with land and funds, contributed two floats. The Moor Quality float featured a Moor harem. Erleen Mills, Jeanette Stallings, Mary Ethel Charles, and Verlin Davis are among the six "harem" girls. Bernard Christenbury is one of three veterans on the float. The second float promoted citizenship and community involvement. A monument honoring mill employees who went to war was erected near the front gate. Most soldiers returned to their jobs at the mill after the war. During the war, mill management sent leather stationery albums to employees wherever they were stationed. With names embossed on the front, they served as a place to keep photographs, memorabilia, and writing paper for letters back home. (Courtesy of Erleen Mills Christenbury.)

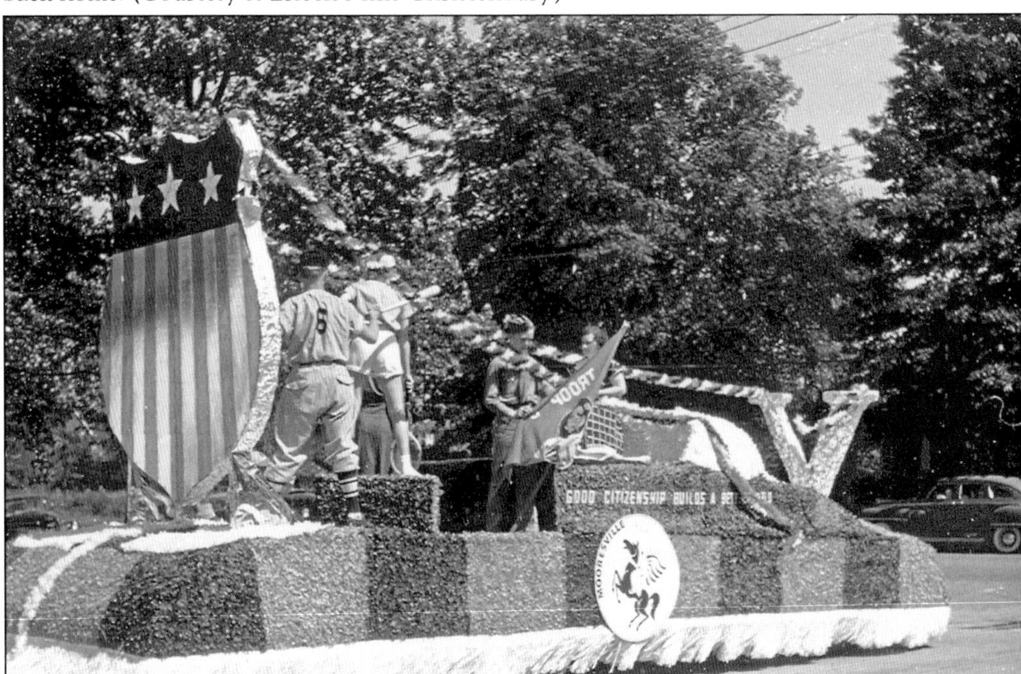

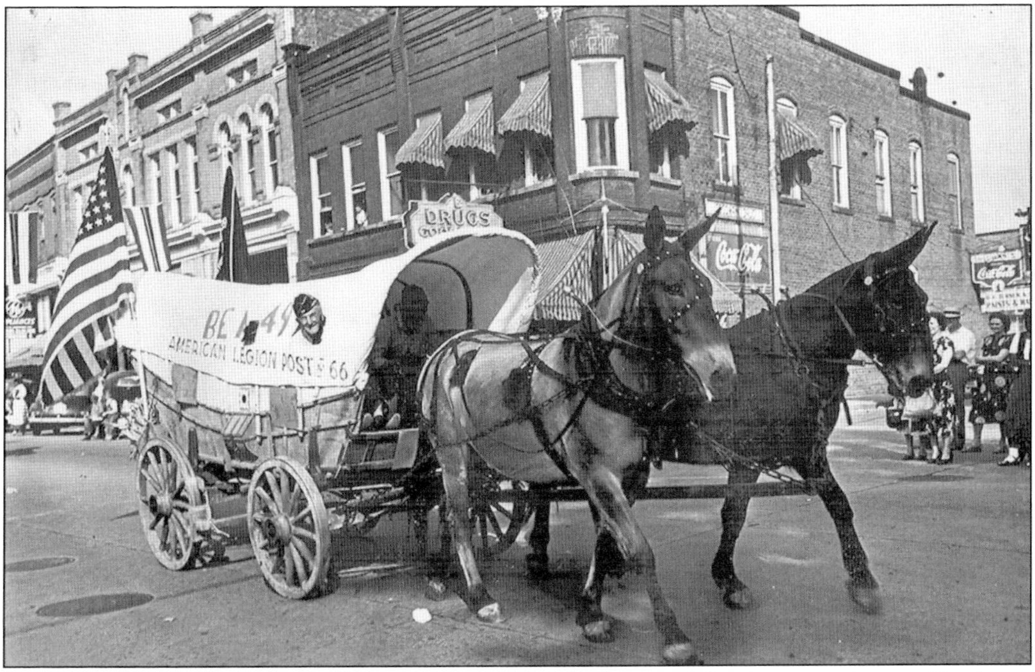

Business and civic organizations joined the campaign in a big way. The American Legion Gresham-Baker Post 66 supported the project heartily. All members joined in working to raise funds for the living tribute to Mooresville's veterans and war heroes. Jimmie Houston represented the group at the ground breaking. (Courtesy of Keith Carpenter.)

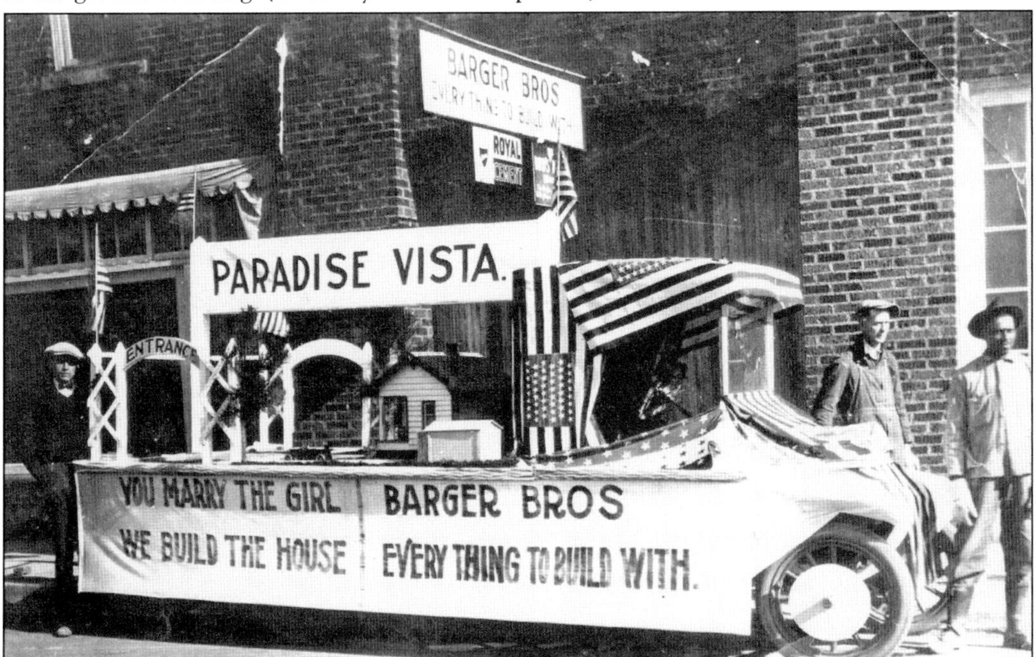

Barger Construction Company got a head start on home building with a message to "boomers." Their participation in the fund-raising campaign was typical of business support for the recreation program and the plan to build a community center to honor veterans and heroes of war.

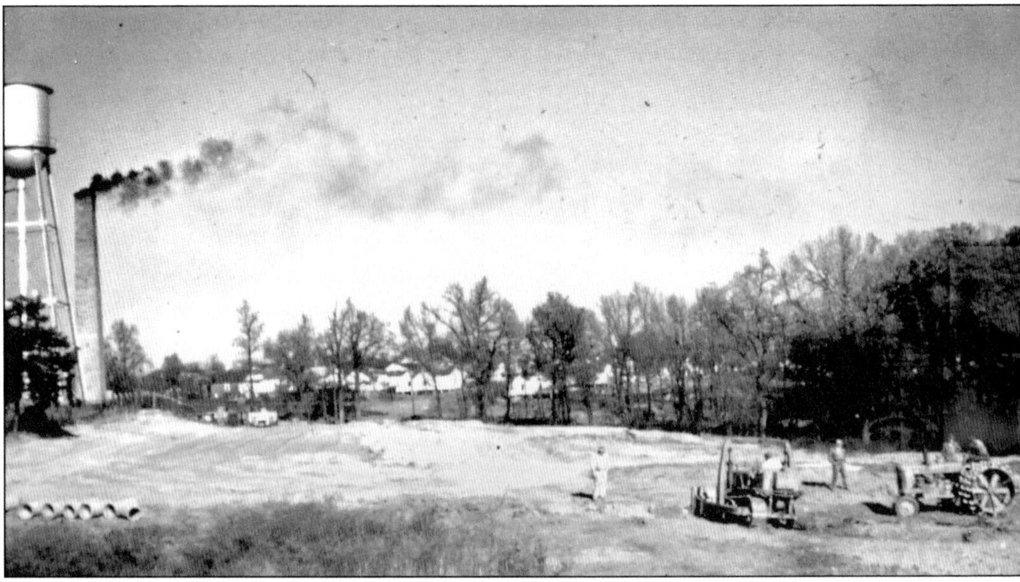

With the donation of land adjacent to Syntex Mill, the town commissioners agreed to enclose a 300-foot portion of Liberty Street to make a playground and baseball field for the War Memorial complex. Work on the outdoor areas of the plan began at the same time as construction of the building in 1948. Known as Liberty Park, the facilities have been improved and modernized over the years. (Courtesy of Marvin Sigmon.)

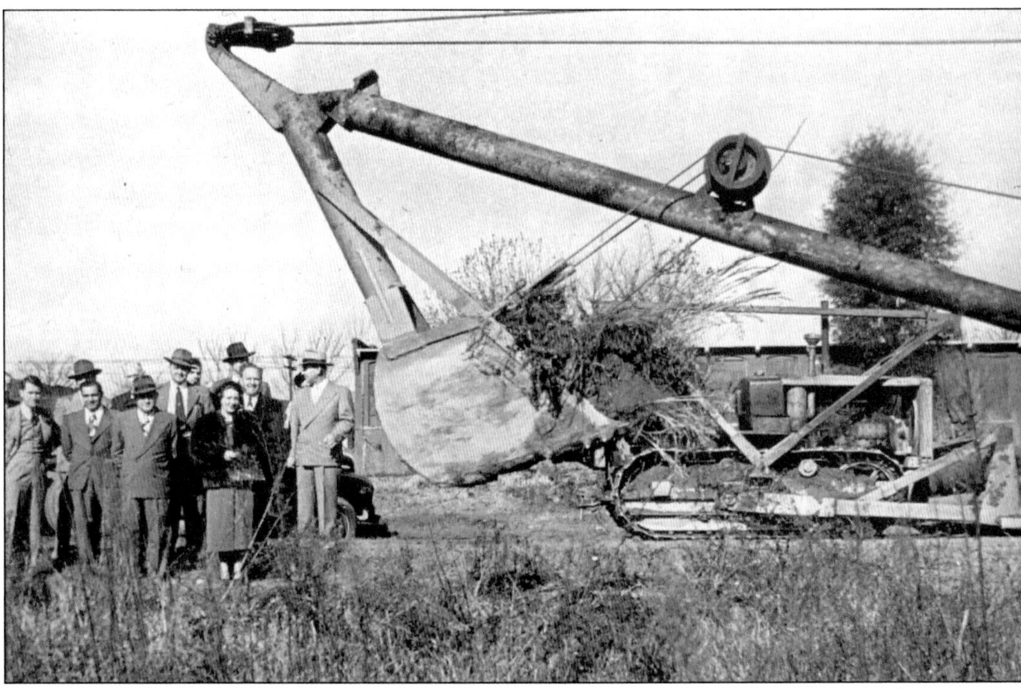

Barger Construction Company was awarded the contract to build the center. They were on site and ready to begin as soon after the ground breaking as possible. Members of the Civic Planning Council and the Recreation Commission were on hand for the festivities. (Courtesy of Marvin Sigmon.)

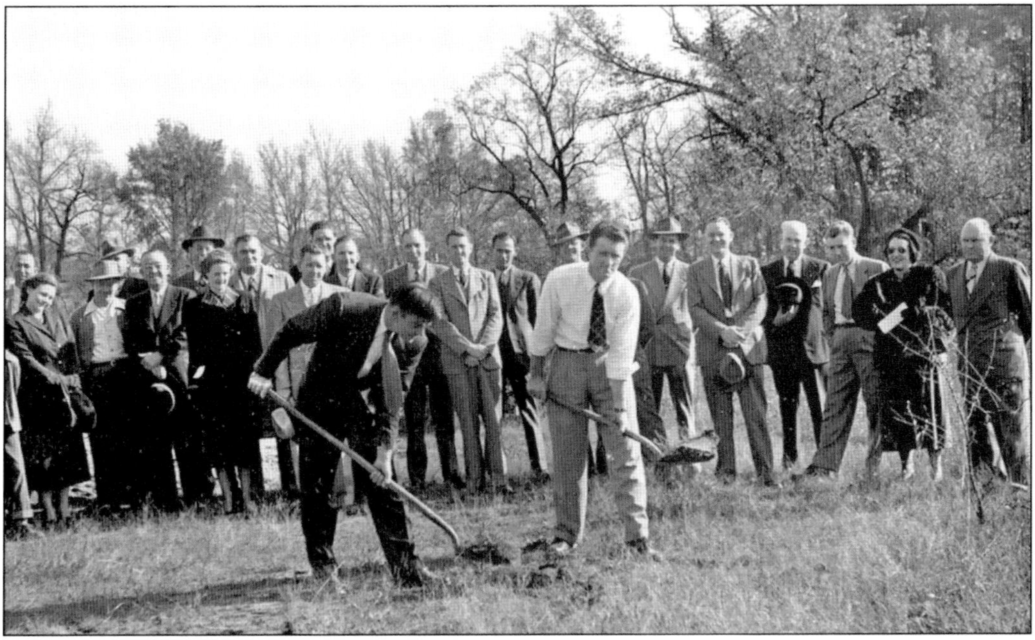

According to all reports, "This event marked the beginning of public recreation in Mooresville as we know it." Jimmy Houston, left foreground, and Marvin Sigmon, right foreground, represented the American Legion and VFW in the planning of the community center. Other "movers and shakers" include, from left to right, Spencer Kirk, Margaret Moore, Tom McKnight, Frank Young, Ben Houston, Margaret Mayhew, Harmon Gillespie, Charlie Gunter, Tom Delk, Rev. Harold Robinson, Fred Hudson, Pete Deaton, Jim Mack Morrow, Jack Scott, W. J. Haselden, Tommy Boyd, Oni Houston, Elmer Turner Jr., Carroll Beatty, Beth Matheson, and Bub McKnight. (Courtesy of Marvin Sigmon.)

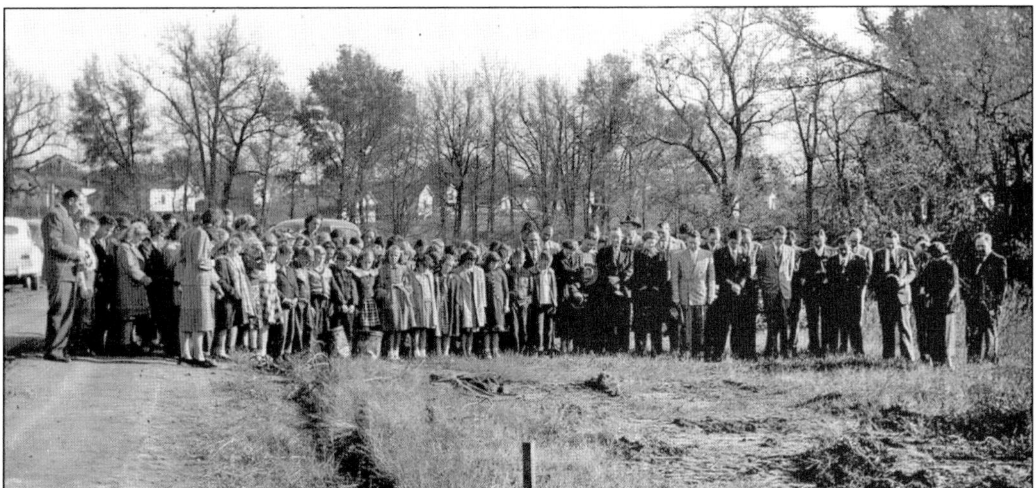

Dr. Roland Morgan accompanied schoolchildren participating in the ground breaking ceremonies. Each school chose representatives to attend. Young people were an important part of the recreation plan and the ultimate beneficiaries of the programs. One of the first events to be held in the War Memorial Teen-Age Club was the Mooresville High School homecoming dance. (Courtesy of Marvin Sigmon.)

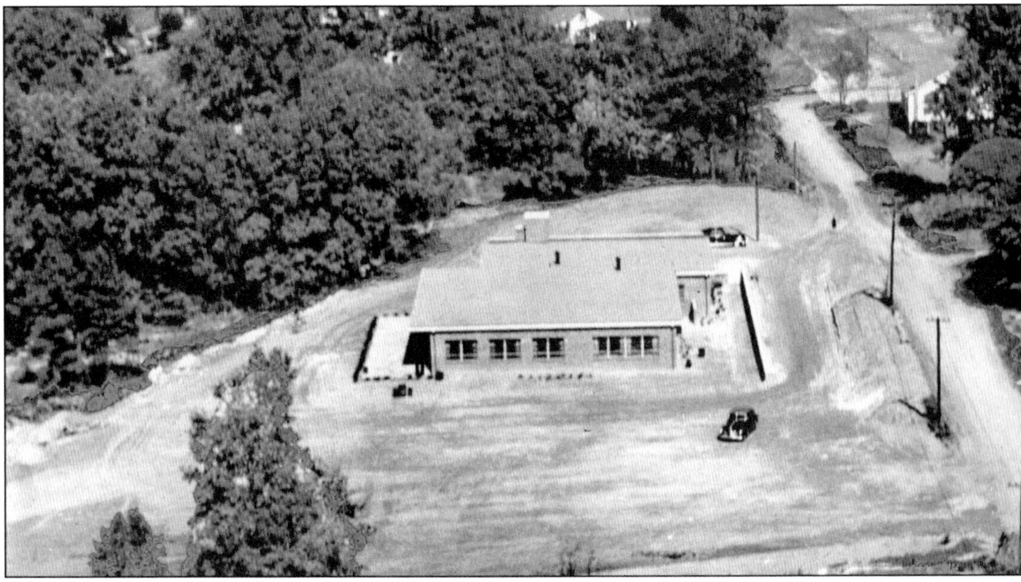

The plan to provide recreation was supported by citizens, business, and government. Town commissioners allocated $8,775 for the Recreation Commission for the year beginning July 1948 to July 1, 1949. This money represented approximately 75 percent of the revenues from parking meters. The funds were used to pay the salaries of the director and clerk and to provide a summer playground and teenage center activities. More than $105,000 was contributed by the community in the fund-raising campaign. Beth Matheson called the contributions of cash, stock, and property a "blazing star in the crown of our community." It meant that a living memorial to veterans and heroes of war would become a reality. The left wing of the building on Maple Street opened on October 14, 1949, to the music of Claude Lytle's orchestra and the aroma of J. W. Oehler's barbeque. Mayor Robert Holthouser led the dignitaries and thanked the Civic Planning Council for their efforts on behalf of the community. The community center events blended into a celebration of homecoming for Mooresville High School. The homecoming dance was held in the Teen-Age Club. (Courtesy of Marvin Sigmon.)

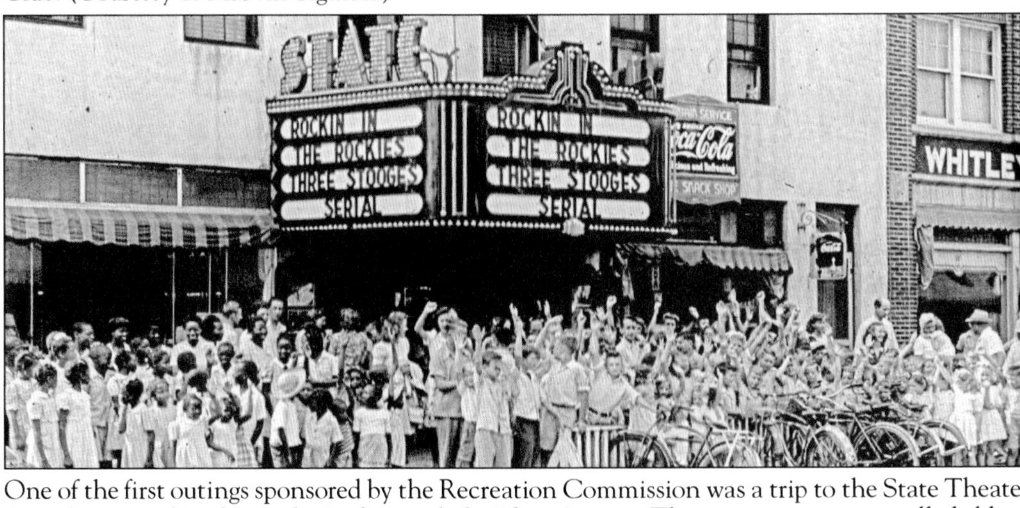

One of the first outings sponsored by the Recreation Commission was a trip to the State Theater for a showing of *Rockin in the Rockies with the Three Stooges*. The event was open to all children in Mooresville. Outings like this and programs at the War Memorial and in Liberty Park became regular events thanks to the efforts of Mooresville's recreation pioneers.

Six

The Mooresville Public Library

By 1897, Mooresville had a successful cotton mill, a solid transportation network to sell goods, churches, newspapers, schools, and the beginnings of paved streets. Mary Jane Grierson, Julia Stirewalt, Bess Hamilton, and others dedicated themselves to providing a library for the community. They opened a subscription library in the Grierson home for a fee of $1.25 per year. The venture proved successful, and people donated books and organized committees for fund-raising events like talent shows, auctions, magazine sales, and silver teas. By 1899, the Mooresville Library Association was organized formally. Still a subscription association, each member paid 10¢ per month to take advantage of books and other materials. When individual interest lagged, books were moved to various locations, including the Central Hotel and the First National Bank. The library took advantage of available space on Main Street and moved several times. Though involvement fluctuated, interest never died thanks to dedicated citizens and supporters. In 1922, the Civic League provided space in the Community House on West Center Avenue for the library. Even then, service hours were limited to a few hours each week. Mrs. J. J. McNeely (Ada Mae) and Nancy McNeely operated the library until the books were moved to Central High School in 1929. The Town of Mooresville withdrew its financial support and the library started a downward spiral, even though interest remained high. The Great Depression took hold of the nation's economy, and funds were not only scarce but needed for other community services. Tragedy struck the library when Maude Creswell was struck and killed by the train on July 25, 1944, as she returned from lunch. DeWitt Mills witnessed the accident, called for an ambulance, and helped put Mrs. Creswell in it for a trip to Lowrance Hospital. According to the recollections of Jimmy Houston and Francella Kerr, Maude Creswell was a woman of great civic energy, working diligently for the Red Cross, Civic League, and the Maids and Matrons Club. Board member John Young Templeton penned a resolution of respect: "She loved our library with unlimited enthusiasm. It seems strange that her life was cut right off when she was so useful and active. However, it is great that we can say that throughout her professional, social and private life that she did nothing to forfeit the esteem of the people among whom she lived and that she carried to the grave a community's love."

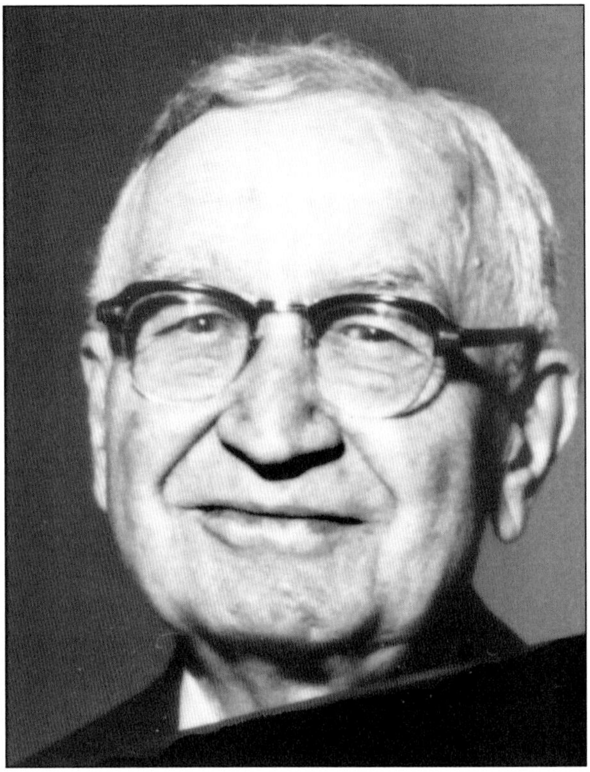

In 1915, lawyer Zeb Turlington got involved in the library movement and offered space in his office above the Goodman Drug Store for the books. He even got involved as a "librarian" by working with patrons to check out books. While serving in the North Carolina Legislature in 1904, he introduced a bill establishing the school district, complete with taxing authority to insure a high level of instruction from exemplary teachers. He served the interests of the Mooresville Public Library throughout his life, working with LuTelle Sherrill Williams to give a building to the community in 1939. (Courtesy of Mitchell Mack.)

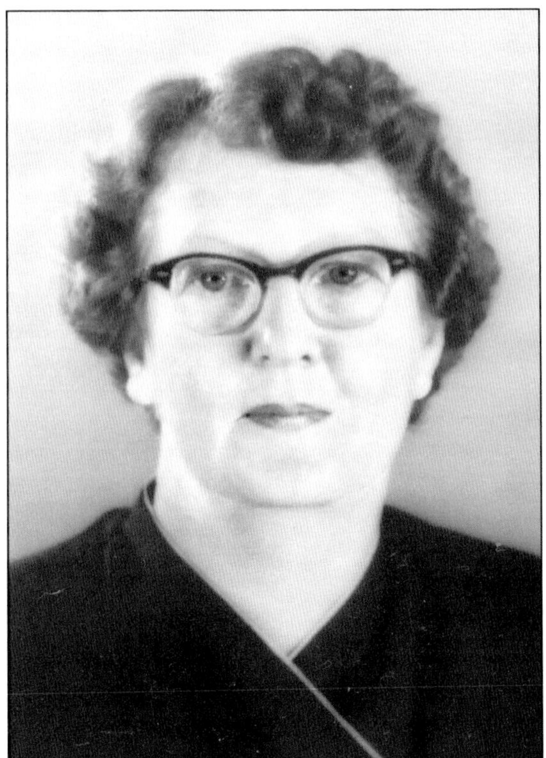

Frances Smith Craven was involved in community life, in particular the Maids and Matrons Club. When the town withdrew its support for the library, she worked with others to move the collection to the Central High School. Later she helped rescue books not damaged by the 1932 fire that destroyed the interior of the school building. When Zeb Turlington asked the Maids and Matrons to sponsor the library, she led the group to get involved. The library, after all, had been an ongoing interest for most community groups in Mooresville, including the United Daughters of the Confederacy, the Daughters of the American Revolution, and the Civic League. (Courtesy of Francella Craven Kerr.)

In July 1936 the Maids and Matrons Club of Mooresville became sponsor for the Mooresville Public Library, in order to comply with the Works Progress Administrations regulations. The Club appointed a committee of three members to serve as a Library Board, these being Mesdames A. C. Craven, Sam Neel and Dick Johnston. The Board promptly secured new quarters for the Library and moved the books, built additional shelves, and reopened the Library to the public. Rent for the new quarters was seven dollars per month, and the Works Progress Administration paid the Librarian's salary of $50.00. The Library is serving the public eighteen hours per week, but the librarian works daily extra hours keeping the books in order, preparing books for circulation, keeping records and making reports.

Mrs D M Creswell

Librarian

In 1936 the Maids and Matrons became the official sponsor of the library to insure financial support from the Works Progress Administration. WPA funds were used to pay librarians and support a book mending group to put existing books back into the collection. Serving on these committees were Maude Creswell, Mary Greenlee, Carol Beatty, Harry Deaton, Mary Templeton, Carey Taylor, Bonté Neel, Frances S. Craven, and Eunice "Jordan" Johnston. (Courtesy of Francella Craven Kerr.)

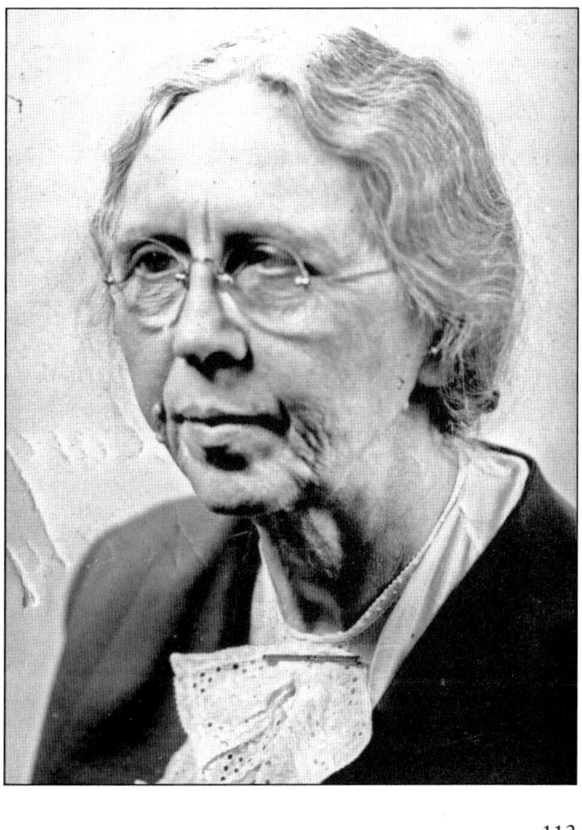

Mary McNeely, a graduate of Emory University, became librarian in 1934. With financial support from the WPA and renewed support from the Town of Mooresville, the collection was moved to rooms over the Moor Theatre. McNeely expanded the hours of operation so that more patrons could be served and offered some programs of special interest to children. The library began its operation as a WPA project, and books were added through loans and gifts. She left the library to work in the Charlotte Public Library and returned to Mooresville to assume teaching duties at the Mooresville Central High School. Ada Mae McNeely was appointed to fill the vacancy. (Courtesy of Lenore McNeely Hathcock.)

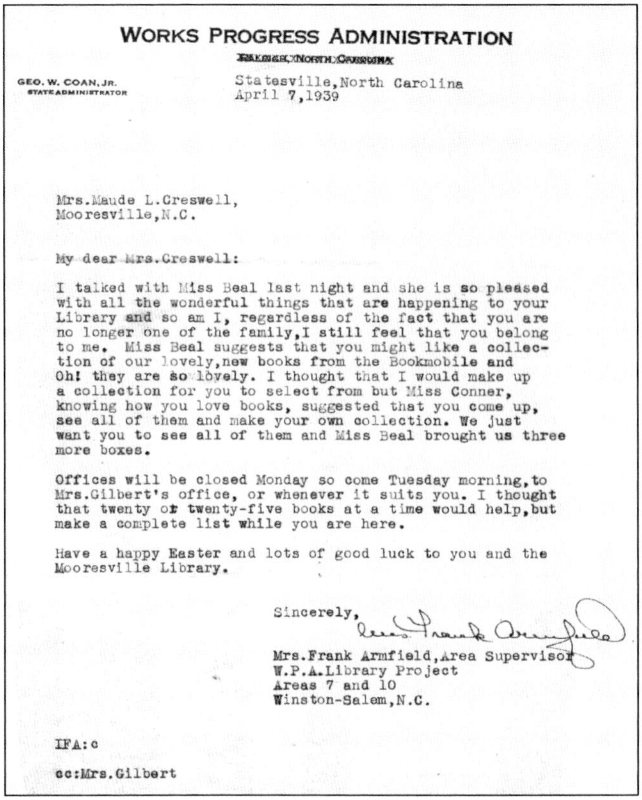

WORKS PROGRESS ADMINISTRATION

GEO. W. COAN, JR.
STATE ADMINISTRATOR

Statesville, North Carolina
April 7, 1939

Mrs. Maude L. Creswell,
Mooresville, N.C.

My dear Mrs. Creswell:

I talked with Miss Beal last night and she is so pleased with all the wonderful things that are happening to your Library and so am I, regardless of the fact that you are no longer one of the family, I still feel that you belong to me. Miss Beal suggests that you might like a collection of our lovely, new books from the Bookmobile and Oh! they are so lovely. I thought that I would make up a collection for you to select from but Miss Conner, knowing how you love books, suggested that you come up, see all of them and make your own collection. We just want you to see all of them and Miss Beal brought us three more boxes.

Offices will be closed Monday so come Tuesday morning, to Mrs. Gilbert's office, or whenever it suits you. I thought that twenty or twenty-five books at a time would help, but make a complete list while you are here.

Have a happy Easter and lots of good luck to you and the Mooresville Library.

Sincerely,

Mrs. Frank Armfield, Area Supervisor
W.P.A. Library Project
Areas 7 and 10
Winston-Salem, N.C.

IFA:c

cc: Mrs. Gilbert

The WPA proved to be a lifesaver for the library. Under the direction of Maude Creswell, new books from the State Library Commission were added to the collection and individuals and civic groups made donations of money and materials. Librarians were paid a total of $803.25 from the WPA in 1936. Children's furniture and books supported the expanding program. WPA funding allowed the library to establish itself as a vital public service, and financial support from Mooresville and Iredell County added to its ability to provide services. After 39 years of struggle mixed with tenacity, the Mooresville Public Library approached institutional stability. In 1938, the library was dealt a blow when WPA funds were withdrawn. Maude Creswell's position was no longer on the funding list. (Courtesy of Maids and Matrons Club minutes.)

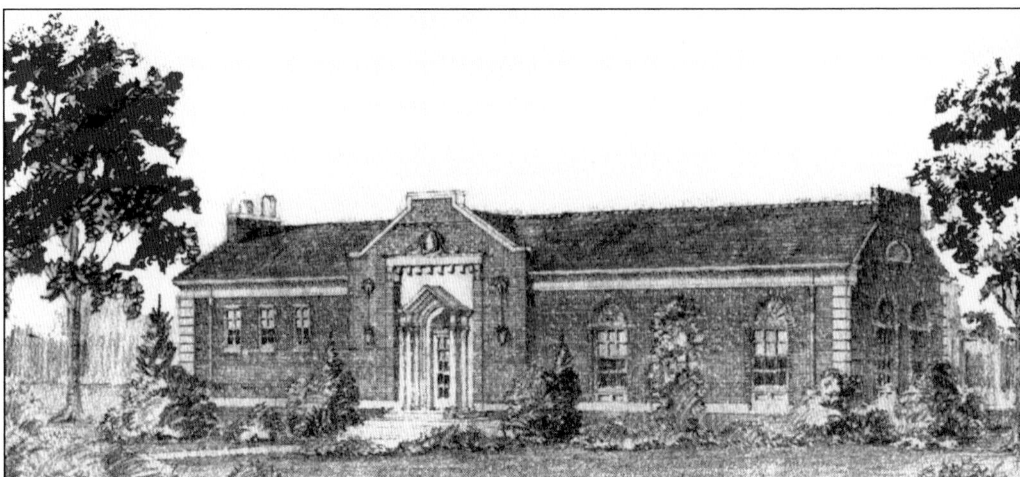

Action to support the library and Mrs. Creswell appeared when LuTelle Sherrill Williams stepped forward in 1938 to add stability to the library by providing a building that would be its first and only permanent home. Williams made a plan to demolish her family home on the corner of South Main Street and Catawba Avenue to make way for a new building for the Mooresville Public Library. Architect Roger McCarl designed the building, a sketch of which was shown at the announcement. (Courtesy of James V. Houston.)

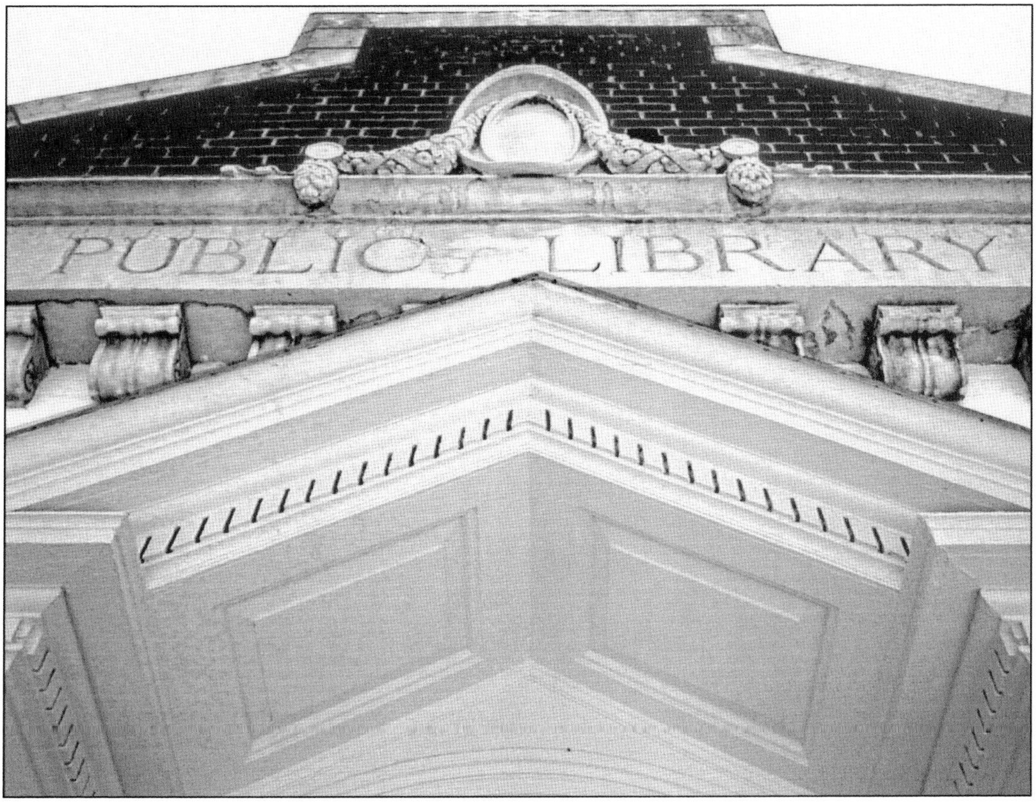

Contracts for the new building were awarded to Barger Brothers construction, George B. Stevens electrical, S. F. Holcomb plumbing, and Gaylord Furniture Company for furnishings. The plans called for a reading room, delivery area, stock room, work room, pergola, children's room, and reference area. At its opening, the shelf capacity was 17,380 volumes.

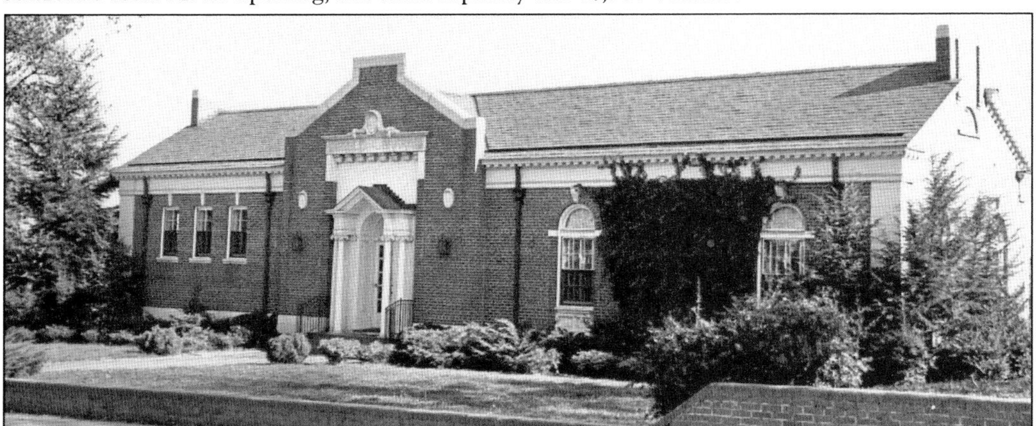

The new Mooresville Public Library was opened to the public on December 12, 1939. *Enterprise* editor Harry Deaton described the callers as "singing praises of the handsome Christmas gift" from LuTelle Sherrill Williams to the citizens of Mooresville. More than 3,500 volumes had been cataloged and made available for circulation. State library officials called it the "handsomest small library in North Carolina." It was a refuge for the bookworms of the community as well as others in search of knowledge, adventure, and information.

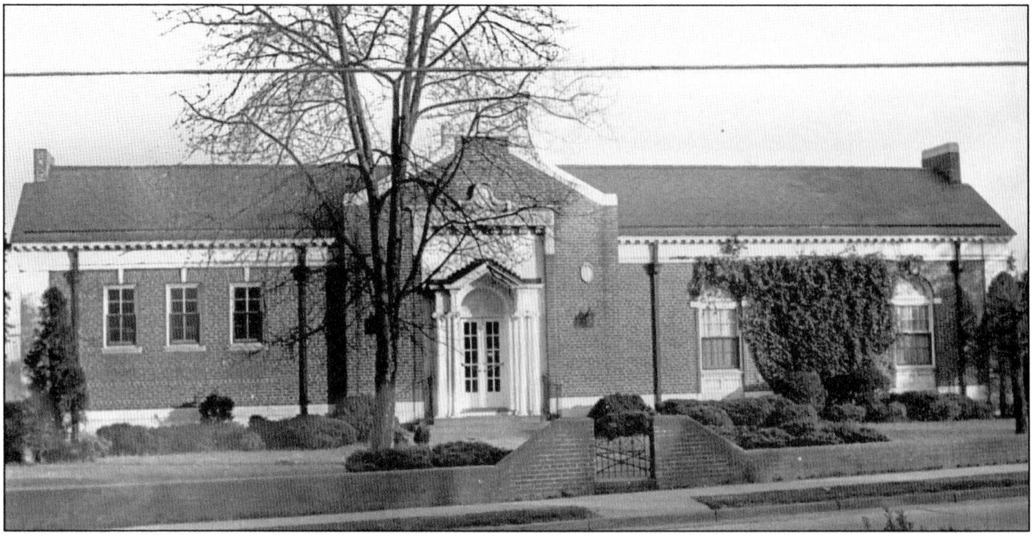

Citizens were welcomed by representatives from local civic organizations as well as the Town of Mooresville: Mayor Claude Mayhew; Betty Mallard and Myrtle Melchor from the American Legion Auxiliary; Lynda Templeton, Ada Veile, and Luetie Johnston from the Womans Club; and Mary Agnes Rogers and Mamie Houston from the UDC. The Maids and Matrons were represented by Nina Black, Frances S. Craven, Maude Creswell, Mrs. Eugene Johnston, Mary Templeton, and Gertrude Norman.

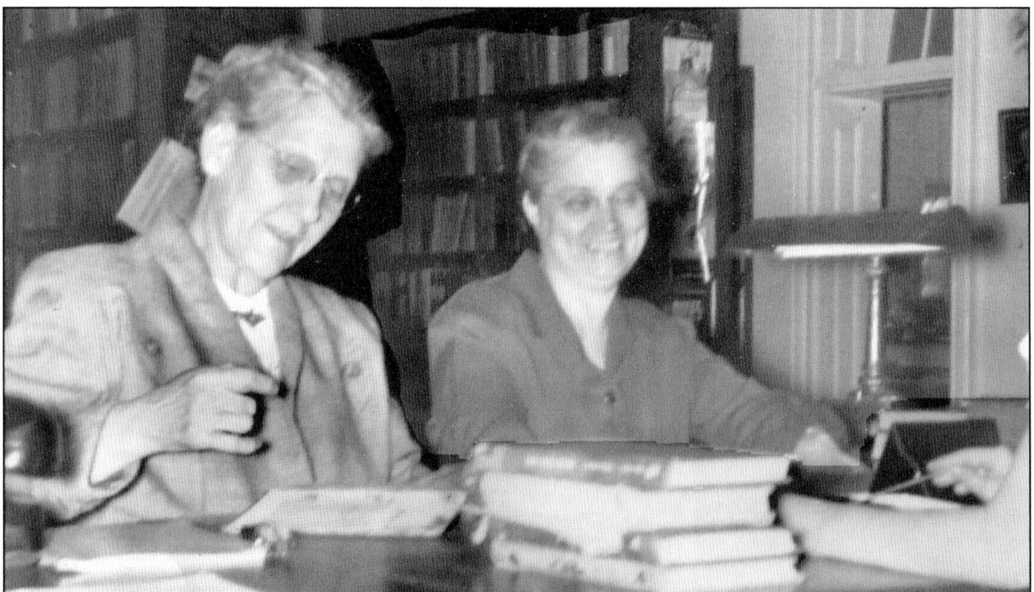

The interior of the building is inviting and comfortable. Mrs. Williams provided all of the furnishings, from shelving to leather sofas and chairs. Work tables and chairs are scattered among the shelves and easy chairs for readers and researchers. A children's area, complete with appropriately sized furniture, is inviting for all kinds of activities. The large circulation desk accommodates easy check out and return, with two librarians available to help patrons. Mrs. J. J. McNeely (left) and Eunice Price were always ready and eager to help readers find books and information. (Courtesy of the Eunice Price family.)

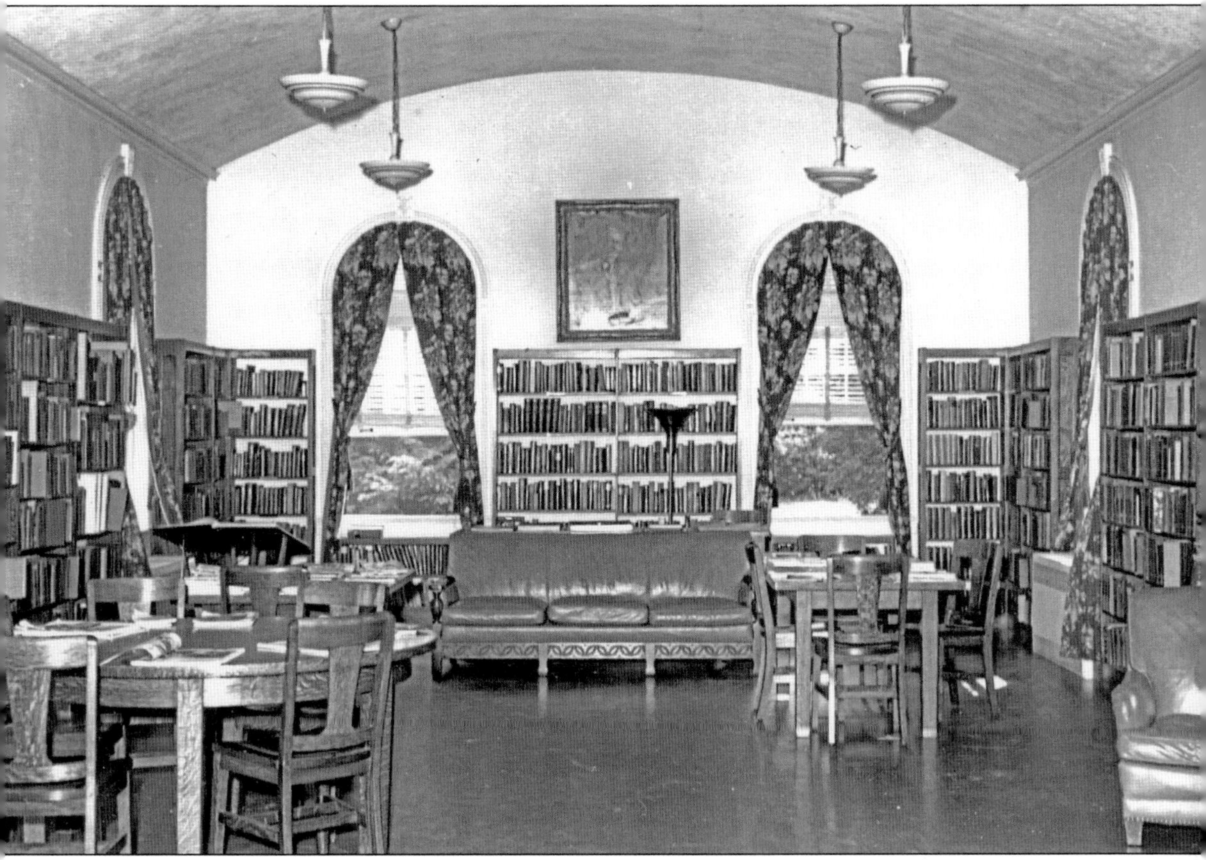

In 1949, LuTelle Sherrill Williams presented a portrait of her father, James Elbert Sherrill, to the Mooresville Public Library. The portrait was hung in the main reading and reference area so that the entire community could enjoy the artwork. The library board placed a bronze plaque at the front entrance commemorating the gift to the community by Williams in honor of her parents, James Elbert and Margaret Emma Harris Sherrill. The Sherrill-Williams gift is unique in Mooresville history and stands out in North Carolina history for its value to a single community. While her gift is the highwater mark, it follows the dedication of a small group of citizens whose love of learning and desire to share the adventure of books with others strengthened them through 42 years of struggle to keep the idea of a library alive in Mooresville. The vision of Mary Jane Grierson; the tenacity of Annie Goodman, Carrie Leazer, and Sallie McPherson; the work of Zeb Turlington; and the creativity of Frances Craven and Maude Creswell make the Mooresville Public Library a community institution in its most perfect form. (Courtesy of the Eunice Price family.)

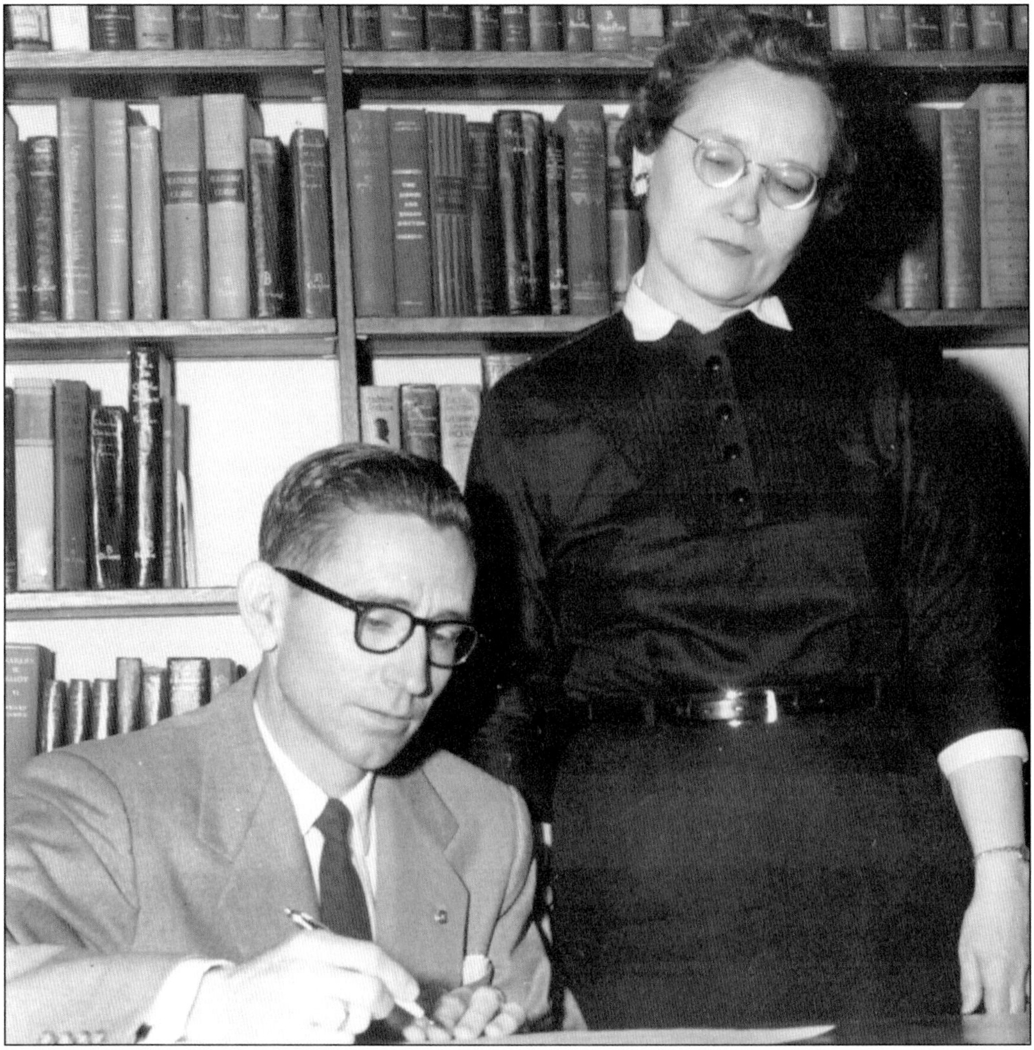

Librarians have worked continuously to make information available to the public about books, activities, and events for readers of all ages. Mayor Boyce Brawley (1953–1960, 1965) was a great supporter of library events and proclaimed National Library Week in Mooresville each year of his tenure. Librarian Florence Johnston (right) worked with all civic groups and schools to make the program meaningful and useful for patrons of all ages. Librarians include Mrs. J. J. McNeely, Mary McNeely, Maude Creswell, Grace Rankin McNeely, Florence Johnston, Hazel Dishman, Toni Reid Couch, Aloma Beaver Hill, Jane Ward, Karen Khan, and John Pritchard. (Courtesy of the Eunice Price family.)

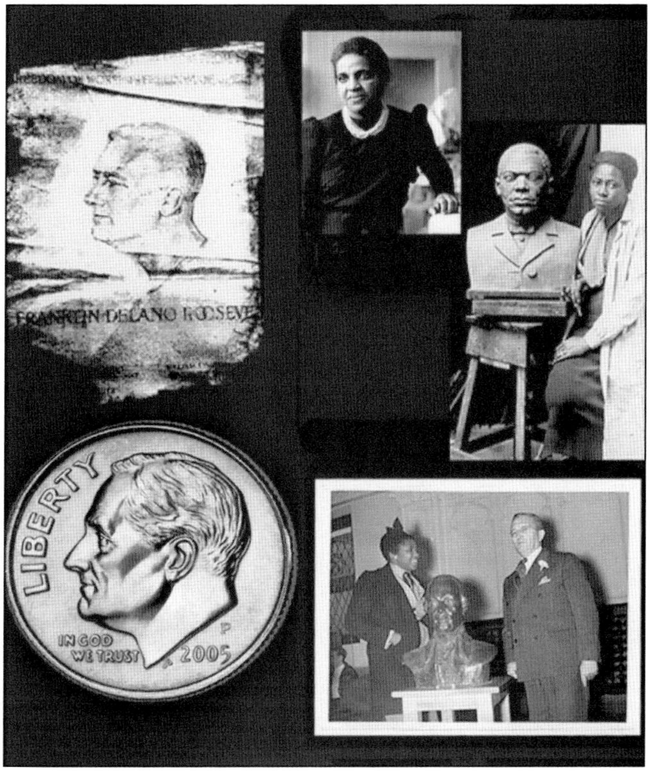

When she was a little girl, Selma Burke played with the clay she found in the creek bed near her parents' home in Mooresville. She knew that she had found her life's calling, creating works of art. In 1943, she won an international competition in Washington, D.C., and was commissioned to sculpt a relief portrait of Pres. Franklin Roosevelt. Pres. Harry Truman unveiled the plaque, which hangs it the Recorder of Deeds Building in Washington. Burke's work is widely believed to be the prototype for the Roosevelt head on the dime. She founded the Selma Burke School of Sculpture in 1947 and in 1968 the Selma Burke Art Center in Pittsburgh. At the age of 70, she completed a Doctorate in Arts and Letters at Livingstone College, Salisbury, North Carolina. (Composite image courtesy of Sylvia Smith.)

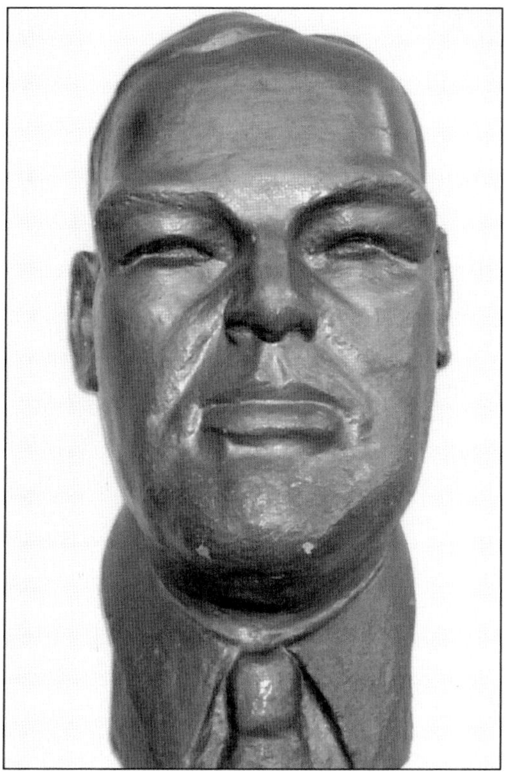

The only example of Selma Burke's art in her hometown is a bust of Dr. Davies McLelland in the Mooresville Public Library. Burke is said to have chosen McLelland as her subject because of his caring attention to all his patients, regardless of their race, creed, or color. (Photograph by Cindy Jacobs.)

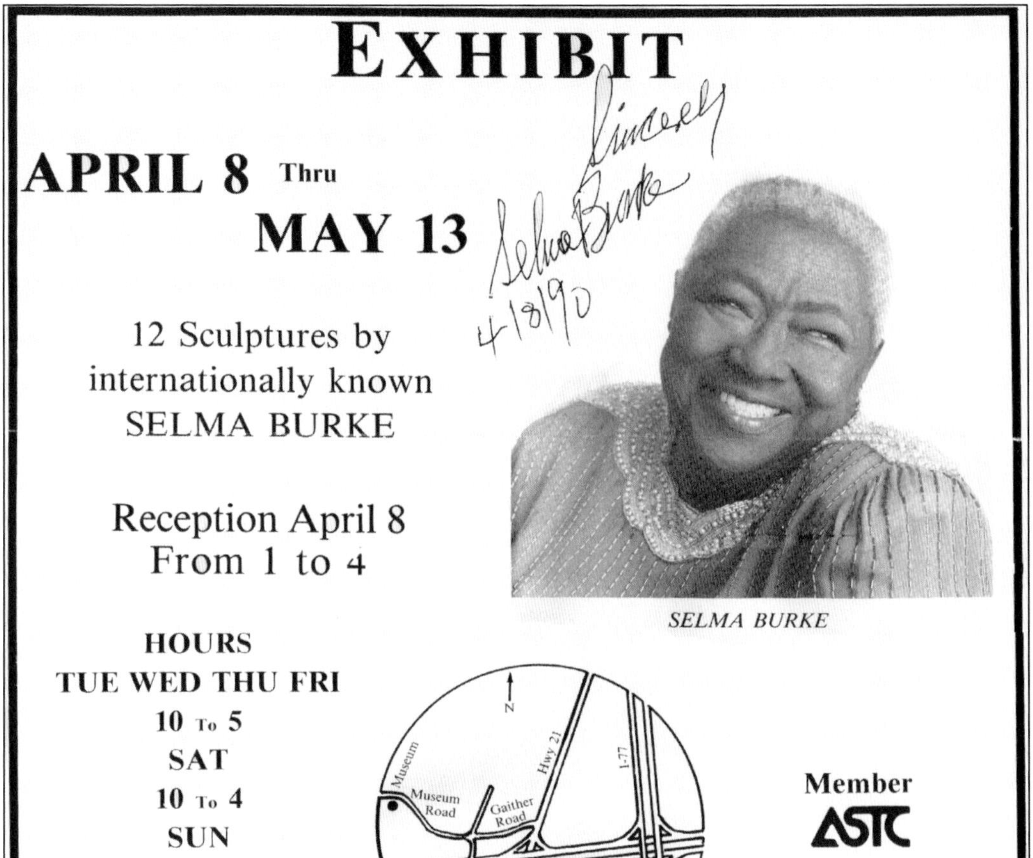

Burke was welcomed home to Iredell County with a showing of her work at the Arts and Science Center in Statesville. Burke's bust of Mary Holliday, the first African American supervisor for the Iredell County Schools, is on display in the Iredell-Statesville Schools office in Statesville.

Seven

The Port City of Lake Norman

In 1957, a plan was developed to build the largest lake in the Duke Power System. A young engineer named William (Bill) States Lee was placed in charge of designing a dam for Cowans Ford. Cowans Ford was the site of a Revolutionary War battle between British general Cornwallis and a band of Catawba Valley farmers led by Gen. William Lee Davidson, a member of the Centre Church community in what is now Mount Mourne. Few events have had more impact on Mooresville than the construction of the Cowans Ford Dam and the creation of Lake Norman. With 520 miles of shoreline, the lake was a recreation mecca from the start. Duke Power president Norman Cocke, for whom the lake is named, put forester Carl Blades in charge of making the land ready for the water. Blades went out into the bottomlands bordering the Catawba River to buy acreage for the new lake. In a 1982 interview, Blades remembered the daunting task of purchasing more than 30,000 acres of family farmland for Duke Power's lake. He said, "I spent many days and nights in this area. We ran into a few difficulties in the negotiations. People were reluctant to sell their family homes where many had lived for generations." Cemeteries were moved and churches were given other land. Duke Power leased a one-acre lake lot to anyone interested for about $120 per year. Those 20th-century pioneers didn't seem concerned by the lack of roads or the land overgrown with trees and underbrush. Weekends were used for clearing brush and building cabins and piers for the water that was slowly approaching the 760-foot elevation. As dam construction progressed, the Catawba River water inundated the land and created waterfront. Mooresville public relations pioneers Fletcher Davis and Tom McKnight decided that Mooresville should take steps to benefit from the growing population of Lake Norman. They developed the idea of the "Port City of Lake Norman" as a marketing slogan for Mooresville. Based on the fact that a portion of Lake Norman reached the town limits through Reed Creek at a point on Highway 21, they named Mooresville as the Port City of Lake Norman. Even though there certainly was no port, the claim to fame stuck. From then on, the name "Port City" was attached to shopping centers, electrical contractors, Mooresville policemen and firemen, and all kinds of small businesses.

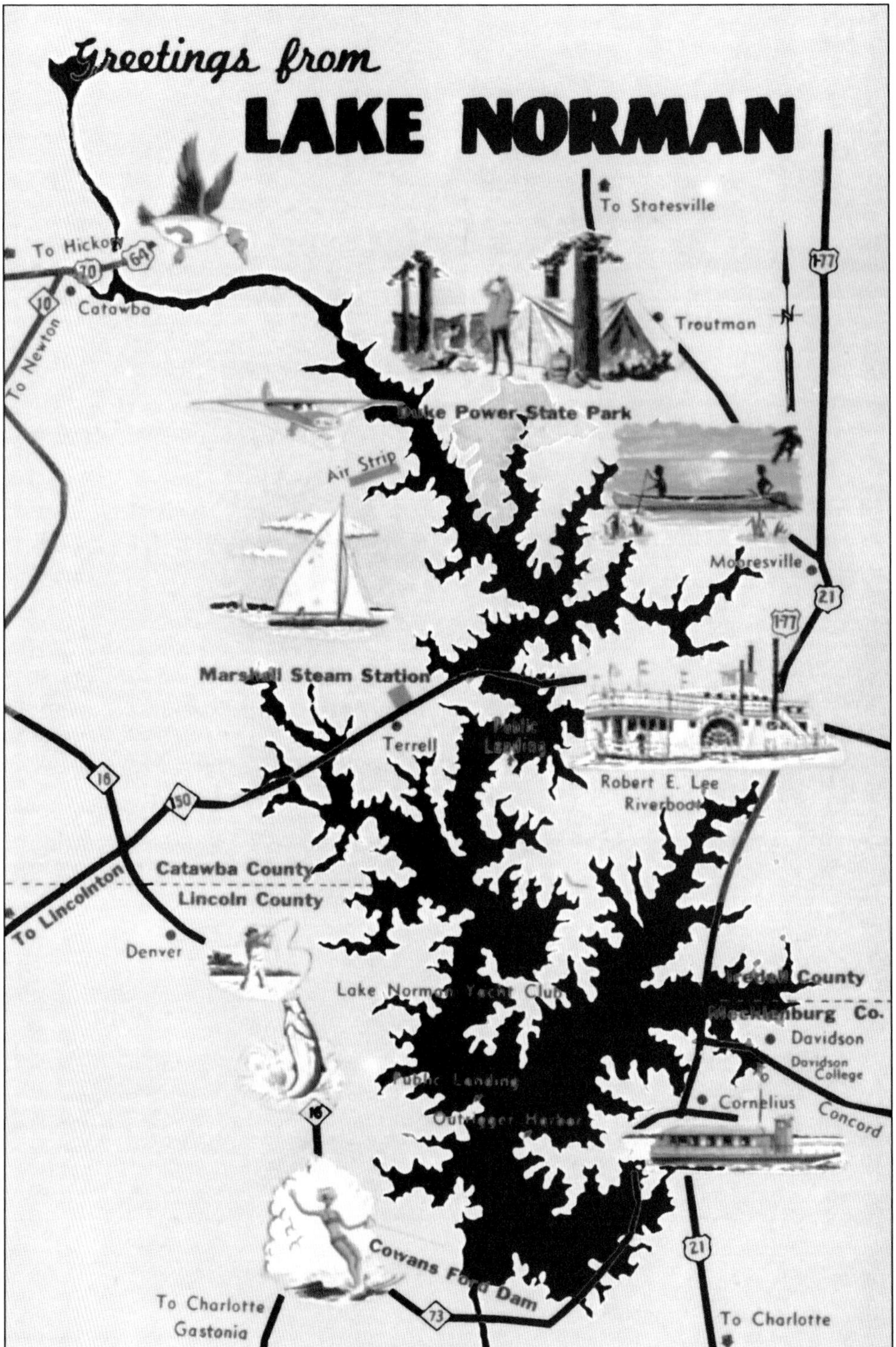

The colorful brochure promoting the Port City made for interesting reading. It highlights all the amenities of Mooresville, from restaurants to golf to shopping for the new lake dwellers.

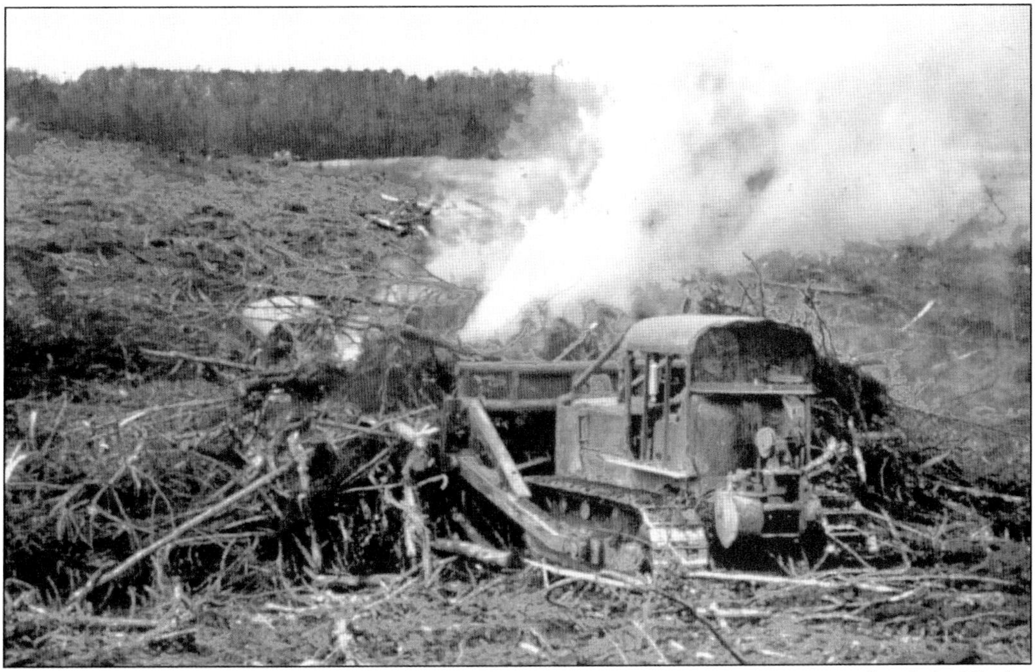

Clearing land of trees, abandoned houses, and other structures was a monumental task for Blades and his crews. Clearing would begin when a property purchase was completed. Clearing the land to insure a safe waterway went on for years as the Cowans Ford Dam was under contraction. (Courtesy of Carl Blades, 1982.)

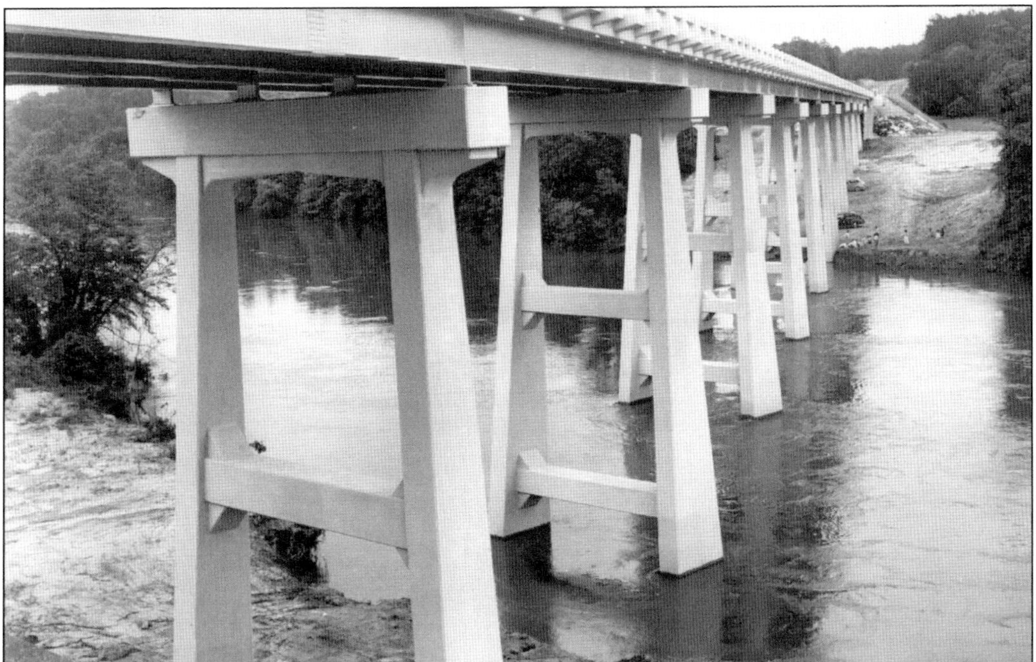

The third bridge across the Catawba River connecting Iredell and Catawba Counties was replaced to accommodate a higher water level. Bridge building started well before the lake filled.

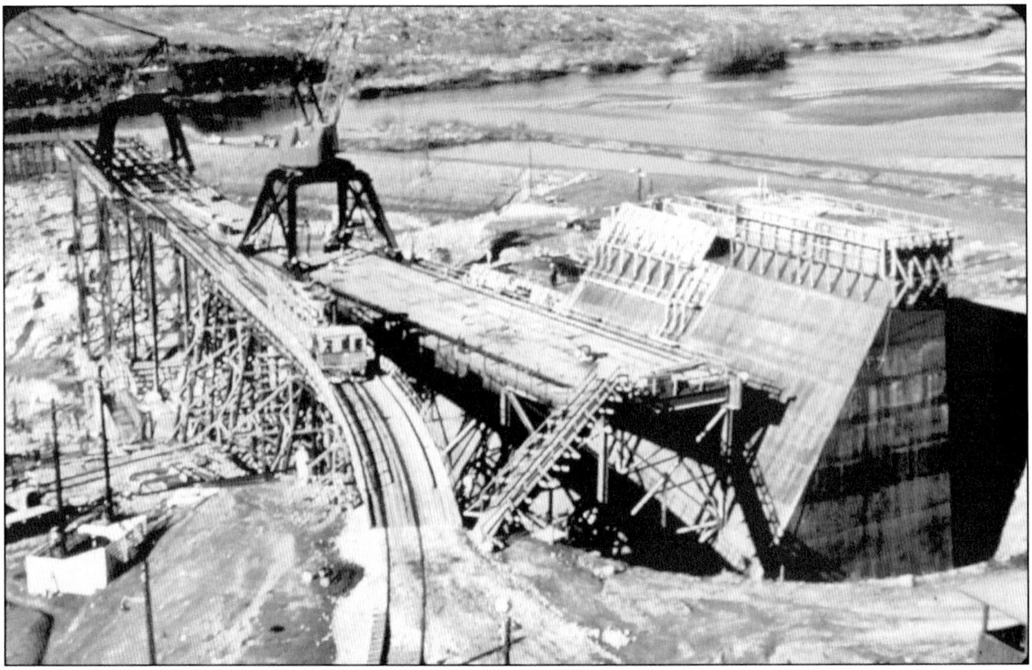

Cowans Ford dam was designed by William Lee and constructed by Duke Power Company to harness the water of the Catawba River for power generation. Additional sites were set aside for power plants like Plant Marshall in Catawba County. With the advent of nuclear power and the McGuire Station, these sites were developed as residential and recreational areas by Crescent Land and Timber (Crescent Recources). (Courtesy of Carl Blades, 1982.)

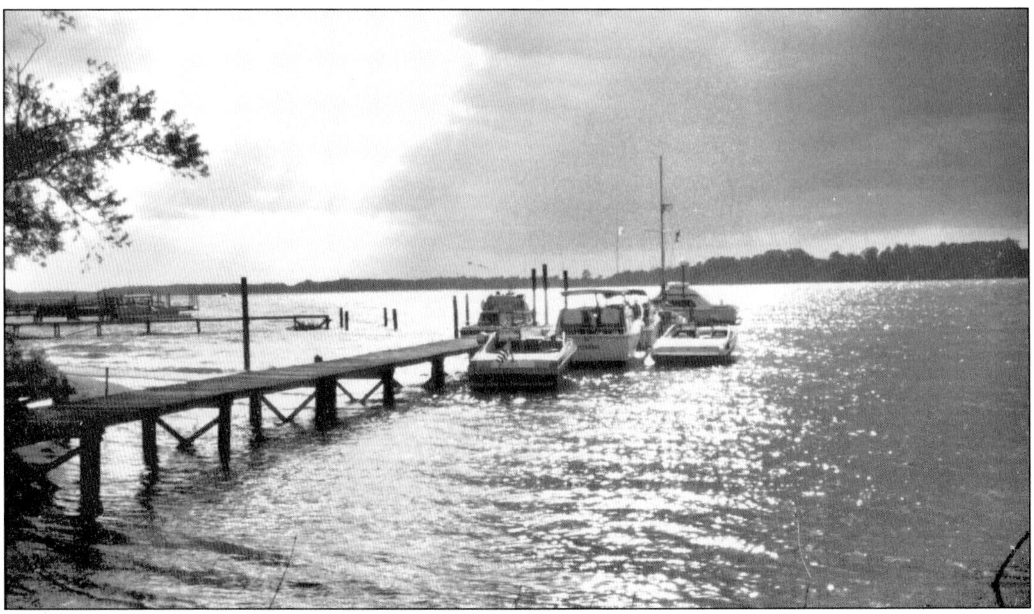

More and more lakedwellers filled the coves with piers and the shoreline with weekend lake homes. The Lake Norman Marine Commission was formed to help set policy for development, with particular emphasis on structures extending into the waters of Lake Norman. Larger docks were built to moor boats of all sizes as larger, more permanent homes were built along the shoreline.

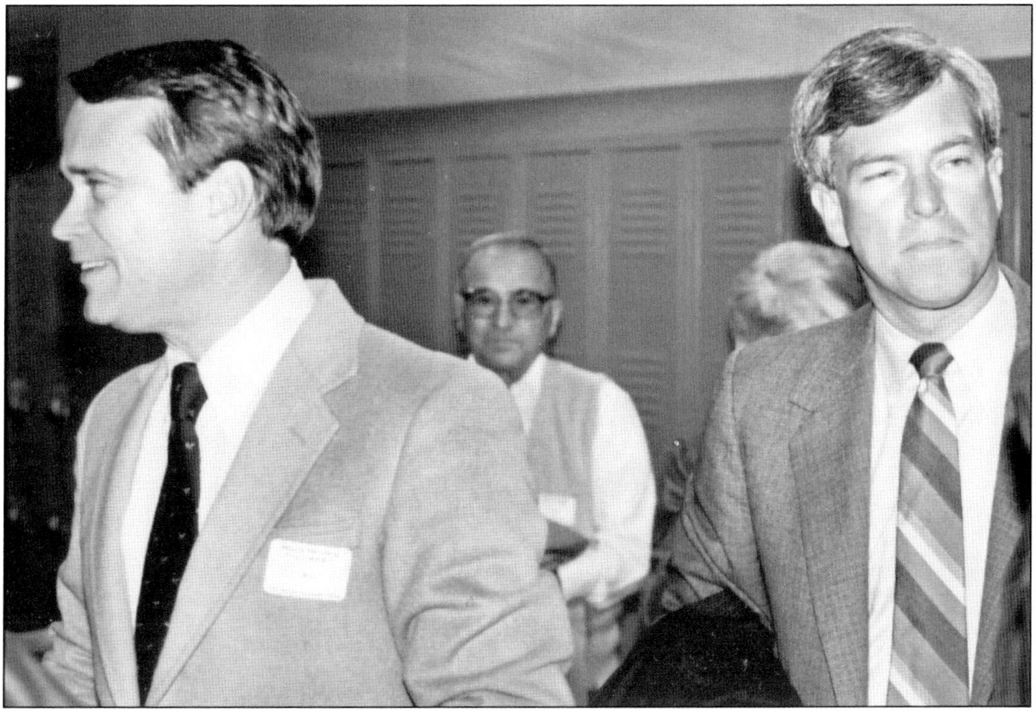

Marine commission chairman Bill Furr, left, and developer James Jennings, right, were active in the work to insure orderly development of Lake Norman property. Both were particularly interested in the safety of the waterway and worked with the Lake Norman Power Squadron to support the installation of aids to navigation. (Photograph by Cindy Jacobs.)

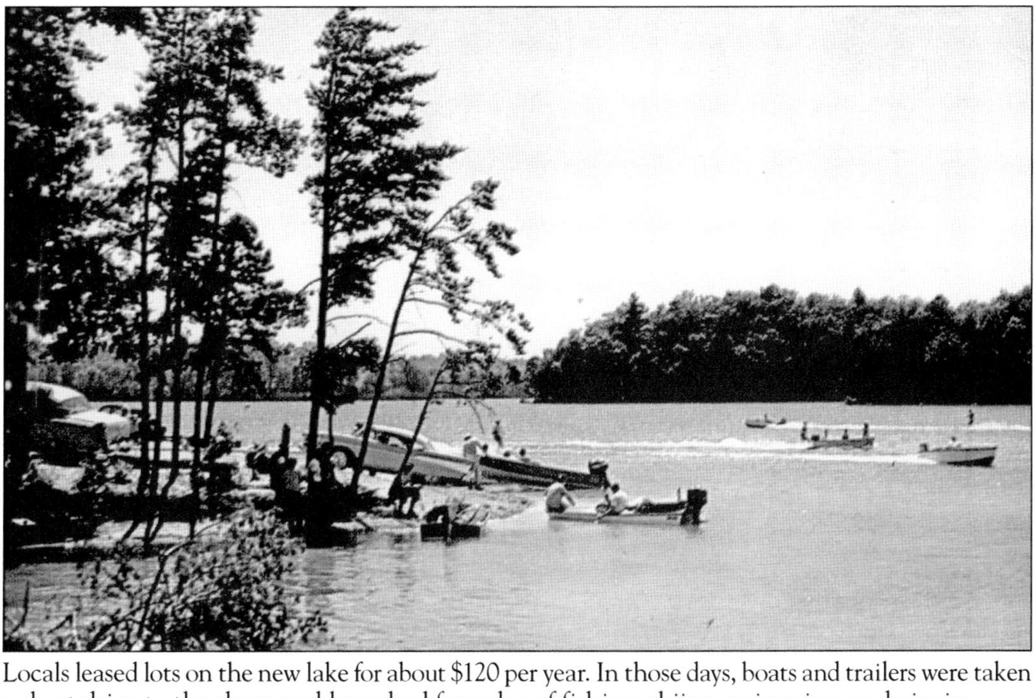

Locals leased lots on the new lake for about $120 per year. In those days, boats and trailers were taken a short drive to the shore and launched for a day of fishing, skiing, swimming, and picnics.

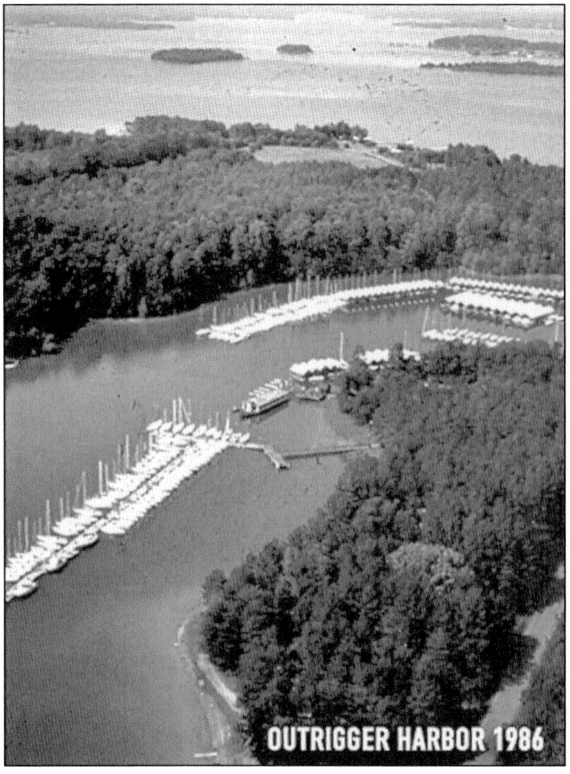

Outrigger Marina was a peninsula leased from Duke Power Company by Earl Teague. He built a Polynesian cruise boat named the *Kon Tiki*. It was docked at the marina, which featured dining onshore and on the boat. Outrigger featured a large campground with leased camping spots.

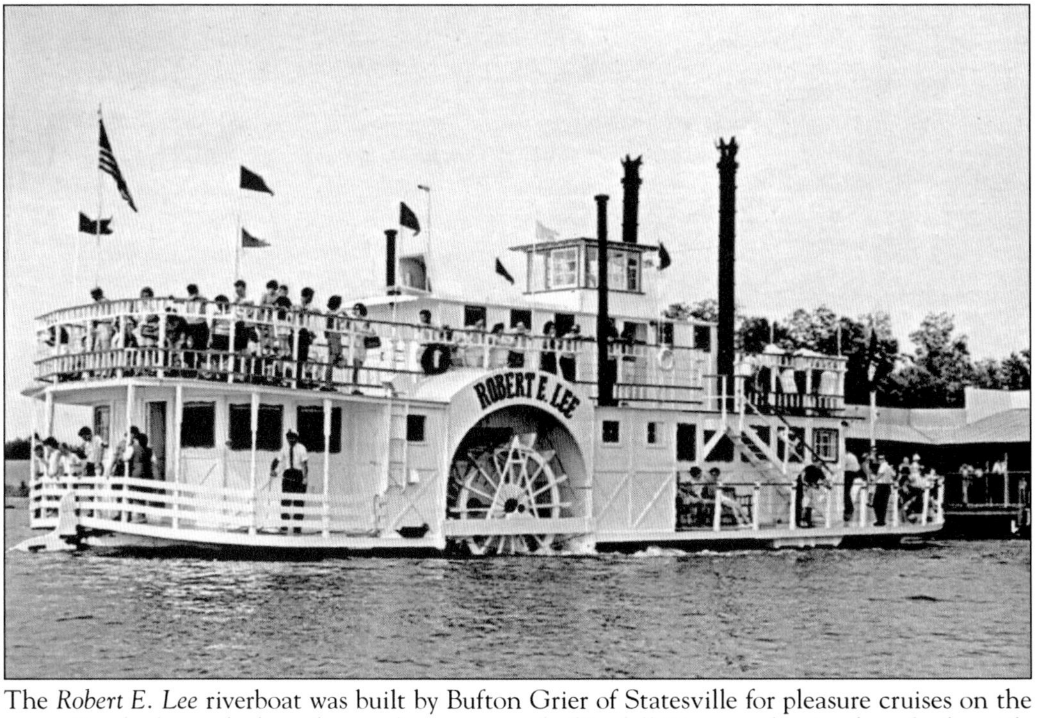

The *Robert E. Lee* riverboat was built by Bufton Grier of Statesville for pleasure cruises on the water. Berthed at a dock at the southernmost end of Iredell County, the riverboat had a wide east-west expanse on which to cruise.

Lake dwellers arrived and many stayed to make beautiful Lake Norman their home.

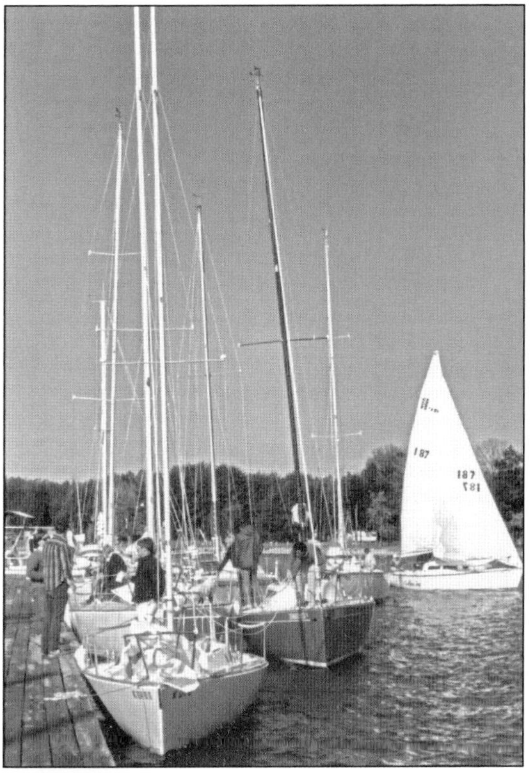

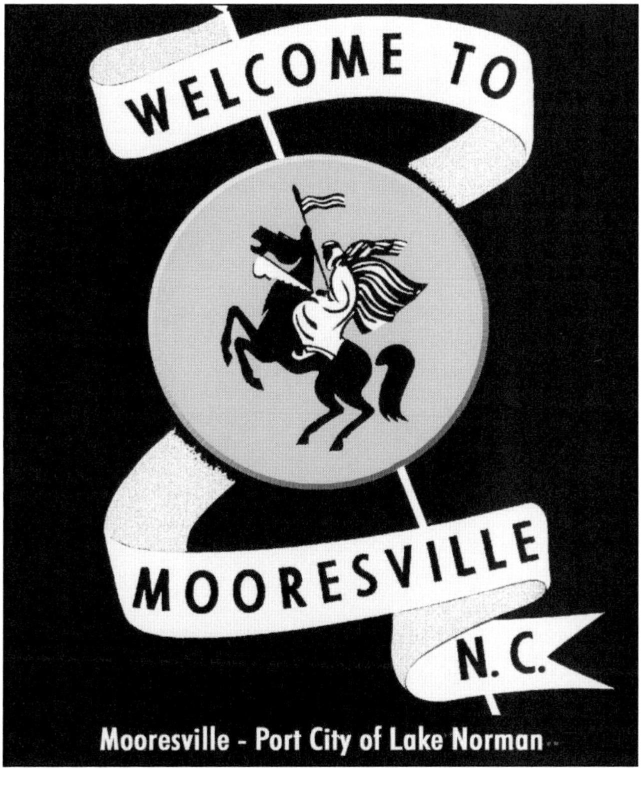

Change came with Lake Norman and made Mooresville a more dynamic community with the diversity among new citizens. The 1960s brought more change and new challenges and opportunities for citizens to take bold steps into the future, always mindful of those who led the way.

Consistent with our mission to preserve history on a local level, this book was printed in South Carolina on American-made paper and manufactured entirely in the United States. Products carrying the accredited Forest Stewardship Council (FSC) label are printed on 100 percent FSC-certified paper.